Bakhtin and his Others

Bakhtin and his Others

(Inter)subjectivity, Chronotope, Dialogism

Edited by
Liisa Steinby and Tintti Klapuri

ANTHEM PRESS
LONDON · NEW YORK · DELHI

Anthem Press
An imprint of Wimbledon Publishing Company
www.anthempress.com

This edition first published in UK and USA 2014
by ANTHEM PRESS
75–76 Blackfriars Road, London SE1 8HA, UK
or PO Box 9779, London SW19 7ZG, UK
and
244 Madison Ave. #116, New York, NY 10016, USA

First published in hardback by Anthem Press in 2013

© 2014 Liisa Steinby and Tintti Klapuri editorial matter
and selection; individual chapters © individual contributors

The moral right of the authors has been asserted.

All rights reserved. Without limiting the rights under copyright reserved above,
no part of this publication may be reproduced, stored or introduced into
a retrieval system, or transmitted, in any form or by any means
(electronic, mechanical, photocopying, recording or otherwise),
without the prior written permission of both the copyright
owner and the above publisher of this book.

British Library Cataloguing-in-Publication Data
A catalogue record for this book is available from the British Library.

Library of Congress Cataloging-in-Publication Data
The Library of Congress has catalogued the hardcover edition as follows:
Bakhtin and his Others : (inter)subjectivity, chronotope, dialogism /
edited by Liisa Steinby and Tintti Klapuri.
pages ; cm
Includes bibliographical references.
ISBN 978-0-85728-308-5 (hardback : alkaline paper)
1. Bakhtin, M. M. (Mikhail Mikhailovich), 1895–1975–Criticism and interpretation.
2. Literature–History and criticism–Theory, etc. 3. Literature–Aesthetics.
4. Subject (Philosophy) in literature. 5. Intersubjectivity in literature.
6. Dialogism (Literary analysis) I. Steinby, Liisa, editor. II. Klapuri, Tintti, editor.
PG2947.B3B325 2013
801'.95092–dc23
2012049649

ISBN-13: 978 1 78308 331 2 (Pbk)
ISBN-10: 1 78308 331 X (Pbk)

Cover image © 2013 Tintti Klapuri

This title is also available as an ebook.

CONTENTS

Acknowledgements   vii

Translation and Transliteration   ix

Introduction   The Acting Subject of Bakhtin   xi
Liisa Steinby and Tintti Klapuri

Chapter 1   Bakhtin and Lukács: Subjectivity, Signifying Form and Temporality in the Novel   1
Liisa Steinby

Chapter 2   Bakhtin, Watt and the Early Eighteenth-Century Novel   19
Aino Mäkikalli

Chapter 3   Concepts of Novelistic Polyphony: Person-Related and Compositional-Thematic   37
Liisa Steinby

Chapter 4   Familiar Otherness: Peculiarities of Dialogue in Ezra Pound's Poetics of Inclusion   55
Mikhail Oshukov

Chapter 5   Author and Other in Dialogue: Bakhtinian Polyphony in the Poetry of Peter Reading   73
Christian Pauls

Chapter 6   Tradition and Genre: Thomas Kyd's *The Spanish Tragedy*   87
Edward Gieskes

Chapter 7   Bakhtin's Concept of the Chronotope: The Viewpoint of an Acting Subject   105
Liisa Steinby

Chapter 8   The Provincial Chronotope and Modernity in Chekhov's Short Fiction   127
Tintti Klapuri

List of Contributors   147

ACKNOWLEDGEMENTS

The idea of this book originated in the research project 'Literature and Time: Time, Modernity and Human Agency in Literature' at the Department of Comparative Literature of the University of Turku, funded by the Academy of Finland (Grant # 2600066111); of the authors, Tintti Klapuri, Aino Mäkikalli and Liisa Steinby are members of the project, while Mikhail Oshukov is closely associated with it. The chapters by Edward Gieskes and Christian Pauls are based on papers given in two Bakhtin workshops organized by the editors of this volume at the conference 'Genre and Interpretation', held as part of the Finnish Doctoral Programme for Literary Studies at the University of Helsinki in June 2009.

The research carried out at the Bakhtin Centre, University of Sheffield, has been a source of great inspiration for our work. We want to thank Prof. Craig Brandist, director of the Bakhtin Centre, for his involvement in our research project and for his continuous interest in our work. In addition, we are grateful to Dr Ellen Valle for language revision and to the two anonymous reviewers of the manuscript for their insightful reading and helpful suggestions.

TRANSLATION AND TRANSLITERATION

Unless otherwise stated, translations are by the authors.

With the exception of some commonly occurring names, Russian words are transliterated in a simplified version of Library of Congress system (without diacritics). The soft sign is not used and ц is transliterated as *c*.

Introduction

THE ACTING SUBJECT OF BAKHTIN

Liisa Steinby and Tintti Klapuri

The international study of the work of Mikhail Bakhtin has recently witnessed a significant reorientation. Bakhtin was originally introduced in the West, from the 1960s to the 1980s, by two important structuralist theoreticians, Julia Kristeva and Tzvetan Todorov, who represented him as a forerunner of structuralist thinking. In Bakhtin's 'dialogism' and 'polyphony' they saw forms of intertextuality (Kristeva 1980; Todorov 1984), defined by Kristeva as follows: 'Any text is constructed as a mosaic of quotations; any text is the absorption and transformation of another. The notion of intertextuality comes to take the place of the notion of intersubjectivity' (Kristeva 1980, 66). In this interpretation, Bakhtin is placed within a framework of thinking in which the constitutive meaning of the interpretative subject is erased and the subject of narration is 'reduced to a code, to a nonperson, to an anonymity' (Kristeva 1980, 74). As an extension of this, it is in the framework of late structuralist discourse pluralism that Bakhtin's concept of 'dialogism' has since the 1980s flourished especially in the United States (Holquist 2002). This interpretation of Bakhtin as a textualist is now recognized as an undue 'familiarization', occurring in an intellectual atmosphere in which structuralism was dominant (cf. Zbinden 2006).

The recent reassessment of Bakhtin's thinking has resulted from the contextualization of his work in its original intellectual background: on the one hand in nineteenth- and early twentieth-century German thought in the areas of philosophy, aesthetics and the theory of the novel, on the other in a Russian and early Soviet context, which itself was in general deeply influenced by German thinking. This work of reassessment, due largely to British scholars – among them David Shepherd (e.g. Shepherd 1998), Ken Hirschkop (1999), Galin Tihanov (2000) and Craig Brandist (2002; see also Brandist and Lähteenmäki 2010) – has contributed to our present new understanding of Bakhtin's thought. The most important German sources of Bakhtin's work are identified in this new scholarship as being Kant and Hegel; the Neo-Kantians; the 'philosophers of life'; Georg Lukács, in both his early, Neo-Kantian–Hegelian and his later Marxist phases (cf. Tihanov 2000); the phenomenologists Edmund Husserl and Max Scheler (cf. Poole 2001; Brandist 2002); and thinkers who, while proceeding from philosophy, figure among the founders of sociology, including Georg Simmel. Among the Neo-Kantians, those most important for Bakhtin are considered to be Hermann Cohen and Ernst Cassirer (cf. Steinby 2011; Poole 1998), while the relevant 'philosophers of life' include such diverse thinkers as Wilhelm Dilthey and Henri Bergson.[1] An essential cause of the earlier misunderstanding was that Bakhtin notoriously tended to leave his sources unmentioned, especially philosophical ones – perhaps primarily because in the Stalinist era it might have been dangerous to quote a 'bourgeois' thinker. The writers he drew upon were in any case most probably familiar to his Russian fellow-intellectuals; when his writings were introduced in the West in the 1960s, however, this background was not recognized by his new audience. He was therefore read as more original than he actually was, even as an entirely unique thinker, without precedent, whose main theoretical concepts – the polyphonic novel, the chronotope, and carnivalism – were entirely his own creation. In addition to the work of British scholars, the studies of Caryl Emerson and Gary Saul Morson (Morson and Emerson 1990; Emerson 1997), working in the United States, and Renate Lachmann (1982) and Matthias Freise (1993) in Germany, have helped to contextualize Bakhtin's thought and have hence contributed to the ways in which Bakhtin's ideas now appear in a new, less unique light.

A fact which comes into sight when Bakhtin is contextualized in German idealist thinking is that he formulates problems and resolves them within the framework of the philosophy of subjectivity, with a strong emphasis on intersubjectivity (cf. Hirschkop 1999, 5, 52, 58, 86, 153, 240; Brandist 2002, 40, 44, 81). Questions of subject and intersubjectivity have been given different interpretations and different weights in understanding Bakhtin.

The Question of Subject(ivity)

Since we are used to reading Bakhtin together with P. N. Medvedev's *Formal Method in Literary Scholarship* (1978 [1928]) and V. N. Voloshinov's *Marxism and the Philosophy of Language* (1986 [1929]) – works that for a long time were attributed to Bakhtin (cf. Brandist 2002, 8–9) – we tend to think about his idea(s) of intersubjectivity in terms of his view of language. Together with his above-mentioned co-workers in the so-called Bakhtin Circle, Bakhtin and his dialogism are seen as a forerunner of the social, or 'sociological', conception of language: speakers use discourse types that are socially and ideologically determined. 'Heteroglossia' then refers to the plurality of socially determined discourses, and 'dialogism' to the encountering or mixing of these discourses in speech. Focusing on the concrete speech situation, however, underlines not only the different sociolects of language but also the active role played by the individual speaker, a view that has affinity to later developments in linguistics. While structuralist theories of language tended to reduce the speaking subject to a position assigned to him by the linguistic system (cf. Benveniste 1966), in linguistic pragmatics – especially following the 'interactional turn' (cf. Tanskanen et al. 2010) – the subject in a speech situation not only makes choices from among a vast number of socially relevant modes of discourse, but also responds individually to the specific content and circumstances of his or her interlocutor's message.[2] In this theoretical framework, 'intersubjectivity' refers to the individual's involvement, in any given encounter with interlocutors, in a process of speech production based on a variety of socially determined discourses.

However, there are also scholars who in view of the newly uncovered German connection doubt whether this social (or 'sociological') emphasis on discourse is Bakhtin's fundamental and original view. In an article published in 1985, Hirschkop writes that 'an idealist conception of the subject – as the primary, irreducible unit of human society, ideally autonomous and free – is ultimately preserved [in Bakhtin's thinking]' (Hirschkop 1985, 770).[3] In their recent, quite fierce attack on Bakhtin, Jean-Paul Bronckart and Christian Bota claim that this 'idealistic' view of the subject is Bakhtin's actual conception; the 'sociological' and truly dialogical view of subjectivity and discourse derives from Voloshinov (see Bronckart and Bota 2011, 185, 293, 539–41). Here some conceptual clarification is needed. To what extent is the 'idealistic' view of subjectivity in the German philosophies in Bakhtin's background contrary to the idea of the social determination of subjectivity? Is intersubjectivity excluded from this view of the individual subject?

In German philosophy, from Johann Gottfried Herder, the Romantics and Wilhelm von Humboldt to Dilthey and Scheler, the individual subject is in no way a self-sufficient atom or monad. For example, when Herder writes of the person acquiring his or her mother tongue that 'he is not only a child of reason, but a nursling of the reason of others. Into whose hands he falls, decides about his forming',[4] he relativizes not only the universal reason of the Enlightenment but also the self-sufficiency of the individual as a subject of cognition and action. Language was for Herder and his follower Humboldt the true realm of intersubjectivity: it is language that endows the linguistic community with its common, shared view of the world. In addition, all cultural products, such as works of art, regardless of their origin in the creative work of the artist, exist as artefacts bearing an intersubjectively attainable import.

Neo-Kantian philosophy saw itself as a whole as a philosophy of culture, comprising science, morality and the arts; this means that culture in its intersubjective existence was at the focus of interest for the thinkers closest to Bakhtin. Thus the revelation of Bakhtin's German intellectual background does not mean that he was confined to an 'idealistic' concept of subjectivity which excludes the social dimension.

However, there is more to Bakhtin's concepts of the individual subject and intersubjectivity. The philosophies of language and of culture were of major interest for Bakhtin; yet his primary interest was in the individual as an ethically acting subject. In this volume, we suggest that the ethical subject is at the core of Bakhtin's thinking about subjectivity and intersubjectivity.

The Acting Subject

Ethics was of course one of the major fields not only in Kant's system of philosophy, but also in Neo-Kantian thought such as that of Cohen. Bakhtin, however, criticized this ethics for its great level of abstraction: it is unable to grasp the concrete acting individual, making ethical decisions in actual life situations. Bakhtin's earliest writings concern precisely this problematic. We have fragments of his unfinished ethical *magnum opus* in his *Toward a Philosophy of the Act* (1993), written around 1920–24 or possibly somewhat later,[5] and in 'Author and Hero in Aesthetic Activity' (1990), written around 1920–23 or possibly 1920–26. Thus the early aesthetics in 'Author and Hero' was planned as part of a major work on ethics (cf. Bakhtin 1993, 54; Bocharov 1993, xxi–xxiv).

Neither of these early texts is among the favourites of readers and scholars. In scholarly works on Bakhtin they are mostly dealt with in passing, often with seeming reluctance and hesitation. The reason for this is obvious: there appears to be an embarrassing discrepancy between these texts of abstract philosophizing and Bakhtin's later, famous texts on more concrete subjects, such as the novels of Dostoevsky and Rabelais or chronotopic forms in the novel. It is in these early texts that the direct influence of German philosophy is at its strongest (e.g. Brandist 2002, 40). Morson and Emerson, for example, point out the Neo-Kantian influence observable in Bakhtin's early writings, but they see this as something that is totally left behind in the 'mature' Bakhtin, and therefore as relatively insignificant. In their *Mikhail Bakhtin: Creation of a Prosaics* (1990), they discuss 'Author and Hero' and *Toward a Philosophy of the Act* briefly in the introductory chapter alone, since according to their view Bakhtin's early manuscripts from the 1920s do not suggest

> a smooth continuity, but something closer to a decisive break – a watershed – between them and the works for which Bakhtin is currently best known […] If all

that Bakhtin had done was to restate and apply the ideas in these manuscripts, he would not have become the original and profound thinker that he later became. (Morson and Emerson 1990, 7)

Some scholars are, however, of the opposite view. Brandist contends that Bakhtin succeeds in adding something new to the ideas of his German predecessors by applying his ethical philosophy 'to the question of art in general and of authorship in particular' (2002, 40). In his book from 1999 Hirschkop goes still further, claiming that Bakhtin 'abandons his philosophical project [in *Toward a Philosophy of the Act*], but then, in effect, rewrites it, and not once, but over and over again, never really moving on to a new problem' (1999, 54). These views imply that one important perspective from which Bakhtin's later work ought to be seen is his continuous commitment to problems of ethics, as presented in his early ethical project. This is something we develop further in the current volume. We also consider *Toward a Philosophy of the Act* as a key text to understanding his concept of intersubjectivity, and consequently to the derivative concepts of polyphony and dialogism.

Toward a Philosophy of the Act was meant to be the introduction and beginning of the first part of the *magnum opus*, dealing with the 'architectonic of the actual world of the preformed act or deed – the world actually experienced, and not the merely thinkable world' (Bakhtin 1993, 54). The work on aesthetics was to be the second part, while the third and fourth parts were to deal with the ethics of politics and with religion, respectively (Bakhtin 1993, 54; Bocharov 1993, xxi–xxiv). The project as a whole thus comprises different fields of philosophy, organized under the ruling perspective of ethics. This dominant position assigned to ethics is new, compared to Bakhtin's Neo-Kantian and other philosophical sources. What is more, Bakhtin's claim that philosophy has to be re-established as the study of the actual human act is not only new compared to Kant and the Neo-Kantians, but actually transgresses the limits of any philosophy. This is because his idea of a non-abstract philosophy is an obvious *contradictio in adjecto*: can philosophy operate otherwise than in abstract concepts? In Bakhtin's view, this is necessary. He criticizes the philosophy of his day, and Neo-Kantianism in particular, for its endeavour to determine the abstract, general laws of different domains of culture, such as Kant's 'categorical imperative' in the realm of ethics. According to Bakhtin, such a philosophy does not deal at all with what actually should be taken as the subject of the 'first philosophy': the unique ethical act of the individual human subject involved in a concrete event of Being (Bakhtin 1993, 19–20).[6]

By 'real' or 'concrete' human act Bakhtin thus refers to the act of an individual participating in a concrete situation or 'event' (cf. Bakhtin 1990a, 14; Bakhtin 1993, 30–33, 56; Morson and Emerson 1990, 46, 98). An 'event' for Bakhtin consists essentially of an encounter between human beings. As Brandist remarks, the Russian word 'event' (*sobytie*) also means 'co-being', and is for Bakhtin closely connected with the joint experience of two or more subjects (cf. Brandist 2002, 39). An event thus never consists of the encounter of a subject with an object alone; it always comprises the encounter with a co-subject, another person considered as a 'thou'. Being is thus basically intersubjective in its character; in the phrasing of Heidegger, Being (*Sein*) is essentially co-Being (*Mit-sein*) (cf. Heidegger 1979, 117–25). This was a common view in German philosophy from Herder onward. Encountering the other person as another subject has been discussed by thinkers from Herder and Friedrich Schleiermacher, through Hegel, to for example Dilthey, Cohen, Martin Buber and Scheler (cf. Hegel 1986, 244–50; Buber 2006; Scheler 1923), and Bakhtin's debt to these thinkers has been widely acknowledged. Bakhtin's emphasis on the ethical aspect of an encounter with the other is particularly strong: being in the world with other human subjects means for Bakhtin first and foremost that we are obliged to show 'responsibility' or 'answerability' (*otvetstvennost*) towards the others.

Thus the individual human being's thinking in a concrete human situation is 'participative' and 'unindifferent' thinking (Bakhtin 1993, 44), in which cognition contains a moment of 'ought', the obligation to perform an ethically responsible act. The individual 'understands the ought of his performed act, that is, *not* the abstract law of his act, but the actual, concrete ought conditioned by his unique place in the given context of the ongoing event' (Bakhtin 1993, 30; emphasis in the original). The subject in which Bakhtin is primarily interested is thus not the socially (or 'sociologically') determined subject but the individual as an ethically acting subject in a concrete human situation. Ethics presupposes a subject who is autonomous in the sense of being able to make choices: a being who lacks any freedom of choice cannot be the subject of an ethical act. It was Kant who first emphasized this aspect of morality: we have to presuppose a freely acting subject to make morality possible (see Kant 1975, 163). In this sense, and only in this one, are subjects for Bakhtin autonomous. This does not mean that as individuals they are free of any social determination; but insofar as we consider them as ethically acting persons, we have to assign to them the freedom of choice. From his early works onward, however, Bakhtin sees the problem of ethical action as lying in the fact that we do not make ethical decisions *in abstracto* but as part of a concrete event, i.e. in real encounters between two or more individuals.

By grounding his ethics, or his philosophy of the act, on the individual's actions in concrete situations in the real world, Bakhtin wanted to avoid the 'fatal theoreticism (the abstracting from my unique self) [which] occurs in formal ethics as well: its world of practical reason is in reality a theoretical world, and not the world in which an act or deed is actually performed' (Bakhtin 1993, 27). That he failed in his attempt to found a new 'first philosophy' was more or less predictable: how could he possibly formulate a theory about the concrete act without relapsing into 'theoreticism'? However, we suggest that he did not abandon his project but found another way to carry it out: he turned to aesthetics and literary theory, because in the arts (more specifically in literature) he found the closest substitute for the longed-for new 'first philosophy'.

On the basis of 'Author and Hero in Aesthetic Activity', it is evident that what art deals with are for Bakhtin human beings, concrete individuals participating in concrete events. The author's task is to create an aesthetic object that is a 'consummated whole' of the hero and his lived life (cf. Bakhtin 1990a, 12, 13, 25). To him- or herself the individual is formless, among other things because he or she is constantly open to new acts (Bakhtin 1990a, 143); only another person, a creative artist who contemplates the person from a distance, is able to bestow upon him or her a 'consummating' or 'meaning-governed form' (Bakhtin 1990a, 25, 138). While abstract theories and concepts of philosophy and the sciences cannot grasp the concrete, acting individual, art seems to achieve what Bakhtin saw as the task of the 'first philosophy': it preserves the individual in his or her concreteness. More precisely, art is the only medium in which the individual is graspable as a whole. In turning to a theorization of art, particularly the novel, Bakhtin has thus not given up his primary interest in ethics: he does so because the ethically acting concrete individual is most completely presented in the arts.

Certain passages in the rather long and repetitive text of 'Author and Hero' show a clear affinity to the efforts of some post-Kantian philosophers to 'save' the unity of a human being in aesthetic perception. For Kant, the human being belongs simultaneously to two realms: the realm of nature and the realm of morality. As a being belonging to nature man is completely determined; as a moral being he is free. It is generally thought that Kant endeavoured to reconcile these contradictory aspects of the human being in his theory of aesthetic experience: aesthetic experience was meant to bridge the gap between 'theoretical reason', whose realm is nature, and 'practical reason', which concerns morality or ethics (cf. e.g. Gasché 2003). However, as the aesthetic experience for Kant excludes both cognition and morality, it is difficult to understand how this could be achieved. Cohen, in contrast, states in his aesthetic theory that both cognition and morality are included in the content of a work of art:

> A work of art must, *first*, be an object of nature and as such an object of the knowledge of nature. *Furthermore*, an artwork must be, along with the first precondition and in inner connection with it, an object of morality and

conceivable as a *pure* object of ethical knowledge. *Both of these conditions remain inescapable preconditions of a work of art and of artistic creativity*. (Cohen 1912, 80; emphasis in the original)[7]

Thus in the signifying aesthetic form a human being can be grasped both as a natural and as an ethical being. We find the very same idea in 'Author and Hero', where Bakhtin writes that 'the center of value for aesthetic objectivity is the *whole* of the hero and of the event of his lived life, and all values that are ethical and cognitive must be subordinated to that whole', and that '[e]very concrete value in an artistic whole is rendered meaningful in two value-contexts: in the context of a hero (the cognitive-ethical context) and in the encompassing and consummating context of an author (the cognitive-ethical plus the formal-aesthetic context)' (Bakhtin 1990a, 13, 230–31; emphasis in the original). 'Cognitive' is here used following the conceptualization in Kant's *Critique of Pure Reason* (1781), referring to the 'pure theoretical reason' by which we grasp natural phenomena; 'cognitive-ethical' thus means a combination of the worlds of nature and of morality. Bakhtin puts it even more clearly in 'The Problem of Content, Material and Form in Verbal Art': it is art that *'creates the concrete intuitive unity of these two worlds'* (1990b, 279; emphasis in the original), i.e. of human beings as naturally determined *and* as free, ethically acting subjects. The content of a work of art comprises both aspects of life, the natural and the ethical, and they are reconciled in the aesthetic form of a work of art. Thus art is not only the 'first philosophy' but also the 'last' or consummative one, a realm of culture which is able to deal with the 'double nature' of man, who as a natural being is determined but whom we nevertheless consider as an autonomous ethical subject.

This interpretation opens up a view not only on Bakhtin's philosophy of art, including his more specific theorizing on the novel, but also on his understanding of intersubjectivity. If the philosophy of the act, i.e. of real human beings making ethical choices in concrete 'events' or encounters with other human beings, is the perspective applied by Bakhtin in his writing on art and language, the most fundamental concepts will be 'subject' and 'intersubjectivity' as understood in the framework of his ethical thinking. Therefore, dialogism and heteroglossia are phenomena on the level of interpersonal relations – in which the social aspect is included – rather than on that of the general social determination of language. Moreover, in the aesthetic creation of forms the ethical aspect of the content is essential. 'Author and Hero in Aesthetic Activity' is Bakhtin's earliest account of how this creation of the meaningful aesthetic form or 'architectonics' of a work of art takes place; *Problems of Dostoevsky's Poetics* (1963) is another (cf. Steinby 2011).

Bakhtin and His Others

The writers in the present volume share this understanding of Bakhtin's thought. We start with two studies in which Bakhtin's thinking is discussed in comparison with some of his 'significant others'. In Chapter 1, Liisa Steinby, supplementing Tihanov's *The Master and the Slave: Lukács, Bakhtin, and the Ideas of Their Time* (2000), explores the relation between Bakhtin and the early writings of Georg Lukács. The concept of 'signifying form' is clarified through the example of Lukács' *Soul and Forms* (*Die Seele und die Formen*, 1911). Lukács' *The Theory of the Novel* (*Die Theorie des Romans*, 1920), presenting a lonely hero's search for authenticity in a world in which he does not feel at home, is compared to Bakhtin's concept of the hero(es) of the novel. Steinby concludes with a comparison of Lukács' and Bakhtin's accounts of temporality in Dostoevsky's novels. In Chapter 2, twentieth-century scholarship on the 'rise of the modern novel' in early eighteenth-century England is compared to Bakhtin's view of these novels. As Aino Mäkikalli states, it appears that Bakhtin did not observe any such 'rise' taking place; rather, he saw the English novel in the first half of the eighteenth century as a continuation of the adventure novel and of the Baroque novel of the preceding century, and the novel of the mid-eighteenth century, such as *Tom Jones* (1759), as a precursor of the *Bildungsroman*, which he saw as the actual turning point in the history of the eighteenth-century novel.

Chapter 3 focuses on different uses of the term 'polyphony' as a characterization or metaphor for the structure of a novel, aiming primarily at conceptual clarification. Steinby juxtaposes Bakhtin's concept of polyphony with two others, those of Thomas Mann and Milan Kundera; these are based on the Romantic view of the construction of a literary work of art in analogy with a musical composition. The essay, however, also presents what the author considers as Bakhtin's subject-philosophical account of Dostoevsky's polyphony in *Problems of Dostoevsky's Poetics*. In the following two chapters, this subject-philosophical view of polyphony, or dialogism, is applied to poetic works. In Chapter 4, Mikhail Oshukov focuses on the presence of 'otherness' in Ezra Pound's *The Cantos* (1970), which are generally viewed as typically authoritative, 'monologic' speech. The 'other' may here represent another culture, such as the Chinese, or another historical period, such as ancient Greece. Oshukov analyses the rather reductive, and therefore 'un-Bakhtinian', manner in which in *The Cantos* another's speech is incorporated into one's own. In Chapter 5, on the poetry of Peter Reading, Christian Pauls questions the Bakhtinian view that lyrical poetry is monologic in character, a view that has recently been challenged by several scholars arguing that a process of 'novelization' has taken place in modern poetry. Through an analysis of the collection of poems *Ukulele Music* (1985), Pauls shows that lyrical texts can emerge at the end of the spectrum of discourse which Bakhtin considered the realm of the novel: the social, dialogic and unfinalizable world of heteroglossia and polyphony. In Chapter 6, after Oshukov's and Pauls' contributions on poetry, Edward Gieskes discusses the English Renaissance dramatist Thomas Kyd. Bakhtin's concept of dialogue operating across generic boundaries is applied in exploring the interaction in the later sixteenth century between Neo-Latin drama at Oxford and Cambridge and the professional stage in London. Drawing on Bakhtin's theory of genre, Gieskes argues that Kyd's *The Spanish Tragedy* (c. 1590) should be seen as a responsive reaction to Neo-Latin Senecan drama.

In Chapter 7, Steinby discusses Bakhtin's concept of the chronotope. This concept is interpreted in connection with Bakhtin's early philosophy of the act. Starting with an analysis of Bakhtin's essay on the *Bildungsroman* and Goethe's 'chronotopic seeing', the writer argues that the chronotope is not, as traditionally conceived, primarily an epistemological but an ethical category, i.e. it is not about different ways of perceiving temporality and spatiality but rather about different possibilities of human action in a concrete situation. This view of the chronotope is then applied in Chapter 8 on the provincial chronotope in a number of Chekhov's short stories. Here Tintti Klapuri suggests that the Chekhovian provincial chronotope is characterized by vulgarity (*poshlost*), repetition and – on a different level – by narrative predictability. These characteristics are associated with authoritative thought and contribute to the non-autonomous subjectivity that can be seen to regulate the action and thought of female characters in particular.

In this volume, Bakhtin appears not quite as 'sociological' as we may have been accustomed to thinking – and which many view as his great merit (e.g. Bronckart and Bota 2011). However, even if we consider that Bakhtin's interest is focused on the ethically responsible individual, this does not abolish the social dimension, since for him the individual is a concrete being acting in concrete situations, i.e. both determined – as a natural and a social being – and simultaneously free as an autonomous ethical subject who is responsible for his or her actions. After structuralism and poststructuralism, which tended to exclude the individual speaker from the domain of research or even deny the individual any autonomy as speaking subject, we have returned to the (ethical) necessity of acknowledging the autonomy of individuals as speaking and acting subjects. The approach which sees the ethical dimension as the most fundamental one in Bakhtin's work can present him as an author or a precedent of the 'ethical turn' – another 'turn' in the humanities and social sciences after the 'linguistic turn' – which likewise made Bakhtin one of its heroes. What makes Bakhtin particularly interesting is his criticism of 'theoreticism' and his insistence on seeing the problems of ethics as necessarily involved with the real individual's concrete being-in-the-world together with others. Moreover, the fact that Bakhtin explores the ethically acting individual, whom he sees as involved in concrete acts, particularly in various forms of literature, above all the novel, makes his work particularly relevant to scholars of literature.

Hence the 'Others' to whom the title of our volume refers is nothing like the 'Other' produced by a process of 'othering', i.e., constructing the 'Other' as the opposite of 'us'; 'Orientalism', as analysed by Edward Said, is a prototype of this kind of producing the 'Other' (cf. Said 1978). Moreover, Bakhtin's 'Other' is not the 'Other' whom we ethically have to recognize, despite his absolute otherness, as is the case in Emmanuel Levinas' ethics. For Levinas, it is the face of another human being that compels us (or rather: ought to compel) to recognize his or her human dignity and our ethical obligation to him or her, despite his or her being absolutely 'other' than ourselves (cf. Levinas 1991). For Bakhtin, the other person is not primarily the object of our gaze – the gaze necessarily objectifies – but a co-subject: one to whom we listen when he speaks, whom we speak to, whose words we include in our own speech. Thus we do not recognize the other's human dignity and our moral obligation to him or her in an abstract way; we are involved in a real encounter with the other person in terms of his own self-understanding and his understanding of the world, as expressed in his or her own words and acts.

As indicated earlier, there is yet another sense we assign to Bakhtin's 'others' in the title of this volume: it also refers to his 'significant others'. What is at issue here is not the question of the authorship of the works of Voloshinov and Medvedev (we consider the matter settled in favour of these two); nor do we wish to take a stand on the more difficult question of who in the 'Bakhtin Circle' was primarily influenced by whom. Our reference point here is the German background of Bakhtin's thinking. We explore this issue, not primarily in the interest of proving that Bakhtin was a less original thinker than previously supposed, but to gain a more sustained understanding of what he actually meant. Research on this background is represented in this book by Steinby's contribution on Bakhtin and the early Lukács. In an extended sense, however, Bakhtin's 'significant others' also include those scholars who, representing views different from his, can help to clarify his thinking, and possibly even his omissions. Such a role is played in Chapter 2 by Anglo-American scholarship in the eighteenth-century English novel.

Moreover, we are not concerned that by emphasizing Bakhtin's ethics and deemphasizing his 'sociologism' we will weaken readers' interest in Bakhtin's work, even if it is his allegedly 'sociological' approach to language and literature that has probably received most attention and praise. We consider that in today's world questions of ethics are pertinent, particularly so when involved in complex cultural situations. The question may arise as to whether with the loss of the former 'sociological' and Marxist emphasis Bakhtin will also be stripped of his guise as an implacable 'democrat' in the harsh circumstances of a political dictatorship or oligarchy – an aspect Hirschkop sees a point that 'should be central to any study of Bakhtin's work' (1999, vii). Bronckart and Bota, for example, seem to think that their 'revelation' of the fact that Bakhtin was an Orthodox Christian and a religious thinker (cf. also Coates 1998), as well as a political reactionary and opponent of the revolution, will necessarily make him unacceptable to Western intellectuals (cf. Bronckart and Bota 2011). However, we do not consider that Bakhtin's political or religious convictions bear any direct relevance on the question of his significance in literary and cultural studies. If he emphasizes the importance of encountering the other person as co-subject, and listening to him, as a human being's most important ethical duty – and if this means 'democracy' – it appears to us as immaterial if this thinking has its roots in Marxism or in Orthodox Christianity.

Notes

1. Cf. Shepherd (1998); Hirschkop (1999); Tihanov (2000); Brandist (2002); Freise (1993).
2. Leslie E. Baxter, for example, has developed on this 'Bakhtinian' ground a 'relational dialectics theory' of interpersonal and family communication, whose core theoretical principle is that 'meaning in the moment is not simply the result of isolated, unitary discourses but instead is the result of the interplay of competing discourses' (Baxter 2011, 2). In addition, Bakhtin's dialogic understanding of language has had a considerable impact on the research of second and foreign language learning (cf. Hall et al. 2005; Vitanova 2010).
3. Hirschkop, however, has reversed his view in his monograph on Bakhtin. Here he contends that it is not the idea of intersubjectivity as such but the manner in which Bakhtin applies it in the discussion of different cultural phenomena that is new (Hirschkop 1999, 5).
4. '[…] nicht nur ein Kind der Vernunft, sondern sogar ein Zögling der Vernunft anderer. In welche Hände er fällt, darnach wird er gestaltet' (Herder 1969, 242).
5. Brian Poole (2001) argues, based on both external and internal evidence, for a later dating; see also Brandist (2002, 27–52).
6. The translation here follows the usage familiar to readers of Heidegger in English, with 'Being', referring (approximately) to 'existence', with a capital B, in distinction to 'being', referring to individual beings.
7. 'Das Kunstwerk muß durchaus *erstlich* als Gegenstand der Natur, und als solcher ein Gegenstand der Naturerkenntnis sein. Und das Kunstwerk muß *ferner*, und zwar neben der ersten Bedingung und im innerlichen Zusammenhange mit ihr, ein Gegenstand der Sittlichkeit sein, und als ein *reiner* Gegenstand der sittlichen Erkenntnis erzeugbar werden. *Diese beiden Bedingungen bleiben unverbrüchliche Grundbedingungen der Kunstwerks und des Kunstschaffens.*'

References

Bakhtin, M. M. 1990a. 'Author and Hero in Aesthetic Activity' ('Avtor i geroi v esteticheskoi deiatelnosti'). In *Art and Answerability: Early Philosophical Essays*. Edited by Michael Holquist and Vadim Liapunov, translated by Vadim Liapunov, 4–256. Austin: University of Texas Press.

———. 1990b. 'The Problem of Content, Material, and Form in Verbal Art' ('Problema soderzhaniia, materiala i formy v slovesnom khudozhestvennom tvorchestve'). In *Art and Answerability: Early Philosophical Essays*. Edited by Michael Holquist and Vadim Liapunov, translated by Vadim Liapunov, 257–325. Austin: University of Texas Press.
———. 1993. *Toward a Philosophy of the Act* ('K filosofii postupka'). Edited by Michael Holquist and Vadim Liapunov, translated by Vadim Liapunov. Austin: University of Texas Press.
Baxter, Leslie A. 2011. *Voicing Relationships: A Dialogic Perspective*. Los Angeles et al.: Sage.
Benveniste, Émile. 1966 [1946]. 'Structure des relations de personne dans le verbe'. In *Problèmes de linguistique générale*. Paris: Gallimard.
Bocharov, S. G. 1993. 'Introduction to the Russian Edition'. In M. M. Bakhtin, *Toward a Philosophy of the Act* ('K filosofii postupka'). Edited by Michael Holquist and Vadim Liapunov, translated by Vadim Liapunov, xxi–xxiv. Austin: University of Texas Press.
Brandist, Craig. 2002. *The Bakhtin Circle: Philosophy, Culture and Politics*. London and Sterling, VA: Pluto Press.
Brandist, Craig and Mika Lähteenmäki. 2010. 'Early Soviet Linguistics and Mikhail Bakhtin's Essays on the Novel of the 1930s'. In *Politics and the Theory of Language in the USSR 1917–1938*. Edited by Craig Brandist and Katya Chown, 69–88. London: Anthem Press.
Bronckart, Jean-Paul and Christian Bota. 2011. *Bakhtine démasqué: Histoire d'un menteur, d'une escroquerie et d'un déliré collectif*. Geneve: DROZ.
Buber, Martin. 2006. *Das dialogische Prinzip*. 10th edition. Munich: Güterloher Verlagshaus.
Clark, Katerina and Michael Holquist. 1984. *Mikhail Bakhtin*. Cambridge, MA: Harvard University Press.
Coates, Ruth. 1998. *Christianity in Bakhtin: God and the Exiled Author*. Cambridge: Cambridge University Press.
Cohen, Hermann. 1912. *Ästhetik des reinen Gefühls*, vol. 1. Berlin: Bruno Cassirer.
Emerson, Caryl. 1997. *The First Hundred Years of Mikhail Bakhtin*. Princeton: Princeton University Press.
Freise, Matthias. 1993. *Michail Bachtins philosophische Ästhetik der Literatur*. Frankfurt am Main and New York: Peter Lang.
Gasché, Rodolphe. 2003. *The Idea of Form: Rethinking Kant's Aesthetics*. Stanford: Stanford University Press.
Hall, Joan Kelly et al. (eds). 2005. *Dialogue with Bakhtin on Second and Foreign Language Learning: New Perspectives*. Mahwah: Lawrence Erlbaum Associates.
Hegel, Georg Wilhelm Friedrich. 1986 [1797–98]. *Entwürfe über Religion und Liebe*. In *Werke*, vol. 1, 239–54. Frankfurt am Main: Suhrkamp.
Heidegger, Martin. 1979 [1927]. *Sein und Zeit*. Tübingen: Niemeyer.
Herder, Johann Gottfried. 1969. *Ideen zur Philosophie der Geschichte der Menschheit*. In *Werke in fünf Bände*, vol. 4. Berlin, Weimar: Aufbau.
Hirschkop, Ken. 1985. 'The Social and the Subject in Bakhtin'. *Poetics Today* 6, no. 4: 769–75.
———. 1999. *Mikhail Bakhtin: An Aesthetic for Democracy*. Oxford: Oxford University Press.
Holquist, Michael. 2002 [1990]. *Dialogism: Bakhtin and His World*. London and New York: Routledge.
Kant, Immanuel. 1974 [1781]. *Critique of Pure Reason*. Translated by J. M. D. Meiklejohn. London and New York: Everyman's Library.

Kristeva, Julia. 1980. 'Word, Dialogue and Novel' ('Bakhtine, le mot, le dialogue et le roman', 1967). In *Desire in Language: A Semiotic Approach to Literature and Art.* Edited by Leon S. Roudiez, 64–91. New York: Columbia University Press.

Lachmann, Renate. 1982. 'Der Potebnjasche Bildbegriff als Beitrag zu einer Theorie der ästhetischen Kommunikation. (Zur Vorgeschichte der Bachtinschen "Dialogizität")'. In *Dialogizität.* Edited by Renate Lachmann, 25–50. Munich: Wilhelm Fink.

Levinas, Emmanuel. 1991 [1969]. *Totality and Infinity: An Essay on Exteriority* (*Totalité et infini: essai sur l'exteriorité,* 1961). Dorcrecht: Kluwer Academic Publishers.

Medvedev, P. N. and M. M. Bakhtin. 1978. *The Formal Method in Literary Scholarship: A Critical Introduction to Sociological Poetics* (*Formalnyi metod v literaturovedenii (Kriticheskoe vvedenie v sociologicheskuiu poetiku),* 1928). Translated by Albert J. Wehrle. Baltimore and London: Johns Hopkins University Press.

Morson, Gary Saul and Caryl Emerson. 1990. *Mikhail Bakhtin: Creation of a Prosaics.* Stanford: Stanford University Press.

Poole, Brian. 1998. 'Bakhtin and Cassirer: the Philosophical Origin of Bakhtin's Carnival Messianism'. *The South Atlantic Quarterly* 97, nos. 3–4: 537–79.

———. 2001. 'From Phenomenology to Dialogue: Max Scheler's Phenomenological tradition and Mikhail Bakhtin's development from *Towards a Philosophy of Act* to his study of Dostoevsky'. In *Bakhtin and Cultural Theory.* Edited by Ken Hirschkop and David Shepherd, 109–35. Manchester: Manchester University Press.

Said, Edward. 1978. *Orientalism.* New York: Pantheon Books.

Scheler, Max. 1927 [1913–16]. *Der Formalismus in der Ethik und die materiale Wertethik: Neuer Versuch der Grundlegung eines ethischen Personalismus.* 3rd edition. Halle a. d. S.: Max Niemeyer Verlag.

Scheler, Max. 1923. *Wesen und Formen der Sympathie.* 2nd, extended and revised edition of *Phänomenologie der Sympathiegefühle* (1913). Bonn: Friedrich Cohen.

Shepherd, David (ed.) 1998. *The Contexts of Bakhtin: Philosophy, Authorship, Aesthetics.* Studies in Russian and European Literature, vol. 2. Amsterdam: Harwood Academic Publishers.

Steinby, Liisa. 2011. 'Hermann Cohen and Bakhtin's Early Aesthetics'. *Studies in Eastern European Thought* 3: 227–49.

Tanskanen, Sanna-Kaisa et al. (eds). 2010. *Discourses in Interaction.* Pragmatics and Beyond New Series, vol. 203. Amsterdam and Philadelphia: John Benjamins.

Tihanov, Galin. 2000. *The Master and the Slave: Lukács, Bakhtin, and the Ideas of Their Time.* Oxford: Clarendon Press.

Todorov, Tzvetan. 1984. *Mikhail Bakhtin: The Dialogic Principle* (*Mikhaïl Bakhtine: le principe dialogique,* 1981). Translated by Wlad Godzich. Minneapolis and London: University of Minnesota Press.

Vitanova, Gergana. 2010. *Authoring the Dialogic Self: Gender, Agency and Language Practices.* Amsterdam: John Benjamins.

Voloshinov, V. N. 1986. *Marxism and the Philosophy of Language* (*Marksizm i filosofiia iazyka,* 1929). Cambridge, MA: Harvard University Press.

Zbinden, Karine. 2006. *Bakhtin between East and West: Cross-Cultural Transmission.* London: Legenda.

Chapter 1

BAKHTIN AND LUKÁCS: SUBJECTIVITY, SIGNIFYING FORM AND TEMPORALITY IN THE NOVEL

Liisa Steinby

Introduction: Bakhtin and Lukács

New research on the German and Russian background of Bakhtin's thinking, and the new perspectives and understanding thus opened up, invite an interest in contributing to this understanding by clarifying some new connection or aspect. Since Bakhtin apparently combined quite freely ideas from a great number of different authors[1] – and notoriously even borrowed directly from their works without indicating the source (e.g. Poole 1998) – it is obvious that a great deal of work remains to be done in this area. My purpose in this chapter is to elucidate one of those connections, namely Bakhtin's debt to the young Georg Lukács, the Hungarian aesthetician and literary scholar. Lukács, who wrote in German, began as a Neo-Kantian and Hegelian, but in the 1930s became immensely influential as a Marxist literary theorist.

The basic study of Bakhtin's relation to Lukács, and of the common intellectual background they shared, is Galin Tihanov's *The Master and the Slave: Lukács, Bakhtin, and the Ideas of Their Time* (2000). Until the publication of Tihanov's work, the connection between Lukács and Bakhtin passed unnoticed in the Bakhtin boom that has been ongoing since the 1970s. There is a natural reason for this: in none of his published writings does Bakhtin ever mention Lukács. Tihanov, however, noticed a reference to Lukács in Bakhtin's unpublished doctoral dissertation (Tihanov 2000, 295). The fact that Bakhtin intended to translate Lukács' *The Theory of the Novel* (*Die Theorie des Romans*, 1920) into Russian, before he found out that the Marxist Lukács himself disapproved of this early work (Clark and Holquist 1984, 99), makes

Lukács' apparent non-presence in Bakhtin's writings even more conspicuous. Tihanov ambitiously investigates these two theoreticians of literature and culture, comparing them not only with each other but also with their common background in German cultural philosophy, aesthetics and literary theory in the nineteenth and early twentieth century.

Tihanov suggests that Bakhtin, in his most original contribution to the theory of the novel, actually takes a stand in the 1930s discussion of the novel and of literary realism, in which the Marxist Lukács played a major role (cf. Tihanov 2000, 140). I argue, however, that there exists an important earlier connection between Bakhtin and the young Lukács that is in need of further clarification, especially with regard to the latter's seminal *The Theory of the Novel*. That Bakhtin never refers to *The Theory of the Novel* in his published writings might be because this idealist (Neo-Kantian–Hegelian) work of the young Lukács would have been an undesirable source for a writer in the Stalinist period. This, however, does not mean that the work ceased to influence Bakhtin's thinking – just as the Marxist Lukács never stopped employing German idealist aesthetics as the basis of his own theory of art. Moreover, we will see that through the young Lukács – though obviously not only through him – Bakhtin's roots reach further back, to Hegelian and Early Romantic thinking about the novel.

Subject and Signifying Form: The Early Bakhtin and the Early Lukács

In 'Author and Hero in Aesthetic Activity', Bakhtin shows how the 'consummating' and 'meaning-governed' form (Bakhtin 1990b, 25, 138) is given to the hero in an act of contemplation and aesthetic creativity by the author. In *Toward a Philosophy of the Act*, he defines this unity-creating aesthetic activity as follows:

> The unity of the world in aesthetic seeing is not a unity of meaning or sense – not a systematic unity, but a unity that is concretely architectonic: the world is arranged around a concrete value-center, which is seen and loved and thought. What constitutes this center is the human being: everything in this world acquires significance, meaning, and value only in correlation with man – as that which is human. (Bakhtin 1993, 61)

The hero and his life deliver the content for the work of art, to which the author gives a form; this form is not a synthesis of meaning or a systematic account of the content, but an 'architectonic' form, organizing the content and thus bearing significance but preserving the genuine concreteness of the individual's experiences (Bakhtin 1993, 61). 'Architectonic form' is thus equivalent for Bakhtin to the consummating, 'meaning-governed' or signifying aesthetic form. He contrasts this with the 'compositional form', referring to the mere technical arrangement of the material (cf. Bakhtin 1990a, 303–4).

The idea of signifying form, one which arises from the content and is not mechanically imposed on it, played a major role in aesthetic thinking in the German tradition since Romanticism. It is obviously an essential element of the young Bakhtin's aesthetics as well, and I would argue that in different, even radical modifications it continues to play an important role in his thinking down to his last writings, such as the essay on speech genres. I therefore suggest that this concept be taken as one of the focal points in analysing Bakhtin's relation to his German background and especially to Lukács. This can be understood as a continuation and narrowing down of what Tihanov perceives as the most important themes which Lukács and Bakhtin share with their German predecessors: the concepts of culture, form and genre (Tihanov 2000, 21–61). All three concepts are both very common and very broad; what is needed is a more specific scrutiny as to how they were used in the German context of the late nineteenth and early twentieth century, before they can be applied in elucidating Lukács' and Bakhtin's thinking. This requirement is not easily accomplished, as the concepts of culture, form and genre are seldom clearly defined and are used in a number of different ways. The concepts of subject, which we consider here primarily in the context of the novel, and of signifying form, may initially not appear much clearer; but I believe that we can clarify them considerably through a contrastive analysis of some of Lukács' and Bakhtin's writings.

The idea that culture is a creation of signifying forms is a tenet in Neo-Kantianism, but it is also important in Hegelianism and the 'philosophy of life'; actually, it is a common philosophical idea at the turn of the century, but we find its roots already in the philosophy of art of Herder, Schiller and Hegel. The form, often conceived as 'inner form', in contrast to any technical devices, is the perceivable *Gestalt* through which the content of the work of art is mediated.[2] In Lukács' *Soul and Forms* (*Die Seele und die Formen*, 1911), the perspective from which a number of authors and thinkers are described is the particular form they give to their experience of living. The form of an experience thus is something that interprets the content of the experience as a whole and determines its significance, while letting the experience retain its concreteness – in contrast to a conceptual definition, which is inevitably abstract. As the signifying form of an individual's life, this concept comes close to Bakhtin's 'consummating' form.

Lukács' essays in *Soul and Forms* suggest that an individual creates signifying forms both in life and in art. For instance, Lukács describes how Kierkegaard, after abandoning his fiancée, purposefully and self-sacrificingly represents himself publicly in 'Diary of a Seducer' (1843) as an unscrupulous libertine, in order to save his fiancée's reputation and let her make a new life as the wife of another man. In this case, the 'form' is the public image that a person creates of himself by means of a literary work. In another essay, Lukács represents the life of Novalis as a realization of the Romantic philosophy of life. These cases might very well illuminate Bakhtin's idea of organizing experience using a person as a 'value centre' – except that here Lukács is speaking of the lives of real people, not of life as represented in a literary work of art. But Lukács also explores how the tragic view of life and the ethics of the tragical are realized in the form of Theodor Storm's short stories. In each case, form is created by viewing and interpreting a person's acts and experiences in terms of a value or an idea, presenting these lived materials as a signifying whole. Since for the young Lukács the state of modern man is tragic, he particularly describes various cases in which life is given a tragic form, both in life and in literature.

For Lukács, then, form is anything but a purely external ordering imposed on a certain content or, in the case of literature, a product of the technical application of a set of devices. Form is in no way an extraneous ingredient added to the content, but is the very essence of content; it is the (quasi-)perceivable overall meaning of the experiences. This concept of form persists throughout Lukács' work. In the Neo-Kantian *Soul and Forms*, an indefinite number of subjectively created forms of experience are supposed to exist, which do not combine to make an overall picture of the world:

> How colourful is the world and how rich in its colourfulness and how strong and rich are we, to whom it is given to become aware of this all. And the forms that are born out of this feeling do not produce a great order, but a great variety: not the great connection of the whole, but a great variety in each of its corners. (Lukács 1911, 308)[3]

This emphasis on the variety of subjective forms of experience and the lack of coherence resembles Bakhtin's presentation of Dostoevsky's 'polyphonic' novel. However, in Lukács' *The Theory of the Novel* only a few years later, this plurality of various subjective truths or views of an experience has been replaced by the search for a meaningful order of existence as a whole, of 'totality' in the Romantic and Hegelian sense of the word.

Bakhtin shares Lukács' concept of form as presented in *Soul and Forms*: the form is a form of human experience which, being meaningful, interprets the content of the experience without removing anything of its concreteness. Lukács is of course not Bakhtin's only source for this conception of form, and it is not only Hegel who in his aesthetics understands artistic form in this manner (e.g. Hegel 1975a, 52; Hegel 1975b, 13, 64); the Neo-Kantians, along with the 'philosophers of life' such as Nietzsche, regarded man essentially as a creator of signifying forms for his experiences.[4] When Bakhtin criticizes the Russian Formalists' understanding of form, he does not intend to disregard the concept of form as a whole but merely a particular understanding of it.

In the essay 'The Problem of Content, Material, and Form in Verbal Art', written during 1923–24, Bakhtin attacks the Formalist notion of the form of a work of art, as created by applying certain technical devices (*priemy*) to the linguistic material. For this Bakhtin uses the term 'compositional form' (e.g. Bakhtin 1990a, 269–70, 303–4). According to Bakhtin, understanding a literary work of art simply as an organization of linguistic materials cannot explain either its aesthetic or its ethical significance (1990a, 261ff.); he states categorically that linguistics cannot grasp the specificity of art (1990a, 294). Rather, the aesthetic form of a literary work of art is to be understood as the form of the concrete human content of the work, i.e. of the persons represented and their actions along with all their cognitive and ethical dimensions.

> The reality of cognition and ethical action that enters (as an already identified and evaluated reality) into the aesthetic object and is subjected there to concrete, intuitive unification, individuation, concretization, isolation, and consummation, i.e., to a process of comprehensive artistic forming by means of a particular material – *this reality we call* (in complete agreement with traditional word usage) *the content of a work of art* (or to be exact – *of the aesthetic object*) [...] *Content* is an indispensable constitutive moment in the aesthetic object, and artistic form is correlative to it; *outside this correlation, artistic form has no meaning at all*. (Bakhtin 1990a, 281; emphasis in the original)

Bakhtin – no doubt quite rightly – finds the reason for the Formalists' misunderstanding in their endeavour to establish a new kind of literary study on a totally scientific basis (1990a, 259): the traditional speculative aesthetics is rejected by the formalists as non-scientific, in favour of an empirical approach which deals only with the perceivable (linguistic) traits of the text. Consequently, aesthetic form, as Klaus Städke (2001, 487) remarks, cannot be anything but a mere configuration of linguistic materials, without any representative or expressive function.[5]

In *Soul and Forms*, form is created by an individual, who can give form either to his or her own life, as do Kierkegaard and Novalis, or to a work of art. Where in *Toward a Philosophy of the Act* cultural forms, which are general, and the lived life in its concreteness, are presented as irreconcilable (e.g. Bakhtin 1993, 2, 30), in 'The Problem of Content, Material, and Form in Verbal Art' and in 'Author and Hero in Aesthetic Activity' content and form, which is now understood as inner or 'consummating' form, can be in harmony. In 'Author and Hero', the author is able to create a signifying form of a person, his world and his story, by contemplating the hero and his life from an aesthetic distance. Bakhtin argues extensively why it is impossible for a character to create an encompassing form for him- or herself: he or she, being part of the world, is constantly involved in making decisions and performing actions, each of which changes what he or she actually 'is'. Only someone contemplating his or her life from an aesthetic distance is able to bestow upon him or her a 'finalized' or 'consummated' form (Bakhtin 1990b). This form shows what a person actually is; in other words, in an artistic creation, the complex phenomenon of a human being and his or her life are given a signifying form.

Likewise in 'The Problem of Content, Material, and Form in Verbal Art' the author is the subject who, out of the content, creates the signifying form of a work of art. Secondarily, the same activity also characterizes the recipient – viewer, reader, listener – of a work of art:

> In form I *find myself*, find my own productive, axiologically form-giving, activity; *I feel intensely my own movement that is creating the object*, and I do so not only in primary creation, not only during my own performance, but also during the contemplation of a work of art. *I must to some extent experience myself as the creator of form, in order to actualize the artistically valid form as such.* (Bakhtin 1990a, 304; emphasis in the original)

That Bakhtin came both in 'Author and Hero' and in 'The Problem of Content, Material, and Form in Verbal Art' to separate action in life or ethical action from artistic activity may be a consequence of the influence of Hermann Cohen's aesthetics, which Bakhtin in several respects follows closely in his discussion of aesthetic creation in 'Author and Hero' (cf. Cohen 1912; Steinby 2011). However, even though Bakhtin questions the individual's capability of creating a signifying form of him- or herself and his or her life, this does not in any way alter his Lukácsian concept of signifying form in art. On the contrary: when Bakhtin in his later ('mature') works turns from ethics and aesthetics to the theory of the novel – where he continues to apply both his ethical and his aesthetic views – the problem of signifying forms becomes relevant in a new manner.

From the German Early Romantics through Hegel to Lukács, the question of how an individual is able to grasp existence in its totality as meaningful is considered to be the main problem of the novel. This problem is closely related to that of signifying form, because search for totality can be understood as the individual's effort to create a signifying form that comprises not only their own life, but – even if symbolically – existence as a whole. This line of thought can be followed clearly down to Lukács' *The Theory of the Novel*. In a sense, this line continues up to Bakhtin's theory of the novel in *Problem of Dostoevsky's Poetics* and beyond.

From the Quest for Totality to a Polyphony of Voices: Hegel, Lukács, Bakhtin

Where in Bakhtin's theory of art (later, the novel) the ethical aspect of a person's being-in-the-world is at the focus of interest, in German theories of the novel it is the cognitive or epistemological aspect that prevails. In fact, it becomes the crucial question in understanding the genre of novel compared to its predecessor in antiquity, the (heroic) epic. For the German Early Romantics, the theory of the novel begins with the contrast between the heroic epic as the epitome of ancient poetry and the novel as the most important modern genre. Where the epic presents the world as it is objectively given for the whole of the community, the novel, which is the most modern and most Romantic of literary genres, is the most subjective, expressing the world view of the creative subject, the poet; but by the same token it is the most inclusive, striving to grasp existence in its entirety, or the Absolute.[6] For Friedrich Schlegel, the novel is 'progressive universal poetry' (*progressive Universalpoesie*; Schlegel 1988a, 114); in other words, the novel's struggle to comprise the totality of existence is a never-ending project.

Hegel and Lukács share with the Romantics the view that the fundamental difference between the (heroic) epic and the novel is the presence or absence respectively of a common, collective understanding of the world; or, as they thought of it, of the meaningful totality of existence. Hegel's aesthetics can be regarded as a continuation, and by the same token a refutation, of the Romantic view of art as the highest form of attaining the totality of being, the Absolute. The function of art, which is to represent the Absolute symbolically in perceivable form, becomes in Modernity more and more difficult to fulfil. This is because the content, which in a work of art has to be expressed in perceivable form (or *Gestalt*), has become too complex. Modern or Romantic art, in its quintessential form, the novel, has already reached the point beyond which the complexity of the modern world can no longer be captured in the signifying form or *Gestalt* of a work of art (Hegel 1975a, 100, 109, 111).

Hegel's viewpoint on the novel is that of a philosopher of history, who sees in the novel a reflection of developments in world history in the era of Modernity. Just like the Romantics, he contrasts the epic with the novel. The epic hero actually represents the totality of the archaic world, incorporating in his deeds the collective world view and moral code of the 'heroic era' (*heroischer Weltzustand*; Hegel 1975b, 236–52). In contrast, the novel is the art form of a 'prosaic era' (*prosaischer Weltzustand*), in which the individual with his or her (for Hegel, it is a he) subjective ideas is opposed to the objective realities of the world (cf. Hegel 1975b, 239–41). The world does not appear as the individual's own, but as a foreign world of senseless accidentality (Hegel 1975c, 140, 198, 211). According to Hegel, the impression of accidentality and disconnectedness stems from the individual's incapacity to conceive of matters in any but a subjectively restricted manner. He is unable to grasp the complexity of the world in its entirety or to recognize the reasonableness of the objective order of things. Hegel's attitude towards the novel is very ironic indeed: that the world appears non-reasonable to the hero ensues from the subjective restrictions in his thinking. What for the hero of a novel appears unattainable, namely the comprehension of the totality of existence, can in Modernity be attained, according to Hegel, by abstract, philosophical thinking.

In his *The Theory of the Novel*, Lukács follows Hegel, except that he does not share Hegel's ironical attitude towards the hero of the novel. Lukács sees the state of modern man as deplorable because the world has become undecipherable to him. Where for the individual of the 'epic era' nothing in the world remained essentially foreign, and the world as a whole appeared to him or her as meaningful and intimately familiar, as 'home' (Lukács 1963, 22), modern man is characterized by a 'transcendental homelessness' (*transzendentale Obdachlosigkeit*; Lukács 1963, 35). The totality, or the meaningfulness of the world as a whole, is lost to the individual, and therefore he or she is in an incessant search for it, even if this totality will never be achieved. According to Lukács, the search for a lost totality is the historical *a priori* of the genre of the novel (1963, 50, 53). Lukács' position here resembles that of the Romantics (and he duly quotes Novalis in this connection; 1963, 22) but he differs from their view in his tragic sense of modern man. In the 1962 preface to *The Theory of the Novel*, Lukács ascribes his despair back then to writing the book in the atmosphere of the catastrophe of World War I.

Lukács describes with sympathetic understanding the efforts of the lonely heroes of novels to decipher their experience in order to grasp the totality of existence. Compared to the unlimited creation of forms for one's life and personality in *Soul and Forms*, in *The Theory of the Novel* the forms given in novels to the hero's attempts to grasp the totality of the world are astonishingly few. Yet there is a line of development in the way in which the protagonist's search is depicted in the modern novel. Lukács draws a trajectory using three points only: Cervantes' *Don Quixote* (1605–15), Goethe's *Wilhelm Meister's Apprenticeship* (1795–96), and Flaubert's *Sentimental Education* (1869). These represent three different forms of the novel respectively: the novel of abstract idealism, the novel of education, and the novel of disillusionment. According to Lukács, Cervantes' hero adheres to the abstract idea of chivalry, which is revealed to be an inadequate guide for encountering the world; as Lukács puts it, the hero's 'soul' is 'narrower' than reality. In *Wilhelm Meister's Apprenticeship*, an equilibrium between the 'soul' and the 'world' is ultimately attained, albeit through a difficult process and partly through artificial constructions designed by the author alone. In the third phase, however, in Flaubert's novel of disillusionment, the hero's 'soul' (his ideas about human possibilities and his own) is 'broader' than the world he experiences, and he ends up with a painful loss of illusions without any positive equilibrium. Thus the various historical forms of the modern novel stem from different attempts to overcome the separation of 'soul' and 'world', the subjective and the objective, the individual and the reality.

Bakhtin shares with the Romantics, Hegel and Lukács the view of the fundamental difference between the epic and the novel, as well as the view of the protagonist of a novel as an autonomous individual. However, he understands the position of the hero in the process of creating signifying forms differently from his predecessors, and in the early 'Author and Hero in Aesthetic Activity' he sees it in a different way than in the first version of the Dostoevsky book (*Problems of Dostoevsky's Art*) from 1929 and his other writings following it. While according to Hegel, and to Lukács in *The Theory of the Novel*, the hero of the novel searches for the meaningful totality of existence but fails, in 'Author and Hero', the hero, an autonomous cognitive and ethical subject in his world, is the 'content' of the work of art, but the 'consummating' or 'meaning-governed' form (his character and life as a whole) is given to him by the author. Thus the cognitive and ethical subject and the subject who gives the former subject and its experiences a meaningful form are separate persons. In contrast, in *Problems of Dostoevsky's Art* the interpretative and form-giving activity is located completely in the characters, and this activity now appears as one aspect of a character's encountering of the world: at issue is no longer the form of one's person and life but rather one's view on the matter at hand, ultimately his or her worldview. For Bakhtin (or rather for Dostoevsky in Bakhtin's account), each person has a 'word' (discourse) or a 'voice' of his or her own, in which they express their view. Bakhtin speaks of Dostoevsky's 'profound personalism': 'Dostoevsky neither knows, nor perceives, nor represents the "idea in itself" in the Platonic sense, nor "ideal existence" as phenomenologists understand it. For Dostoevsky there are no ideas, no thoughts, no positions which belong to no one, which exist "in themselves"' (Bakhtin 1989, 31). In other words, the signifying forms assigned to matters and to the world as a whole cannot be detached from the concrete person to whom they belong. The encounter between the characters is then always an encounter between different views – not in a theoretical dispute but in concrete, ethically laden situations of life. 'Every thought of Dostoevsky's heroes' is, according to Bakhtin, 'a rejoinder in an unfinalized dialogue'; 'It is oriented toward an event in its own special way and is inseparable from a person' (Bakhtin 1989, 32).

Bakhtin follows the Romantics in believing that the novel, in contrast to epic or actually any other literary genre, is a 'genre-in-the-making' and 'one in the vanguard of all modern literary development' (Bakhtin 2008b, 11).[7] The difference between the views of Bakhtin and the Romantics lies in their understanding of the 'non-finality' of the form of the novel. For the Romantics, the creative subject (i.e. the author) never actually attains totality, even though this is 'progressively' approached. Bakhtin, in contrast, conceives the novel as an unending encounter of individuals who do bear different views of the world, however 'unfinalized' these might be, involved in concrete events in which they participate as ethically responsible subjects. Rather than unending 'progress', Bakhtin's 'polyphonic' novel thus presents a plurality of voices or different points of view. This plurality of voices does not display merely a 'colourful' and 'rich' variety of forms which 'do not produce a great order', as Lukács describes the variety of human creations of signifying forms in *Soul and Forms*; 'polyphony' arises from persons with different world views encountering each other in the concrete events of life.

In a sense, Bakhtin's view is more modern than that of Lukács in *The Theory of the Novel*: where the latter mourns the 'homelessness' of the individual caused by the lack of a common, comprehensive view of the world, Bakhtin values the process whereby human beings in open dialogue try to understand each others' viewpoints and submit their own viewpoint to the challenge presented by the encounter with others. Certainly, even here everyone is in search of *the* truth; yet no common consent as to the nature of that truth is attained, and each individual has to act according to his or her own truth and is therefore regarded as an autonomous ethical subject.

Most probably one of the reasons for Lukács' and Bakhtin's opposing stances derives from the different political connotations they associate with the term 'totality'. For Bakhtin, the word has come to mean a petrified cultural hierarchy attached to a hegemonic or even totalitarian power structure. It is precisely against this kind of culture that Bakhtin mobilizes the novel, which now means for him a kind of rebellious counter-culture. He locates the prehistory of the novel in the tradition of the Greek Menippea and other forms of satire as well as in the carnivalistic folk culture of the Middle Ages and the Renaissance; hence, parody, satire and laughter are for him essential constituents of the novel (cf. Bakhtin 1968; 1989; 2008a; 2008b). Bakhtin's view of the novel as the epitome of a carnivalistic and satiric counter-culture is in direct opposition to Lukács' tragic view of the novel.

We can see that Bakhtin's definition of the novel takes place in the framework of the understanding of the novel established by the German Early Romantics and continued by Hegel and Lukács, anchored in a philosophy of the subject; with the difference that in the polyphonic, polysubjective or dialogic novel, the single subject is replaced by a number of autonomous subjects engaged in action and mutual dialogue. We can even say that Bakhtin's contribution means a turn from subject philosophy to the philosophy of intersubjectivity. This turn, however, is also, if not anticipated, nevertheless so to speak opened up by Lukács in his *The Theory of the Novel*: some of the ideas introduced here may have induced Bakhtin to seek in Dostoevsky a way out from the cul-de-sac of the novel of a single subject.

Lukács concludes *The Theory of the Novel* by asking whether Tolstoy or Dostoevsky in their works might possibly have initiated a new phase in the history of the novel, or whether on the contrary they transgressed the limits of the novel by regaining something of the unity and totality typical for the epic. The question as such shows that Lukács saw modern authors as seeking a way out of the novel, because the individual's inability to grasp the world as a meaningful whole made the genre as such problematic. Lukács then describes Tolstoy as striving to find a way back from the individualism of the novel to the collectivism of the epic by returning to the natural order of things. Tolstoy's means of doing so, however, is to oppose nature to culture, which according to Lukács is an opposition not recognized by the ancient epic (Lukács 1963, 150). Thus an epic unity of the modern world cannot be regained by this means.

The Theory of the Novel ends with the claim that Dostoevsky has created something that does not describe the lonely struggle of a hero and that therefore is no longer a novel. The question of what this new kind of writing is, Lukács (1963, 158) leaves open to be answered by later research.[8] It is of course tempting to wonder whether this ending, suggesting nothing less than that a new era in the history of the novel might have begun with Dostoevsky, or a completely new genre arisen, was the source of inspiration for Bakhtin in his study of Dostoevsky's novels (cf. Freise 1993, 59; Pechey 1998, 175).

Bakhtin's answer to Lukács' question, as to whether Dostoevsky's work marks a turning point in the history of the novel by providing a new way of dealing with subjectivity, is in the affirmative. The Dostoevskyan novel represents a subject-philosophical turn from the lonely 'I': not back to the collective 'us' of epic, but to the necessity of genuine encounter with other subjects, just as autonomous and individual as oneself. In the polyphonic novel, co-subjectivity is assigned to other persons outside oneself:

> *A plurality of independent and unmerged voices and consciousnesses, a genuine polyphony of fully valid voices is in fact the chief characteristic of Dostoevsky's novels.* What unfolds in his works is not a multitude of characters and fates in a single objective world, illuminated by a single authorial consciousness; rather *a plurality of consciousnesses,*

with equal rights and each with its own world, combine but are not merged in the unity of the event. (Bakhtin 1989, 6; emphasis in the original)

Compared to any possible attempt to regain epic unity by means of a new collectivism, Dostoevsky's polysubjective novel (which is what Bakhtin's 'polyphonic novel' actually means; see Chapter 3) is definitely a modern genre. It identifies the existence of modern men and women as a state of being responsible for one's worldview and acts based on it, even though one is aware of the fact that there are other positions and views and we have to act without having reached the 'final' truth about matters.

Subjectivity and Temporality in the Novel

Bakhtin's distinction between the monologic and the polyphonic novel – as discussed later in Chapter 3 – is based on the different positions of the subjects in them. Later Bakhtin endows chronotopes with the function of distinguishing between different subgenres of the novel; and in Chapter 7 I endeavour to show that the acting subject is an essential aspect of Bakhtin's concept of chronotope as well. Before introducing the concept of the chronotope in 'The *Bildungsroman* and Its Significance in the History of Realism (Toward a Historical Typology of the Novel)', Bakhtin discusses the temporality in the novel in the context of Dostoevsky's novels, and it is here that an affinity to Lukács' thoughts in *The Theory of the Novel* is clearly discernable.

In *The Theory of the Novel*, Lukács considers temporality to be an essential constitutive element of the novel. Time becomes essential in a narrative when the events no longer express a totality which gives them their meaning; or, as Lukács puts it, 'when the attachment to the transcendental home no longer exists' (1963, 125). We can rephrase this as follows: while in the epic the meaning of any event is given 'vertically', by its being a part of the metaphysical world order, in the novel it is determined 'horizontally', in the continuum of successive acts and events and their interpretations (cf. Saariluoma 1982, 70). In the novel, the essential and the temporal thus fall apart (Lukács 1963, 125ff.). Life is reality experienced at certain moments of time, and the individual cannot tell the definitive meanings of his or her experiences. Remembering the past and anticipating the future are means of overcoming the ephemeral in temporal experience, and they thus create the basis for one's efforts to interpret one's experiences (Lukács 1963, 126ff.).

Lukács analyses the different temporal structures occurring in the novels of Cervantes, Goethe, Flaubert and Tolstoy. For him, it is Dostoevsky alone who does not fit the frame of temporal orientation (1963, 157–8).

Lukács regards this as an indication that Dostoevsky's works are no longer novels – which may be the reason why he does not discuss them in *The Theory of the Novel*. It remains for Bakhtin to describe the temporal structure in Dostoevsky's polysubjective novels.

Bakhtin agrees with Lukács that Dostoevsky 'saw and conceived his world primarily in terms of space, not time'. He 'strives to organize all available meaningful material, all material of reality, in one time-frame, in the form of a dramatic juxtaposition, and he strives to develop it extensively' (Bakhtin 1989, 28). In this respect Dostoevsky is the opposite of Goethe, whose *Wilhelm Meister's Apprenticeship* Bakhtin, like Hegel and Lukács, adopts as a paradigm of the modern novel. In the *Bildungsroman*, things – both the hero and the world around him – develop in time (Bakhtin 1989, 28; 2007). However, the condition of modern man, according to Bakhtin, is no less adequately rendered in Dostoevsky's novels:

> In contrast to Goethe, Dostoevsky attempted to perceive the very stages themselves in their *simultaneity*, to *juxtapose* and *counterpose* them dramatically, and not stretch them out into an evolving sequence. For him, to get one's bearings on the world meant to conceive all its contents as simultaneous, and *to guess at their interrelationships in the cross-section of a single moment*. (Bakhtin 1989, 28; emphasis in the original)

By concentrating different elements in a single moment of time, Dostoevsky in a sense achieves a 'triumph over time': what is essential and significant is contained in a single moment of time. Consequently, Dostoevsky's characters have no biography, representing the whole of their lives; moreover, 'there is no causality in Dostoevsky's novels, no genesis, no explanations based on the past, on the influences of the environment or of upbringing, and so forth'. The lack of causal or genetic explanations foregrounds the characters' ethical responsibility. 'Every act a character commits is in the present, and in this sense is not predetermined; it is conceived of and represented by the author as free' (Bakhtin 1989, 29). Thus the temporal structure focuses the reader's attention on the characters' cognitive and ethical autonomy.

In the first version of his study of Dostoevsky, Bakhtin does not yet apply the concept of the chronotope; the essay 'Forms of Time and of the Chronotope in the Novel' was written from 1937 to 1938, between the two versions of the Dostoevsky book (appearing in 1929 and 1963). The concept of the chronotope is applied in chapter four of the 1963 version, dealing with the historical roots of Dostoevsky's novels. The carnivalistic Menippea is here regarded as having essentially 'set the tone for Dostoevsky's entire work' (Bakhtin 1989, 138), and Bakhtin now connects temporality in Dostoevsky's novels with the carnivalistic experience of time. Time in Dostoevsky's novels is defined as a time of crisis, in contrast to the biographical time of being born, growing up, aging and dying (Bakhtin 1989, 169ff.). Dostoevsky 'concentrates actions at *points of crisis, at turning points and catastrophes*, when the inner significance of a moment is equal to a "billion years", that is, when the moment loses its temporal restrictiveness'. Action takes place 'on the *threshold* (in doorways, entrance ways, on staircases, in corridors, and so forth), where the crisis and the turning point occur, or in the *public square*, whose substitute is usually the drawing room (the hall, the dining room), where the catastrophe, the scandal take place' (Bakhtin 1989, 149; emphasis in the original). The threshold, the transition between two states, and the public square, where the carnival takes place, belong to the carnivalistic chronotopes. It is as if a concrete (social) place, such as a public square or a drawing room, brings about a certain kind of action and a time experience connected to it. This concreteness – the combination of certain kinds of actions with certain kinds of time experiences and places – is characteristic of Bakhtin's concept of the chronotope.

Thus enquiring into time and space in the novel is for Bakhtin not enquiring merely about the co-ordinates of events in (physical) space and time, as was typical of classical narratology (cf. Genette 1980). On the contrary: literary chronotopes determine the signifying forms of time and space in connection with human action (see Chapter 7). Literature appears then as a repertoire of such forms, transformed into a common cultural inheritance and made available to all.

We may ask whether anything comparable to Bakhtin's chronotope is found in Lukács' discussion of the temporality of the novel. Lukács asks how novelists tried to solve the problem of the disconnection between experience and meaning. According to him, in Flaubert's *Sentimental Education* reality appears as a sequence of scattered pieces of experience. The protagonist cannot eliminate this disconnectedness of events, hence the irrationality experienced in their succession. Yet beside and beyond this feeling of lacking coherence in one's experiences, a continuous 'current of living' is sensed, which supports the protagonist and lends the whole of the novel a kind of unity, even if it cannot obliterate the incoherence of surface experience (Lukács 1963, 128–9). This 'current of living', of course, indicates Lukács' indebtedness to Bergson (cf. Bergson 1991). These two forms of the individual's temporal experience – the disconnectedness of events and the 'current of living' – do not resemble Bakhtin's chronotopes, which are likewise subjective modes of experience but which refer to human action in specific socio-cultural contexts.

In his analysis of Tolstoy's novels, where he distinguishes between three forms of temporality, Lukács comes closer to Bakhtin's concept of the chronotope (Lukács 1963, 153–5). First, there is the time of social conventions, which means no temporal change at all but a perpetual repetition of the same which has lost its meaning long ago; therefore this form of temporality is experienced as boredom. The second form of temporality consists of the recurrence of the cycles of life, the passing by of seasons and generations; this kind of time is irrevocable, and according to Lukács does not answer any questions concerning the meaning of events. The third is the time of weighty moments, in which the meaning of existence is suddenly revealed to an individual. But the insight vanishes when the moment has passed by, and the third kind of temporality is thus unable to furnish one's temporal experience as a whole with meaning.

In this analysis, Lukács distinguishes between different fields of experience in Tolstoy's novels – social life, natural life, individually experienced meaningful moments – each of which is characterized by a different temporal structure and a different way of creating meaningfulness (or its absence). The similarity to Bakhtin's chronotopes lies in the fact that in defining a chronotope, Bakhtin as well often applies criteria which refer to a certain topic, a realm of life or an attitude toward the world. For example, the chronotope of the idyll is defined first in terms of social space and time: in it life and events are bound to a homely location, and temporally events appear in the frame of the succession of generations, entailing a sense of a cyclically rhythmic nature of time. Bakhtin subdivides this chronotope according to the different spheres of life depicted in the idyll: there are 'the love idyll (whose basic form is the pastoral); the idyll with a focus on agricultural labour; the idyll dealing with craft-work; and the family idyll' (Bakhtin 2008a, 224–5). The chronotope of provincial town, characterized likewise by a cyclical everyday time and a limited locality, comes in some cases close to the idyll, but in the 'Flaubertian type of provincial town chronotope', the recurring of the same has the character of triteness: 'Time here is without event and therefore almost seems to stand still. [...] It is a viscous and sticky time that drags itself slowly through space' (Bakhtin 2008a, 224; see also Chapter 8). These kinds of chronotopes have some affinity with Lukács' idea of the experience of time as determined by social conventions or natural (biological) necessities, although Bakhtin's chronotopes are far more specific and are bound to concrete socio-historical environments.

To conclude: Bakhtin's ideas on the signifying form, on the position of the subject(s) in the novel and on time-space in the novel, when contextualized in the German tradition of the theory of the novel and especially in the thinking of the young Lukács, become not only more easily approachable but also weightier; they now appear as proposals as to how to solve, or at least how to approach, certain crucial problems uncovered by the preceding theory of the novel. Both young Bakhtin's exploration into the relationship of the hero and the author and his later idea of a polyphonic novel appear as approaches to the problem of subjectivity in the novel, which is the focal issue of the theory of the novel from Early German Romanticism onward. In his mature and most original period, Bakhtin's answer is an approach which replaces the hero who alone faces an indecipherable world with a number of equally autonomous cognitive and ethical subjects in a genuine encounter with each other. The chronotope is Bakhtin's answer to the problem of temporality in the novel, a problem developed sketchily in Lukács' *The Theory of the Novel*. Not only the early 'Author and Hero', but also the concepts of polyphony and chronotope present certain forms or 'architectures' of the novel. Here the concept of form is the Neo-Kantian, or Romantic, Hegelian or Lukácsian, concept of signifying form, as opposed to the Russian Formalists' concept of form as a technical device independent of content. The elucidation of Bakhtin's German background prevents the confusion which might follow when similar terms – such as form – are applied in reference to completely different matters.

Notes

1 E.g. Shepherd (1998); Hirschkop (1999); Tihanov (2000); Brandist (2002, 2004, 2006).
2 See Herder (1994); Schiller (1989); Hegel (1975a, 20–21).
3 '[W]ie bunt doch die Welt ist und wie reich in dieser ihrer Buntheit und wie stark und reich wir sind, denen gegeben ist, alles dessen inne zu werden. Und die Formen, die aus diesem Gefühl geboren sind, geben nicht die große Ordnung, sondern die große Vielheit; nicht die große Verknüpfheit des Ganzen, sondern die große Buntheit jedes seiner Winkel.'
4 In *The Birth of Tragedy*, Nietzsche calls such signifying forms created by man 'Apollonian dream images' (*apollinische Traumbilder*, Nietzsche 1999, 23–31).
5 We may add that in narratology as well form is conceived as a linguistic organization of materials, although nothing is said about its aesthetic effect any longer; the narratological project comprises only the description of perceivable structures (cf. Genette 1980).
6 Schlegel (1988a, 1988b, 1988c); Uerlings (1991, 158, 197); cf. also Lacoue-Labarthe (1978). Through the 'poetization' or 'romanticization' performed by a poet, the particular matters of reality appear in a poetic work as symbols which reveal the innermost essence of things and their unity with the Absolute (cf. Novalis 1999).
7 Cf. Schlegel (1988a, 115): 'Andre Dichtarten sind fertig, und können nun vollständig zergliedert werden. Die romantische Dichtart ist noch im Werden; ja das ist ihr eigentliches Wesen, daß sie ewig nur werden, nie vollendet sein kann.' ('Other kinds of poetry are finished and can be completely defined in their parts. Romantic poetry is still becoming; in fact, it is its essential character that it can always be only becoming, never accomplished.')
8 Tihanov (2000, 171ff.) mentions that from 1914 to 1915 Lukács wrote notes for a monograph on Dostoevsky which, however, was never completed.

References

Bakhtin, M. M. 1968. *Rabelais and His World* (*Tvorchestvo Fransua Rable i narodnaia kultura srednevekovia i renessansa*, 1965). Translated by Hélène Iswolsky. Cambridge, MA and London: MIT Press.

———. 1989 [1984]. *Problems of Dostoevsky's Poetics* (*Problemy poetiki Dostoevskogo*, 1963). Edited and translated by Caryl Emerson. Minneapolis: University of Minnesota Press.

———. 1990a. 'The Problem of Content, Material, and Form in Verbal Art' ('Problema soderzhaniia, materiala i formy v slovesnom khudozhestvennom tvorchestve'). In *Art and Answerability: Early Philosophical Essays by M. M. Bakhtin*. Edited by Michael Holquist and Vadim Liapunov, translated by Vadim Liapunov, 257–325. Austin: University of Texas Press.

———. 1990b. 'Author and Hero in Aesthetic Activity' ('Avtor i geroi v esteticheskoi deiatelnosti'). In *Art and Answerability: Early Philosophical Essays by M. M. Bakhtin*. Edited by Michael Holquist and Vadim Liapunov, translated by Vadim Liapunov, 4–256. Austin: University of Texas Press.

———. 1993. *Toward a Philosophy of the Act* ('K filosofii postupka'). Edited by Michael Holquist and Vadim Liapunov, translated by Vadim Liapunov. Austin: University of Texas Press.

———. 2007. 'The *Bildungsroman* and Its Significance in the History of Realism (Toward a Historical Typology of the Novel)' ('Roman vospitaniia i ego znachenie v istorii realizma'). In *Speech Genres and Other Late Essays*. Edited by Caryl Emerson and Michael Holquist, translated by Vern W. McGee, 10–59. Austin: University of Texas Press.

———. 2008a [1981]. 'Forms of Time and of the Chronotope in the Novel: Towards a Historical Poetics' ('Formy vremeni i khronotopa v romane: Ocherki po istoricheskoi poetike'). In *The Dialogic Imagination*. Edited by Michael Holquist, translated by Caryl Emerson and Michael Holquist, 84–258. Austin: University of Texas Press.

———. 2008b [1981]. 'Epic and Novel: Toward a Methodology for the Study of the Novel' ('Epos i roman [O metodologii issledovaniia romana]'). In *The Dialogic Imagination*. Edited by Michael Holquist, translated by Caryl Emerson and Michael Holquist, 3–40. Austin: University of Texas Press.

Bergson, Henri. 1991. *Matter and Memory* (*Matière et mémoire: Essai sur la relation du corps à l'esprit*, 1896). Translated by Nancy Margaret Paul and W. Scott Palmer. New York: Zone Books.

Brandist, Craig. 2002. *The Bakhtin Circle: Philosophy, Culture and Politics*. London and Sterling, VA: Pluto Press.

———. 2004. 'Mikhail Bakhtin and Early Soviet Sociolinguistics'. In *Proceedings of the Eleventh International Bakhtin Conference*. Edited by C. A. Faraco et al., 145–53. Curitiba: Universidade Federale do Paraná.

———. 2006. 'Early Soviet Research Projects and the Development of "Bakhtinian" Ideas: The View From the Archives'. In *Proceedings of the XII International Bakhtin Conference*. Edited by M. Lähteenmäki et al., 144–56. Jyväskylä: University of Jyväskylä, Department of Languages.

Clark, Katerina and Michael Holquist. 1984. *Mikhail Bakhtin*. Cambridge, MA and London: Harvard University Press.

Cohen, Hermann. 1912. *Ästhetik des reinen Gefühls*, 2 vols. Berlin: Bruno Cassirer.

Freise, Matthias. 1993. *Michail Bachtins philosophische Ästhetik der Literatur*. Frankfurt am Main: Peter Lang.

Genette, Gérard. 1980. *Narrative Discourse* ('Discours du récit', 1972). Translated by Jane E. Lewin. Oxford: Basil Blackwell.
Hegel, Georg Wilhelm Friedrich. 1975 [1831]. *Vorlesungen über die Ästhetik*, vols 1–3 [a, b, c]. In *Werke*, vols 13–15. Frankfurt am Main: Suhrkamp.
Herder, Johann Gottfried. 1994 [1778]. 'Plastik'. In *Werke*, vol. 4, 243–326. Frankfurt am Main: Deutscher Klassiker Verlag.
Hirschkop, Ken. 1999. *Mikhail Bakhtin: An Aesthetic for Democracy*. Oxford: Oxford University Press.
Lacoue-Labarthe, Philippe and Jean-Luc Nancy. 1978. *L'absolu littéraire: Théorie de la littérature du romantisme allemand*. Paris: Seuil.
Lukács, Georg. 1911. *Die Seele und die Formen. Essays*. Berlin: Egon Fleischle Co.
———. 1963 [1920]. *Die Theorie des Romans: Ein geschichtsphilosophischer Versuch über die Formen der großen Epik*. Neuwied am Rhein and Berlin-Spandau: Luchterhand.
Nietzsche, Friedrich. 1999 [1872]. *Die Geburt der Tragödie*. In *Sämtliche Werke*, vol. 1. Edited by Giorgio Colli and Mazzino Montinari, 9–156. Munich: Deutscher Taschenbuch Verlag.
Novalis. 1999 [1799]. *Heinrich von Ofterdingen*. In *Schriften*, vol 1. Edited by Paul Richard Samuel, 237–413. Darmstadt: Wissenschaftliche Buchgesellschaft.
Pechey, Graham. 1998. 'Modernity and Chronotopicity in Bakhtin'. In *The Contexts of Bakhtin: Philosophy, Authorship, Aesthetics*. Edited by David Shepherd, 173–82. Amsterdam: Marwood.
Poole, Brian. 1998. 'Bakhtin and Cassirer: The Philosophical Origins of Bakhtin's Carnival Messianism'. *South Atlantic Quarterly* 97, nos. 3–4: 537–78.
Saariluoma [Steinby], Liisa. 1982. 'Aika struktuuritekijänä 1700-luvun saksalaisessa romaanissa: barokin historiallinen hoviromaani, Wielandin *Geschichte des Agathon*, Goethen *Wilhelm Meisters Lehrjahre*'. ['Time as a structural factor in the German eighteenth-century novel: The high Baroque novel, Wieland's *Geschichte des Agathon*, Goethe's *Wilhelm Meisters Lehrjahre*']. In '*Siivilöity aika' ja muita kirjallisuustutkielmia*. Edited by Eino Maironiemi, 60–104. Joensuu: University of Joensuu.
Schiller, Friedrich. 1989 [1795]. *Über die ästhetische Erziehung des Menschen in einer Reihe von Briefen*. Stuttgart: Reclam.
Schlegel, Friedrich. 1988a [1798]. 'Athenäums-Fragmente'. In *Kritische Schriften und Fragmente [1798–1801]*, vol. 2. Edited by Ernst Behler and Hans Eichner, 105–56. Munich, Paderborn, Vienna, Zurich: Schöningh.
———. 1988b [1800]. 'Gespräch über die Poesie'. In *Kritische Schriften und Fragmente [1798–1801]*, vol. 2. Edited by Ernst Behler and Hans Eichner, 186–222. Munich, Paderborn, Vienna, Zurich: Schöningh.
———. 1988c [1797]. 'Kritische Fragmente'. In *Kritische Schriften und Fragmente [1794–1797]*, vol 1. Edited by Ernst Behler and Hans Eichner, 239–50. Munich, Paderborn, Vienna, Zurich: Schöningh.
Shepherd, David (ed.) 1998. *The Contexts of Bakhtin: Philosophy, Authorship, Aesthetics*. Amsterdam: Marwood.
Städke, Klaus. 2001. 'Form'. In *Ästhetische Grundbegriffe*, vol. 2. Edited by Karlheinz Barck et al. Stuttgart and Weimar: Metzler.
Steinby, Liisa. 2011. 'Hermann Cohen and Bakhtin's Early Aesthetics'. *Studies in Eastern European Thought* 3: 227–49.
Tihanov, Galin. 2000. *The Master and the Slave: Lukács, Bakhtin, and the Ideas of Their Time*. Oxford: Clarendon Press.
Uerlings, Herbert. 1991. *Friedrich von Hardenberg, genannt Novalis: Werk und Forschung*. Stuttgart: Metzler.

Chapter 2

BAKHTIN, WATT AND THE EARLY EIGHTEENTH-CENTURY NOVEL

Aino Mäkikalli

In a number of his studies Mikhail Bakhtin pays attention to the history of the novel, identifying various traditions of the genre and naming them so as to create a typology for the novel and define the characteristics of these types.[1] What is palpable in Bakhtin's view of the history of the novel is his firm emphasis on certain authors and phases of the genre. On the one hand he emphasizes Renaissance folklore and the carnival tradition as represented in particular by Rabelais; on the other, his interest lies in the *Bildungsroman*, the late eighteenth-century novel of education. Bakhtin highlights in particular two of Goethe's novels, *Wilhelm Meister's Apprenticeship* (1795–96) and *Wilhelm Meister's Journeyman Years* (1821–29), which represent for Bakhtin a seminal turning point in the history of the novel. In addition, we recognize Bakhtin as a theorist – and devotee of – Dostoevsky's novels, in which he perceived the polyphonic novel in its most possible perfection. Bakhtin seemed to focus specifically on these writers in order to emphasize their position as the crowning literary representatives of their respective historical ages (cf. Brandist 2002, 133). All in all, the novel was for Bakhtin not merely one literary genre among others: it stood for a profound form of thinking that represented the prevalent views and ideas of the historical period in question (Burton 1996, 44).

Although Bakhtin concentrates mainly on novelists of the early modern and modern period, he also explores the ancient novelistic tradition of the Hellenistic period, i.e. the 'prehistory' of the modern novel. Thus, his writings cover the whole history of the novel genre, from its very beginnings to the twentieth century. Yet, it is obvious that he could not explore and write meticulously about every phase of the history of the novel, and there are important periods and phases of the genre which he does not discuss to any great extent.

One of the key turning points in many theories of the novel, English literature in the first part of the eighteenth century, is not foregrounded in Bakhtin's writings. It is interesting to note Bakhtin's inattentiveness, if not pure lack of interest, with regard to the novel of the early eighteenth century. In his writings Bakhtin refers to the novels of this period mainly as examples of something that he does not consider particularly interesting. In this chapter, I pose two questions: how did Bakhtin view the early eighteenth-century English novel, and why do these novels play such a minor part in his writings on the novel genre?

In Anglo-American literary scholarship the early eighteenth century is considered to be a pivotal period of the genre; it is identified with the 'rise of the novel', as used in the title of Ian Watt's influential book from 1957, The *Rise of the Novel*. This has by now become a classic study, which cannot be ignored in any discussion of the central elements of the early modern novel. It is noteworthy that whereas Bakhtin considers for example Charles Dickens as one of the major realistic novelists of the Victorian era, his comments on earlier English novelists, such as Defoe, Richardson, Fielding or Sterne – not to mention even earlier ones, such as Aphra Behn – do not express similar appreciation. We may thus ask: how did Bakhtin actually perceive the novels published in the first half of the eighteenth century? What was their function for him? How do Watt's key arguments as to the development of 'formal realism' and individualism in the early eighteenth-century novel, and the debate following the publication of his book, relate to Bakhtin's main views of the novel genre?

My purpose here is to compare Bakhtin's and Watt's theories of the novel, so as to cast light on the reasons why they differ in so many cases. What motivates this comparison is their mutual background in Lukács' *The Theory of the Novel* (1920), which they were both aware of while working on their own studies. The connections between the two thinkers are illuminated in Galin Tihanov's *The Master and the Slave* (2000) and in Chapter 1 in this volume. With regard to Watt, we also have an interesting essay, originally delivered as a plenary lecture in 1978 and published in 2000, in which Watt gives an account of how elements in *The Rise of the Novel* came into being, mainly through the German intellectual tradition. Watt describes spending several months after the war reading Lukács' *Die Theorie des Romans* and Erich Auerbach's *Mimesis* (1946), and notes that these contributed much more to his book 'than the few references in the text suggest' (Watt 2000, 149–50).

I first take a brief look at Bakhtin's views on the major turning points of the novel genre, followed by a discussion of the position and function in this scheme of the novels of the late seventeenth and early eighteenth century. In the second part of the chapter, I survey Anglo-American criticism concerning the early eighteenth-century novel and the question of the origins of the modern novel. I focus on Watt's pivotal concepts of individualism and formal realism, with a brief discussion of the tenability of his ideas in the light of later criticism. Against this background, in the final part of the chapter I consider the role played by the period between Rabelais and Goethe in Bakhtin's theory of the novel, especially the period commonly referred to as the 'rise of the novel'.

Novelistic Turning Points and the Eighteenth-Century Novel According to Bakhtin

As shown elsewhere in this collection, Bakhtin's intellectual formation was above all in classic German philosophy, especially in Neo-Kantianism, and his views on the novel have their roots in German Romanticism.[2] As Tzvetan Todorov has put it, 'Bakhtin never breaks his ties with the Romantic aesthetic (particularly in his theory of the novel)' (1988, 74). This partly explains Bakhtin's admiration for the novel; for Romantics the novel was the genre of genres, and as a hybrid form it was considered to incorporate a mixture of genres: dialogue, poetry, philosophical meditation, letters. The novel was not only an art form but also a forum for critical reflection. According to Friedrich Schlegel, the theory of the novel had to be included in a novel itself (e.g. Schlegel 1988, 114–15). Another context which should be kept in mind is Bakhtin's position as a scholar working under the totalitarian revolutionary and Stalinist regime. It has been suggested, for instance, that his doctoral study on Rabelais, and the procedures concerning its examination, were influenced by contemporary political circumstances (Holquist 1981, xxv–xxvi; Holquist 1983; Tihanov 2000, 264–5).

It is thus clear that the novel was at the centre of Bakhtin's work on genres, but one of the difficulties in studying and comprehending Bakhtin's views of the novel, particularly those in his essays of the 1930s and 1940s, is their lack of systematic coherence. Simon Dentith suggests that this general problem is the result of a contradiction between historical and ahistorical views: 'the account provided of the novel is at once a substantive historical one, which locates the novel in particular linguistic and cursive situations, and a more abstract, ahistorical account, which sees the novelistic as a universal relativizing principle which battens upon and subverts all discursive authority' (1995, 58). Bakhtin accentuates the historical contexts of the genre, yet according to him the novel emerged as a dominant genre several times in the course of its history; in the Hellenistic period, again during the late Middle Ages and the Renaissance, but most clearly in the end of the eighteenth century. Bakhtin argues that one of the core elements of these periods is a knowledge of the present: the focus of new, creative work is not in past models and traditions but in the present world, in its ideas and possibilities, which give rise to innovative and future-oriented literary forms (Bakhtin 2008b, 5, 38). Furthermore, from the very beginning, the novel 'developed as a genre that had at its core a new way of conceptualizing time' (Bakhtin 2008b, 38). Time is therefore for Bakhtin the very essence of the novel form, and in the course of history the genre has taken on new forms in step with changing conceptions of time. In terms of fiction, such works as Apuleius' *The Golden Ass* (c. 170), Rabelais' *Gargantua* and *Pantagruel* (1532–64) and Goethe's *Wilhelm Meister's Apprenticeship* and Dostoevsky's polyphonic novels constitute a canon in this continuum and turning points in the generic history of the novel.

In the background of Bakhtin's theory of the novel lie differences between the epic and the novel; especially how the two genres, through their form, structure and characters, differ in their representation of time. For Bakhtin, the epic seems to have represented a form similar to the ideas earlier introduced by the young Georg Lukács, who in his *The Theory of the Novel* saw the epic as a form of literature embodying the totality of existence.[3] Bakhtin agrees with Lukács in maintaining the epic to be a manifestation of a static world. In this world the hero represents the whole people rather than his personal self (Lukács 1971, passim, 56–69).[4]

In the antique novel tradition, especially in the case of Apuleius' *The Golden Ass*, the epic began to be transformed into a novelistic form. Yet the temporal aspect remains primarily static; the world's diversity is viewed purely spatially, and the hero is a point moving in space, without essential distinguishing characteristics. The relevant temporal aspect is adventure-time, which allows the hero to move from place to place and from one episode to another without causing any essential change in the character (Bakhtin 2007, 10–11).

In *Rabelais and His World* (1968), the first book by Bakhtin to be translated into English, he notes how the hierarchical picture of the world bequeathed by Aristotle was called into question in the Renaissance (Bakhtin 1968, 362–4). Rabelais' work represents for Bakhtin the maturation of the new sense of being: it is 'the greatest attempt at constructing an image of *man growing* in *national-historical time*', in which the individual is 'on the border between two epochs, at the transition point from one to the other' (Bakhtin 2007, 23–5; emphasis in the original).[5] For Bakhtin, this means a shift in understanding man's existence. Man was not something complete and finished but open and uncompleted: 'he is not only being but becoming' (Bakhtin 1968, 363–4), leading towards a horizontal line of time, from past to future. An essential aspect in this process was a new awareness of the temporal present. The present dimension began to be felt as more connected to the future than to the past. Bakhtin (2007, 40) observes that the cultures of antiquity lacked any real concept of the future;

the reorientation occurred for the first time in the early modern period. In his comprehensive history of the European consciousness of time, *Zeit und Kultur: Geschichte des Zeitbewusstseins in Europa*, Rudolf Wendorff (1980, 152–4, 198) writes of the new possibility of elementary human experience emerging in the Renaissance: the consciousness of being in the world independently of theological constructions. This generated an existential experience of being in the world, of the presence of time, and of a detached relation to the past. This echoes Bakhtin's views: 'It was in the Renaissance that the present first began to feel with great clarity and awareness an incomparably closer proximity and kinship to the future than to the past' (2008b, 40).

The early modern period showed, as illustrated by Rabelais' novels, that the absolute epic distance had now disappeared and the hero had been transferred 'from the distance plane to the zone of contact with the inconclusive events of the present' (2008b, 35). According to Bakhtin, folklore and popular comedy played a significant role in re-structuring the human image in the novel: it was 'laughter [that] destroyed epic distance' (2008b, 35). In the Renaissance the integral social whole begins to break down, and different spheres of life, in relation to which individual identity can be identified, begin gradually to emerge (Brandist 1999, 22–3). For Bakhtin, Rabelais' novels represent the idea of the carnivalesque, the varied life of popular festivals of the period. Laughter expresses an anti-authoritarian attitude to life. According to Bakhtin, Rabelais articulated an aesthetic which celebrates the grotesque, body-based aspects of popular culture, and turned this against the solemnity and humourlessness of official culture (Bakhtin 1968, passim). In very general terms, it can be argued that the element of popular laughter in Rabelais' work also represents a twofold understanding of the novel: it brings forward the popular, folkloric element in the history of the novel genre and, secondly, it conveys the idea of the possibility of action, through the medium of the novel, against the oppression emanating from official power. The novel thus presents its heteroglossic aspect, the conflict between different social forces.

The *Bildungsroman* is an important form of the novel for Bakhtin. As pointed out earlier, in his essays Bakhtin classifies different novelistic forms in a way which does not seem fully coherent. Of all of the various categories and typologies of the novel proposed in his essay 'Discourse in the Novel', Bakhtin (2008c, 392–3) considers the *Bildungsroman* the most developed and modern type insofar as the protagonist and his place in the novel are concerned. The key figure for Bakhtin is the evolving central character, whose identity interacts with the world. Bakhtin establishes the same criterion for the modern novel as Lukács: the world of the protagonist is not pre-established or settled, and his perception and understanding of it is shaped through his own thoughts and experiences. In the *Bildungsroman*, priority is given to the development and change of the character: transformations in the character of the protagonist parallel changes in the world around him (Bakhtin 2008c, 392–3; Bakhtin 2007, 23–4). According to Bakhtin (2008c, 392–3), novels containing the idea of development and of man's becoming depict events in the protagonist's life as experiences crucial to the formation of the hero's character and worldview. Unlike the novels of the seventeenth century, in the *Bildungsroman* life itself is thus not an ordeal but also an education, shaping one's character and worldview. Time is the element through which alterations and development in the protagonist are seen (Bakhtin 2007, 23–5). This also implies that space does not appear as a meaningless field of action. On the contrary: specific locations and milieus have an impact on man's actions and character.

This overview shows how subjectivity defines the basis of the novel for Bakhtin. The integral social whole begins to collapse in the early modern period, and by the late eighteenth century the subject has become active and reflective. Bakhtin elaborates upon Rabelais and Goethe; but how does the early eighteenth century, with Defoe, Richardson and Fielding among others, fit into this perception? In an unfinished essay on the *Bildungsroman*, 'The *Bildungsroman* and Its Significance in the History of Realism (Toward a Historical Typology of the Novel)', Bakhtin presents one of his typologies of the novel. He divides the genre into four categories, according to how the image of the main hero is constructed and how this is related to the type of plot (*siuzhet*), to the conception of the world, and to the composition of a given novel. His categories consist of the travel novel, the novel of ordeal, the biographical (autobiographical) novel, and the *Bildungsroman* (Bakhtin 2007, 10). In this typology the novels of the first half of the eighteenth century are principally assigned to the first three categories, which all precede the fourth type, the *Bildungsroman*, although Bakhtin's typology does not tend to be fully chronological. These first three categories share certain common denominators, such as heroes who are shown as complete and unchanging. The world in which they live is also, according to Bakhtin, unchanging, static, and lacking in historicity (Bakhtin 2007, 10–19).

For Bakhtin, the category of the travel novel includes such works as Daniel Defoe's *Captain Singleton* (1720) and *Moll Flanders* (1722), which he defines as 'adventure-picaresque', and Tobias Smollett's adventurous *Roderick Random* (1748) and *Peregrine Pickle* (1751). The novel of ordeal is represented on the one hand by the eighteenth-century descendants of the Baroque novel, such as Ann Radcliffe's and Horace Walpole's gothic fiction – the 'adventure-heroic novel' is Bakhtin's term – on the other by 'the pathos-filled psychological, sentimental novel' represented by Samuel Richardson and Jean-Jacques Rousseau (Bakhtin 2007, 10–14).[6] Finally, the biographical novel, which due to its characters' biographical presence in the actual world includes a more realistic temporal representation than the two other types, is exemplified by Henry Fielding's *Tom Jones* (1749). These subgenres are swiftly passed over in Bakhtin's writings, with the emphasis on the *Bildungsroman* and its significance for the later realist novel.[7]

Bakhtin's categorizations suggest that he viewed one form of the early eighteenth-century English novel primarily in terms of the tradition of the adventure novel, which began with Apuleius and Petronius and continued in the heroic novels of the Baroque. 'Adventure novel of everyday life' is the term used by Bakhtin in his essay 'Forms of Time and Chronotope in the Novel' (2008a, 111). In this type of novel the transformation of the hero takes the form of metamorphosis, and adventure-time – referring to the episodic structure of the novels – is mixed with everyday time: 'Metamorphosis has become a vehicle for conceptualizing and portraying personal, individual fate, a fate cut off from both the cosmic and the historical whole' (2008a, 114). However, this transformation presents the destiny of a man in its life-long entirety, 'at all critical *turning points*', and shows '*how an individual becomes other than what he was*' (2008a, 114–15; emphasis in the original). What is important is that for Bakhtin this does not mean evolution but rather crisis and rebirth, and unusual events are determined by chance. Here we can see for example Defoe's youthful and curious characters: they seek adventure, whether at sea or in marriage, take the initiative, and ultimately find out they have made a mistake. In the end they repent and atone for their mistakes, making the structure irreversible. Yet, according to Bakhtin, in this type of the novel the temporal sequence leaves no traces in the surrounding world, and the connection between the individual's fate and the world is an external one (2008a, 119). The hero does not interact with the world, nor is he reflective; thus he remains outside historical time.

In the essay 'Discourse in the Novel' Bakhtin explores heteroglossia and its evolution in the course of the genre's history. Bakhtin sees the English comic novel of Fielding, Smollett, Sterne, Dickens, Thackeray and others as one form of heteroglossia. In these novels he finds 'a comic-parodic re-processing of almost all the levels of literary language [...] that were current at the time' (Bakhtin 2008c, 301). These novelists use various styles together with the authorial voice within a novel, thereby foregrounding different perspectives. This method is dialogic; as Bakhtin points out, however, the primary source of language usage in the comic novel is specifically the use of 'common language', which 'is taken by the author precisely as the *common view* [...] as the *going point of view* and the going *value*' (2008c, 301–2; emphasis in the original). This implies that social and historical voices do not differ enough to allow 'an authentic heteroglossia' (2008c, 308). Bakhtin considers Fielding, Smollett and Sterne parodists in the narrow sense: their literary parody serves to distance the author further from language, and the novelistic discourse itself is turned into an object (2008c, 309).

Another aspect of this type of novel is their biographical structure, which has some consequences for the representation of subjectivity. Bakhtin (2007, 24) identifies *Tom Jones* as an early biographical novel of emergence. In novels such as *Tom Jones*, emergence is 'the result of the entire totality of changing life circumstances and events, activity and work'. Human destiny and character is created simultaneously, and the 'emergence of life-destiny fuses with the emergence of man himself' (Bakhtin 2007, 22). According to Bakhtin (2008c, 393), the novels of both Fielding and Sterne include the theme of becoming and *Bildung* and that of the testing of the hero; these also influenced the continental type of the *Bildungsroman*. Yet, in the early eighteenth-century biographical novel the individual's emergence takes place against the static and ready-made background of the world; here it differs from *Bildungsroman* of the later eighteenth century, where emergence is accomplished in real historical time, 'with all of its necessity, its fullness, its future, and its profoundly chronotopic nature' (Bakhtin 2007, 23). In Fielding the individual can emerge, but the world itself cannot.

Another case is the sentimental novel of Richardson, which according to Bakhtin was an offshoot of the Baroque novel. Bakhtin sees Richardson's novels as characterized by psychology and pathos; their epistolary form is genetically connected with the epistolary expression of love in the Baroque novel. The sentimental novel takes the reader into intimate situations, into family life, combined with a didactic approach to everyday moral choices: 'What emerges is a specific-temporal zone of Sentimental pathos associated with the intimacy of one's own room' (Bakhtin 2008c, 397). Although literary language is brought closer to conversational form, this does not entail heteroglossia. Conversational language merely becomes a unitary language for the direct expression of authorial intention, therefore representing one-sided dialogism (Bakhtin 2008c, 398).

The Early Eighteenth-Century Novel: Watt and Anglo-American Criticism

It makes sense that literary theoreticians of the genre date the birth of the modern novel according to different approaches and points of view. For Lukács and Bakhtin, one of the most important aspects seems to be the individual and his inner development, which changes reciprocally with the surrounding world; this form became prevalent in the *Bildungsroman*. According to the Anglo-American scholarly tradition, on the other hand, the first stages of the modern novel arose in the first few decades of the eighteenth century, for some scholars even earlier, and the place for this process was obviously not Germany but England. A new phase in literary scholarship regarding the early eighteenth-century English novel began with Watt's *The Rise of the Novel*, in which he emphasized important social and economic processes in English society which formed the context for the rise of the English novel: the rise of capitalism, bourgeois culture and literacy, and changes in the idea of reality brought about by rationalism and empiricism. These wide-ranging socio-cultural changes facilitated the birth of a new kind of realistic narration, which at the same time placed a focus on individualism (Watt 1983, 9–65).

Watt's study established 'formal realism' and individualism as key concepts in the theory of the novel; through these he illuminated the uniqueness not only of the eighteenth-century English novel, but indeed of the genre of the modern novel in general. Watt described formal realism as a mode of narration which is already partly present in the novels of Defoe, Richardson and Fielding. Formal realism was based on the idea of empiricism: the view that reality is conceived through the senses and that this reality can be represented in the form of prose fiction. In contrast to the seventeenth-century romance tradition, the events of the eighteenth-century novel were credible and probable, for two reasons: the setting of the story was usually created so to resemble the writer's own historical time and place, and the writer described things, events and characters which were familiar to the contemporary reader. According to Watt, the special feature of the genre of the novel is that it depicts particular characters and their particular experiences under particular circumstances, at a specific time and place; in consequence the characters and events become individualized (Watt 1983, 34–5).

Watt's idea of formal realism has similar aspects as Bakhtin's views of Richardson as a describer of sentimental and private experience or Fielding as a representative of social-historic repertoire of voices or biographic structures. According to Watt, unlike earlier prose fiction, the characters of the early eighteenth-century novels already hold a certain personal identity, enabling the writer to present them more as individuals than as mere types. Rather than having recourse to traditional mythological stories or plot lines based on legends, writers increasingly created characters whose personal history and course of life functioned as a source for the plot line (Watt 1983, 12–28). Bakhtin does not talk so much about plots, but he (2008a, 118) discusses the biographical novel of trial in which the adventure sequence is subordinated to another sequence which interprets it: guilt – punishment – redemption – blessedness. Here the episodic but irreversible plot line also is structured in the form of one person's course of life.

Watt considers Defoe, Richardson and Fielding the most important developers of the modern novel, since according to him they were the first writers to realize these aspects of 'modern realism' in their novels. Watt's study explores, first of all, the reasons for the appearance of this new form of narration and discovers the answers in the historical changes of the period: the emergence of rationalism and empiricism in Western thought, the new meanings of time and space, the strengthening of the middle class, and the appearance of a new reading public. However, as Michael Seidel has noted, Watt's major contribution remains his recognition that 'formal realism begins not so much in the actual work-horse novels of the early eighteenth century as in the general attitude towards representation developing throughout the seventeenth century in Europe and in England' (2000, 206). However, where for Watt a character like Robinson Crusoe represents *homo economicus*, a person making individual economic decisions, for Bakhtin Defoe's character is a mere curious adventurer. Economic individualism is not an aspect that Bakhtin took into consideration. Characters like Crusoe, Moll Flanders or Roxana appear as representatives of common denominators; Bakhtin does not discuss their possible roles as active subjects. For Watt, in contrast, it is important as a signifier of individualistic representation that a character is positioned in a certain time and location and thus has a personal history. One key to understanding the differences between these views could be Bakhtin's and Watt's dissimilar conceptions of temporal representation in this type of novel.

It is obvious that Bakhtin considers time as an essential element of the novel, but *The Rise of the Novel* too deals with the relationship between time and the novel. According to Watt, the novel is a representation of the modern world with respect to temporality as well. Plots were created in which present action was caused by past experience; the earlier tradition of fragmented episodes and coincidences was replaced by temporal causality and continuity. Not only did causality give the novels more coherence, but – as Watt points out – the new application of temporality also offered the possibility of depicting developing characters and of describing events in more detail than earlier. This also meant representing them in specific locations, places and milieus (Watt 1983, 24). All in all, Watt seems not to have considered temporality as deeply as Bakhtin in his studies on the chronotope. There appears an obvious shift in the representation of time and place between the novels of the Baroque and the work of Defoe, but what Watt misses is the impact of modern historicity on every aspect of the novel.

What seem to be shared pivotal aspects of the novel genre for Watt and Bakhtin are thus the rise, in the course of the eighteenth century, of individualism and modern temporality but with somewhat diverse substances. Interestingly, as mentioned earlier, they also have at least one common context for their studies: Lukács' *The Theory of the Novel*. We know that at the time he was planning and writing *The Rise of the Novel* Watt had read Lukács' work on the theory of the novel (Watt 2000, 149–50). He nevertheless chose another point of view as to the origins and development of the genre than Lukács and Bakhtin. Where Lukács and Bakhtin placed emphasis on 'hero', Watt focused on the issue of narration in a context of contemporary history. Yet there seem to be similarities in the realistic, verisimilar narration of the individual's everyday life and the protagonist's development in a changing world.

In his *Origins of the English Novel, 1600–1740* (1987), Michael McKeon briefly compares the theories of Bakhtin and Watt, criticizing both of them from the point of view of genre. Where he sees Watt as giving undue weight to alterity and difference, thus ignoring previous traditions and influences, Bakhtin is judged as a scholar seeking a 'total' theory of genre (McKeon 2002, 10–11). McKeon considers the problem to derive from Bakhtin's overall praise for the novel as a genre above others and from his view of historical change itself: 'Rather than permit antecedent genres to manifest in their own, precursory form elements that will become dominant in "the novel", Bakhtin digs an implausible gulf between the "rigid", "fixed", "sealed-off", "straightforward" closure of traditional genres and the "openended" "flexibility" and "indeterminacy" of the novel' (2002, 13). Furthermore, he claims, Bakhtin's tendency to speak as though 'novelistic discourse' was not only quite separable from other discourse but also something like 'an "authentic" literary language' prevents him from considering Defoe or Richardson as models of novelistic prose (McKeon 2002, 14).

Since the original publication of Watt's book, however, enormous attention has been paid in Anglo-American criticism to the period and its significance for the novel genre. Ever since its first appearance Watt's theory has been much debated, and in the last two decades several new approaches and viewpoints have been developed in literary scholarship concerned with the modern novel in general. The Anglo-American discussion has called attention especially to early phases of the modern novel, i.e. to prose fiction written during the late seventeenth and early eighteenth century (cf. McKeon 2002, 1–4).

Where earlier theories – those of Lukács, Bakhtin and Watt – focused primarily on changes in worldview and the notion of reality, the individualistic protagonist and the importance of the *Bildungsroman* as the important novel form of the eighteenth century, the scholarly debate of the last thirty years has stressed the multiplicity and complexity of the early phases of the modern novel and has laid emphasis on the broadening of the novel canon, for example by including forgotten or previously ignored women writers. The idea of the development of the modern novel as a counterpart to the epic or the seventeenth-century romance tradition has been challenged. Instead, various types of texts, or rather discourses – e.g. early journalism, historiography, religious autobiography, travel literature or the prose of amorous intrigue – have been discovered standing in the background of the appearance of the modern novel.[8] It is surprising that this discussion has failed to relate to Bakhtin's views on popular folklore and the novel, or on the novel's dialogic elements.

A central theoretical influence on Anglo-American criticism dealing with the early phases of the modern novel has been exercised by Michel Foucault's concepts of discourse and power and the new approach to historical change (cf. Warner 1991, 185–203). At the heart of Lennard J. Davis' study *Factual Fictions: The Origins of the English Novel* (1983) is the view that in the early modern novel a large number of different types of texts come together to form a specific discourse. Like Watt, Davis maintains that there exists a clear rupture between the seventeenth-century romance tradition and the modern novel. Rather than having developed out of the romance, the novel emerged from within the realm – or rather the discourse – of contemporary prose fiction, its criticism, newspapers, advertisements and publishers' letters. Through a close study of the ideas, opinions and views of the historical period, Davis strives to uncover the interaction between various texts and the contemporary society, placing special emphasis on the relationship between the rise of journalism and prose writing and the effects of this relationship on the genre of the novel. Finally, Davis claims that the genre of the modern novel took shape from the separation of two discourses, factual journalism and the fictional novel, which during the early phases of the modern novel were still indistinguishable (Davis 1983, 42–70).

Nancy Armstrong's study *Desire and Domestic Fictions: A Political History of the Novel* (1987) approaches the history of the genre from a feminist point of view, viewing literature as a representation of the world of women and stressing that the history of the novel is also a history of love and sexuality. Armstrong shares Watt's view of the importance of female readership of the novel, but she also points out that *The Rise of the Novel* gives no explanation for the fact that many eighteenth-century novels were written by women. It is not Armstrong's primary aim, however, to do justice to forgotten women writers.[9] Rather, she claims that the ideal role, tasks and duties assigned to women during the eighteenth century, just like the most highly valued female traits and characteristics of the age, ought to be seen as an inseparable part of the rise of both the middle class and the novel. The novel penetrated primarily into the private sphere of daily life, associated with the world of women, in contrast to the public sphere controlled by men. Therefore, according to Armstrong, the study of the early modern novel should take into consideration the crucial role that women played in its rise, as both readers and writers. This also obviously influenced the content of novels, which in the course of the eighteenth century richly represented issues primarily associated with the feminine sphere: everyday domestic life, family affairs, personal relationships and the psychology of love (Armstrong 1987, 3–27; especially 7–8).

The studies by Davis and Armstrong define the novel as a culturally determined discourse, containing references to diverse texts and areas of knowledge. Consequently, the novel as a discourse ultimately enhances and consolidates certain issues and ideologies, its formulation being thus connected to power relations: the novel emerges as a political discourse, as a voice of the contemporary culture. We might add, however, that the novel is not only a symptom of its own time but also functions as a vehicle generating ideas and ideologies for the future.[10] It is interesting to see how these ideas echo Bakhtin's theories of the novel as a verbal discourse and social phenomenon:

> The novel can be defined as a diversity of social speech types [...] and a diversity of individual voices, artistically organized. The internal stratification of any single national language into social dialects, characteristic group behaviour, professional jargons, generic languages, languages of generations and age groups, tendentious languages, languages of the authorities, of various circles and of passing fashions, languages that serve the specific socio-political purposes of the day [...] – this internal stratification present in every language at any given moment of its historical existence is the indispensable prerequisite for the novel as a genre. (Bakhtin 2008c, 262–3)

Moreover, Armstrong's ideas echo those of Bakhtin on private experience and depictions of family life for instance in Richardson. As mentioned, Bakhtin's views have rarely been taken into account in Anglo-American studies dealing with the early eighteenth-century novel from a discursive point of view. Davis, for instance, does not mention Bakhtin at all and Armstrong in passing, in two footnotes.[11]

During the last decades of the twentieth century, as scholarly interest came to be increasingly focused on the cultural history of the genre, the early modern novel was more and more clearly defined in Anglo-American criticism as part of the culture of its own time. Two studies in particular focused on this point of view. The first was J. Paul Hunter's *Before Novels: The Cultural Contexts of Eighteenth-Century English Fiction* (1990), which criticizes eighteenth-century studies for their lack of a historical perspective and calls for placing the novel in a wider context of cultural history. Hunter (1990, 5) sets the novel in the same context as popular print products and popular thought, journalism, private papers and histories, and calls attention to such factors as contemporary patterns of literacy, reading habits, the availability of reading materials and the interrelationship between oral expression and writing.

An approach arising out of cultural history is also explicit in the second study, William B. Warner's monograph *Licensing Entertainment: The Elevation of Novel Reading in Britain, 1684–1750* (1998). In the foreword, entitled 'From a Literary to a Cultural History of the Early Novel' Warner urges scholars studying the early modern novel to turn from the discourse of literary history to that of cultural history. He criticizes the tendency which, following in Watt's footsteps, from a twentieth-century perspective legitimizes 'the novel' already in its early phase as an aesthetic cultural object, taking it for a closed form or genre. He extends his own study to the reception and reading culture of novels, suggesting that early novels should be examined as a phenomenon in the history of media culture (Warner 1998, 2). Especially before the 1740s, i.e. before the appearance of *Pamela*, *Joseph Andrews*, *Clarissa* and *Tom Jones*, prose fiction was considered a form of leisure entertainment, and popular writers – such as Mary Delarivier Manley, Daniel Defoe and Eliza Haywood – were according to Warner in practice 'media workers' creating entertainment. He also notes that the new literary form provoked contradictory opinions and harsh debates, not least for its alleged demoralizing influence on readers, particularly women (1998, xi–xvi).

One common point made in these studies is the pluralistic character of the early modern (English) novel and of the historical period in which this new literary form took shape. The contemporary Anglo-American discussion, however, has not really denied the central aspects of the modern novel articulated by Bakhtin or Watt: claims concerning the rise of the new realism, temporality, individualism and subjectivity, and the idea that the novel depicts the contemporary, everyday life of ordinary people.[12] While the early eighteenth-century novel cannot be defined in terms of concepts so closely related to Bakhtin as carnival, *Bildung* or polyphony, as a theoretician of dialogism and heteroglossia of the novel genre Bakhtin may also have offered a rich and constructive theoretical starting point for the above-mentioned investigations.

Thus those approaches that rest on the discursive formation of the genre might have been based specifically on Bakhtinian theories. In a fairly recent study, *Making the Novel: Fiction and Society in Britain, 1660–1789* (2006), Brean Hammond and Shaun Regan introduce Bakhtin as a key theorist in exploring the development of the novel genre. They note that for Bakhtin the emergence of the modern novel was not an eighteenth-century English phenomenon, yet they consider his ideas on the nature of the novel and on the cultural conditions in which it flourished valuable (Hammond and Regan 2006, 19). Hammond and Regan use Bakhtin's term *novelization* 'to refer to a cultural process which […] took place in post-1660 England, making for the mingling and mixing of different literary modes within and between all the major genres' (2006, 21). I understand their use of this term to refer to Bakhtin's idea of the dominant tendencies of the novel form. In his essay 'Epic and Novel', Bakhtin writes: 'In an era when the novel reigns supreme, almost all the remaining genres are to a greater or lesser extent "novelized": drama [...], epic poetry [...], even lyric poetry' (2008b, 5–6). In England the period between 1660 and around 1750 has been defined as the beginning of a mass market for literature, and the growth of this market also had an effect on what was written. Hammond and Regan specify their use of Bakhtin's term to mean 'altering standards of plausibility' (2006, 22). New readers put aside implausible heroic tales and wanted instead to read a new kind of story, with familiar characters and humour. Hammond and Regan write: 'The kinds of stories that Aphra Behn, Delarivier Manley, Eliza Haywood, Daniel Defoe and others wanted to tell, do differ from epic stories in the ways described by Bakhtin' (2006, 22).

Conclusion

For Bakhtin, the seminal novelistic turning points were the ages of Rabelais and Goethe, which offered valuable innovations for the treatment of the individual in novelistic discourse. In the case of the early eighteenth-century adventure novel and of the sentimental and biographical novel as represented by Defoe, Richardson, Fielding and Sterne, Bakhtin sees extensions and offshoots of the earlier Baroque novel. Despite the fact that Bakhtin did not especially underline the early eighteenth-century novel, his views of the novel could be put to more use in studies dealing with the early stages of the modern English novel. Combining Watt's emphasis on formal realism and Bakhtin's vision of the novel as a dialogic and heteroglossic discourse would be a productive approach in exploring the prose fiction of the seventeenth and early eighteenth century.

According to Craig Brandist (1999, 23), Bakhtin viewed the novel as a form of literature, an 'organ', through which culture reaches self-awareness. On the other hand, Gary Saul Morson has attested to Bakhtin's idea of the novel genre as the most 'casuistical' of genres. 'Casuist' here means that one insists on the specificity of each case on which an ethical choice can be based. The novel expresses the complexity of daily circumstances and choices, and it also represents a form of thinking 'that is wisest about temporality and development' (Morson 1991, 1076). These definitions privilege the novel as the genre through which culture can reflect itself. It is quite another question whether the novel still holds this key position today. In any case, for Bakhtin the novel genre was not only a literary form but also a weighty form of thinking. He emphasized the historical periods 'between two epochs' in which the novel form proved to be the preeminent cultural form to reflect ongoing changes. In this light, the last decades of the seventeenth century and the first decades of the eighteenth offered a favourable period, particularly in England, after the nation underwent substantial changes in politics, economics and religion.

Notes

1. According to Simon Dentith (1995, 41), Bakhtin's writings on the novel can be grouped into four sections: (1) the book on Dostoevsky first published in 1929 and republished in 1963 (*Problems of Dostoevsky's Poetics*, 1984), (2) the essays of the 1930s and 1940s most of which appear in English translation in *The Dialogic Imagination* (1981), (3) the remaining sections of the lost book on the *Bildungsroman*, and (4) the work on Rabelais and carnival (*Rabelais and His World*, 1968).
2. Cf. Holquist (1990, 16–18); Dentith (1995, 11–13); Emerson (1997, 248–9); Brandist (2002, 15–24); see also Chapter 1 in this volume.
3. In his views on the epic and the novel Lukács follows Hegel's ideas, which he also points out in his study (Lukács 1971, 15). See also Holquist (1990, 73–4).
4. See also Tihanov (2000, 10–13), and Chapter 1.
5. In his essay on the significance of Renaissance to Bakhtin, Craig Brandist (1999, 19) has used a rather different translation of the 'national-historical time'. He uses the expression 'folkloric popular-historical time', which seems to have a slightly different meaning from the former. Whereas 'national' refers to the whole nation as a representative of its people, 'folkloric popular' is associated with common folk tradition.
6. The actual novels that Bakhtin refers to are Radcliffe's *The Mysteries of Udolpho* (1794), Walpole's *The Castle of Otranto* (1764), Richardson's *Pamela* (1740) and *Clarissa* (1748), and Rousseau's *Julie ou La nouvelle Héloïse* (1761).
7. Bakhtin writes: 'But of special importance for the realistic novel [...] is the *Bildungsroman*, which appeared in Germany in the second half of the eighteenth century' (2007, 19). Yet for instance in his study of Dostoevsky, Bakhtin (1984, 102–6) acknowledges the impact of adventure novel on Dostoevsky's plot compositions.
8. On the connection between journalism and the novel, see Davis (1983); on historiography and the novel, see Mayer (1997); on the links between the religious autobiography and the novel, see Starr 1965; on travel and adventure literature and the novel, see Green (1980) and Adams (1983); on popular amorous prose fiction and the novel, see Warner (1998) and Richetti (1999, 18–51).
9. Such studies as Jane Spencer's *The Rise of the Woman Novelist* (1986), Dale Spender's *Mothers of the Novel: 100 Good Women Writers before Jane Austen* (1986) and Janet Todd's *The Sign of Angellica: Women, Writing and Fiction, 1660–1800* (1989) are among the first major efforts to revise the novel canon.
10. On ideologies and power relations, see Davis (1983, 9); Bender (1987, 3–4, 8–9); Warner (1991, 185–203).
11. An exception would be for example John Bender's study *Imagining the Penitentiary: Fiction and the Architecture of Mind in Eighteenth-Century England* (1987), which uses Bakhtin's terminology in investigating novelistic representations of the eighteenth-century penitentiary prison.
12. Cf. Hunter (1990, 30); Richetti (1998, 4–6); Hunter (1998, 9–10); Seidel (2000, 194).

References

Adams, Percy G. 1983. *Travel Literature and the Evolution of the Novel*. Lexington: University Press of Kentucky.
Armstrong, Nancy. 1987. *Desire and Domestic Fictions: A Political History of the Novel*. New York and Oxford: Oxford University Press.
Bakhtin, M. M. 1968. *Rabelais and His World* (*Tvorchestvo Fransua Rable i narodnaia kultura srednevekovia i renessansa*, 1965). Translated by Hélène Iswolsky. Cambridge, MA and London: MIT Press.
———. 1984. *Problems of Dostoevsky's Poetics* (*Problemy poetiki Dostoevskogo*, 1963). Translated and edited by Caryl Emerson. Manchester: Manchester University Press.
———. 2007. 'The *Bildungsroman* and Its Significance in the History of Realism (Toward a Historical Typology of the Novel)' ('Roman vospitaniia i ego znachenie v istorii realizma'). In *Speech Genres and Other Late Essays*. Edited by Caryl Emerson and Michael Holquist, translated by Vern W. McGee, 10–59. Austin: University of Texas Press.
———. 2008a [1981]. 'Forms of Time and of the Chronotope in the Novel: Towards a Historical Poetics' ('Formy vremeni i khronotopa v romane: Ocherki po istoricheskoi poetike'). In *The Dialogic Imagination*. Edited by Michael Holquist, translated by Caryl Emerson and Michael Holquist, 84–258. Austin: University of Texas Press.
———. 2008b [1981]. 'Epic and Novel: Toward a Methodology for the Study of the Novel' ('Epos i roman [O metodologii issledovaniia romana]'). In *The Dialogic Imagination*. Edited by Michael Holquist, translated by Caryl Emerson and Michael Holquist, 3–40. Austin: University of Texas Press.
———. 2008c [1981]. 'Discourse in the Novel' ('Slovo v romane'). In *The Dialogic Imagination*. Edited by Michael Holquist, translated by Caryl Emerson and Michael Holquist, 259–422. Austin: University of Texas Press.
Bender, John. 1987. *Imagining the Penitentiary: Fiction and the Architecture of Mind in Eighteenth-Century England*. Chicago and London: University of Chicago Press.
Brandist, Craig. 1999. 'Bakhtin's Grand Narrative: The Significance of the Renaissance'. *Dialogism: An International Journal of Bakhtin Studies* 3: 11–30.
———. 2002. *The Bakhtin Circle: Philosophy, Culture and Politics*. London and Sterling, VA: Pluto Press.
Burton, Stacy. 1996. 'Bakhtin, Temporality, and Modern Narrative: Writing "the Whole Triumphant Murderous Unstoppable Chute"'. *Comparative Literature* 48, no. 1: 39–64.
Davis, Lennard J. 1983. *Factual Fictions: The Origins of the English Novel*. New York: Columbia University Press.
Dentith, Simon. 1995. *Bakhtinian Thought: An Introductory Reader*. London and New York: Routledge.
Emerson, Caryl. 1997. *The First Hundred Years of Mikhail Bakhtin*. Princeton: Princeton University Press.
Green, Martin. 1980. *Dreams of Adventure, Deeds of Empire*. London and Henley: Routledge.
Hammond, Brean and Shaun Regan. 2006. *Making of the Novel: Fiction and Society in Britain, 1660–1789*. Basingstoke and New York: Palgrave Macmillan.
Holquist, Michael. 1981. 'Introduction'. In M. M. Bakhtin, *The Dialogic Imagination: Four Essays*, xv–xxxiv. Austin: University of Texas Press.
———. 1983 (1982). 'Bakhtin and Rabelais: Theory as Praxis'. *Boundary 2* 11, nos. 1–2: 5–19.
———. 1990. *Dialogism: Bakhtin and His World*. London and New York: Routledge.

Hunter, J. Paul. 1990. *Before Novels: The Cultural Contexts of Eighteenth-Century English Fiction*. New York and London: W. W. Norton.

———. 1998. 'The Novel and Social/Cultural History'. In *The Cambridge Companion to the Eighteenth-Century Novel*. Edited by John Richetti, 9–40. Cambridge: Cambridge University Press.

Lukács, Georg. 1971. *The Theory of the Novel: A Historico-philosophical Essay on the Forms of Great Epic Literature* (*Die Theorie des Romans: Ein Geschichtsphilosophischer Versuch über die Formen der grossen Epik*, 1920). Translated by Anna Bostock. London: Merlin Press.

Mayer, Robert. 1997. *History and the Early English Novel: Matters of Fact from Bacon to Defoe*. Cambridge: Cambridge University Press.

McKeon, Michael. 2002 [1987]. *The Origins of the English Novel, 1600–1740*. Baltimore and London: Johns Hopkins University Press.

Morson, Gary Saul. 1991. 'Bakhtin, Genres, and Temporality'. *New Literary History* 22, no. 4: 1071–92.

Richetti, John J. 1998 [1996]. 'Introduction'. In *The Cambridge Companion to the Eighteenth-Century Novel*. Edited by John Richetti, 1–8. Cambridge: Cambridge University Press.

———. 1999. *The English Novel in History, 1700–1780*. London and New York: Routledge.

Seidel, Michael 2000. 'The Man Who Came to Dinner: Ian Watt and the Theory of Formal Realism'. *Eighteenth-Century Fiction: Reconsidering the Rise of the Novel* 12, nos. 2–3: 193–225.

Schlegel, Friedrich. 1988 [1798]. 'Athenäums-Fragmente'. In *Kritische Schriften und Fragmente [1798–1801]*, vol. 2. Edited by Ernst Behler and Hans Eichner, 105–156. Munich, Paderborn, Vienna, Zurich: Schöningh.

Starr, G. A. 1965. *Defoe & Spiritual Autobiography*. Princeton: Princeton University Press.

Tihanov, Galin. 2000. *Lukács, Bakhtin, and the Ideas of Their Time*. Oxford: Clarendon Press.

Todorov, Tzvetan 1988. *Literature and Its Theorists: A Personal View of Twentieth-Century Criticism* (*Critique de la critique*, 1984). Translated by Catherine Porter. London: Routledge & Kegan Paul.

Warner, William B. 1991. 'Social Power and the Eighteenth-Century Novel: Foucault and Transparent Literary History'. *Eighteenth-Century Fiction* 3, no. 3: 185–203.

———. 1998. *Licensing Entertainment: The Elevation of Novel Reading in Britain, 1684–1750*. Berkeley and London: University of California Press.

Watt, Ian. 1983 [1957]. *The Rise of the Novel: Studies in Defoe, Richardson, and Fielding*. Harmondsworth: Penguin.

———. 2000 [1978]. 'Flat-Footed and Fly-Blown: The Realities of Realism'. *Eighteenth-Century Fiction: Reconsidering the Rise of the Novel* 12, nos. 2–3: 147–66.

Wendorff, Rudolph. 1980. *Zeit und Kultur: Geschichte des Zeitbewusstseins in Europa*. Wiesbaden: Westdeutscher Verlag.

Chapter 3

CONCEPTS OF NOVELISTIC POLYPHONY: PERSON-RELATED AND COMPOSITIONAL-THEMATIC

Liisa Steinby

Introduction: Polyphonies of the Novel

Chronotope, carnivalism and polyphony, or rather the polyphonic novel, are the three concepts which have made Bakhtin famous as a theoretician of the novel and which have been widely adopted in contemporary literary scholarship. Once become part of the toolkit of literary scholars, Bakhtin's concepts have taken on an academic life of their own: they have often been used in an approximate way, even misleadingly. Of these, 'carnivalism' and 'chronotope' are exclusively Bakhtinian while 'polyphony' has been applied as a musical analogy to literary structures by others as well.

That a literary work may be composed in analogy with a musical work is an idea beloved by the German Early Romantics. In this tradition the term 'polyphony' is used to refer to a literary structure considered as analogous to the structure of polyphonic music. Today, however, 'polyphony' is often seen as an exclusively Bakhtinian concept, overlooking the fact that the term has been used to refer to quite different aspects of a literary work of art. The *Routledge Encyclopedia of Narrative Theory*, as well as Vladimir Biti's dictionary of literary and cultural theory, for example, do not recognize any use of the term other than the Bakhtinian (Aczel 2005, 443–4; Biti 2001, 627–9). In this chapter I compare the Bakhtinian concept of novelistic polyphony to other cases where the term is used to refer to the structure of a novel. I start with a brief discussion of the polyphony which Bakhtin has in mind; I then define other types of polyphony, which derive rather from the Romantic idea of literary composition as analogous to a musical one, or at least show a close affinity to this idea.

Bakhtin: Polyphony as Polysubjectivity

In 'Author and Hero in Aesthetic Activity' (1990, written about 1920–23), Bakhtin develops an aesthetic theory according to which the content of a literary work of art – a novel – is primarily made up of its hero, his acts and experiences, whereas the aesthetic form derives from the author (e.g. Bakhtin 1990, 83). As a concrete individual, the hero is part of the natural and cultural world in which he lives, but simultaneously he is the autonomous subject of ethical acts. He experiences a multitude of things, he makes ethical decisions, and he often in self-reflection ponders upon his experiences and doings, but he never conceives of his life and himself in consummated, finalized form; only the author is capable of doing so: 'The author stands totally over against this activity of the hero, the activity of living his life, and translates it into aesthetic language, i.e., produces a transgredient artistic determination for every constituent moment in the hero's activity of living' (Bakhtin 1990, 174).

Thus, '[f]orm expresses the author's self-activity in relation to a hero – in relation to another human being' (Bakhtin 1990, 84). This form can only be created in aesthetic contemplation, in which the author sympathetically co-experiences the hero's life but still remains at the distance of another human being to him:

> Sympathetic co-experiencing of the hero's life means to experience that life in a form completely different from the form in which it was, or could have been, experienced by the *subiectum* of that life himself. Co-experiencing in this form does not in the least strive toward the ultimate point of totally coinciding, merging with the co-experienced life [...] A sympathetically co-experienced life is given form not in the category of the *I*, but in the category of the *other*, as the life of *another* human being, another *I*. In other words, a sympathetically co-experienced life is the life of another human being (his outer as well as his *inner* life) that is essentially experienced *from outside*. (Bakhtin 1990, 82; emphasis in the original)

In his early aesthetics, Bakhtin is indebted above all to Hermann Cohen. Just like Cohen in his *Ästhetik des reinen Gefühls* (*Aesthetics of Pure Feeling*, 1912), Bakhtin distinguishes between the hero, his acts and his experiences, which make up the content of the novel, and the manner in which this is 'consummated' in an aesthetic form created by the author (cf. Steinby 2011). The hero as the object of the author's contemplation appears very much like an individual in real life: Bakhtin – like Cohen – does not distinguish between the 'consummating form' bestowed upon the hero by the author and the form of the work of art. Since Bakhtin's later interest was focused particularly on the novel, it is worth noting that the idea of the novel as dealing primarily with the hero and his experiences was familiar to Bakhtin from the German tradition of the theory of the novel going back to Friedrich von Blanckenburg, Early Romanticism, Hegel, and Lukács.[1] Bakhtin, however, seems to have completely abandoned the aesthetics of 'Author and Hero' only a few years later in his study of Dostoevsky's novels, novels which he calls polyphonic.

In the first version of what later became famous as *Problems in Dostoevsky's Poetics* (1929; 1963), Bakhtin considers the author's objectifying relationship to the characters in a novel no longer as a necessity for the creation of the aesthetic form of a work of art, but merely as typical of the main tradition of the novel. In *Problems of Dostoevsky's Poetics* (1963), a novel in which the author is the central subject who gives the consummative definition of the hero and whatever exists in his world, or who is 'a monologic authorial consciousness' behind the whole of the work, is called monologic (cf. Bakhtin 1989, 8–14; cit. 11). This is juxtaposed with the polyphonic novel, which in the first version of the Dostoevsky study Bakhtin considers to be unique to this author. In contrast to what is customary, the characters in Dostoevsky's novels are not subdued to the author's definition but appear as autonomous subjects:

> Dostoevsky, like Goethe's Prometheus, creates not voiceless slaves (as does Zeus), but *free* people, capable of standing *alongside* their creator, capable of not agreeing with him and even of rebelling against him [...] *A plurality of independent and unmerged voices and consciousnesses, a genuine polyphony of fully valid voices is in fact the chief characteristic of Dostoevsky's novels*. What unfolds in his works is not a multitude of characters and fates in a single objective world, illuminated by a single authorial consciousness; rather a plurality of consciousnesses, *with equal rights and each with its own world*, combine but are not merged in the unity of the event. (Bakhtin 1989, 6–7; emphasis in the original)

Thus Dostoevsky presents his readers with a new kind of fictive world, which is 'a world of autonomous subjects, not objects' (Bakhtin 1989, 7). Whereas the novel as presented in the 'Author and Hero in Aesthetic Activity' is monosubjective in the sense that the world of the novel here appears 'finalized' in the form the author gives to the materials, the polyphonic novel which Bakhtin finds in Dostoevsky's works is a polysubjective one in which each individual's subjective viewpoint is presented without any intervention from the author. The polyphonic or polysubjective novel is thus defined by the manner in which the characters, or 'heroes', appear in the novel: the ethically acting individuals do not have any 'finalized form' given to them by another subject (the author), but they appear only through their action and their consciousness, as expressed in their speech. A polyphonic novel contains several 'voices' which are on a par with each other. Thus 'polyphonic' here refers literally to the equality of the 'voices' of acting persons. This concept of polyphony can therefore be characterized as person-related.

The polyphonic novel is characterized, first, by the presence of a number of 'heroes', in contrast to the single hero in *Author and Hero*. Second, from the retreat of the author from his former position as the central subject in the novel there ensues a fundamental alteration in its architecture. Third, the idea of polyphony implies not only a plurality of voices, but also a genuine encounter among the various subjective points of view.

In the Dostoevskyan novel, there is nothing above the consciousness of the characters:

> This is a very important and fundamental feature of the way a fictional character is perceived. The hero as a point of view, as an opinion on the world and on himself, requires utterly special methods of discovery and artistic characterization. And this is so because what must be discovered and characterized here is not the specific existence of the hero, not his fixed image, but the *sum total of his consciousness and self-consciousness*, ultimately *the hero's final word on himself and his world*. (Bakhtin 1989, 48; emphasis in the original)

Bakhtin speaks of 'a small-scale Copernican revolution' brought about by Dostoevsky, 'when he took what had been a firm and finalizing authorial definition and turned it into an aspect of the hero's self-definition' (Bakhtin 1989, 49). A definition from outside, which in 'Author and Hero' is described as an act of sympathy and love (Bakhtin 1990, 82), now appears suspicious and even reprehensible:

> [A] living human being cannot be turned into the voiceless object of some secondhand, finalizing cognitive process. *In a human being there is always something that only he himself can reveal, in a free act of self-consciousness and discourse, something that does not submit to an externalizing secondhand definition.* (Bakhtin 1989, 58; emphasis in the original)

Where in 'Author and Hero' the author was able to see in the hero something that transcends his self-understanding, now on the contrary the individual's self-understanding transcends what others can see of him or her.

Bakhtin calls the 'new artistic position' in Dostoevsky's novels, in which the main characters are assigned 'independence, internal freedom, unfinalizability, and indeterminacy', a *'fully realized and thoroughly consistent dialogic position'* (Bakhtin 1989, 63; emphasis in the original). Bakhtin understands this as a dialogic position between the author and the hero: 'For the author the hero is not "he" and not "I" but a fully valid "thou", that is, another and other autonomous "I" ("thou art")' (Bakhtin 1989). In other words, the hero is seen as another subject, a co-subject whom we encounter in speech:

> The consciousness of other people cannot be perceived, analyzed, defined as objects or as things – one can only *relate to them dialogically*. To think about them means to *talk with them; otherwise they immediately turn to us their objectivized side*: they fall silent, close up, and congeal into finished, objectivized images. (Bakhtin 1989, 68; emphasis in the original)

The structure of the novel remains thus constantly open for the new that is revealed in the speech of the characters.

The same principle of dialogism, which determines the author's relation to the hero in a 'polyphonic' novel and therefore the structure (or 'architecture') of the novel as a whole, also determines the relations between the autonomous subjects in the world of the novel. In Dostoevsky's polyphonic or polysubjective novels, the characters acknowledge to each other the same position of an autonomous subject that they themselves occupy. This means that his characters encounter each other with openness to each others' 'truths': 'Whenever someone else's "truth" is presented in a given novel, it is introduced without fail into the *dialogic field of vision* of all the other major heroes of the novel' (Bakhtin 1989, 73; emphasis in the original). The other one is then not defined as an object in my world, but is encountered as a co-subject in the dialogue. The other's 'voice' or 'word' (discourse) expresses that person's view of the world, which is received as a challenge to one's own 'word': '[T]he orientation of one person to another person's discourse and consciousness is, in essence, the basic theme of all of Dostoevsky's works' (Bakhtin 1989, 207). In fact, a person's inner life can be described only through his or her dialogical relation with others: 'A single person, remaining alone with himself, cannot make ends meet even in the deepest and most intimate spheres of his own spiritual life, he cannot manage without *another consciousness*' (Bakhtin 1989, 177; emphasis in the original). Polyphony thus means dialogism (cf. Clark and Holquist 2002, 242). One's 'word' is constantly directed to that of another person and bears in itself a reaction to it: speech is 'internally dialogized' (Bakhtin 1989, 138). Each 'word' is actually double-voiced, a microdialogue between two or more interlocutors (Bakhtin 1989, 74). As a whole, a polyphonic novel is structured as a 'great dialogue' (Bakhtin 1989, 40).

Despite one's openness to other persons' voices or words (discourses) and the inherent dialogism of each person's 'word', in the polyphonic novel the voices do not merge but remain separate: according to Bakhtin, Dostoevsky's artistic idea is 'the fundamental plurality of unmerged consciousnesses' (1989, 9). It is precisely this encounter without merging which makes the structure polyphonic: 'The essence of polyphony lies precisely in the fact that the voices remain independent and, as such, are combined in a unity of a higher order than in homophony [...] [T]he artistic will of polyphony is a will to combine many wills, a will to the event' (Bakhtin 1989, 21); 'event' referring here to the encounter of two or more individuals conceived as autonomously acting ethical subjects (cf. Brandist 2002, 39 and the introduction to this volume). That the 'voices' remain separate and do not merge follows, of course, from the fact that they are the voices of concrete individuals: a synthesis of the ideas which they represent would be possible only if these ideas were treated as abstractions, separate from the characters. 'Polyphony' thus in a sense ensues from the fact that for Dostoevsky, according to Bakhtin, ideas cannot be separated from characters.

A novel in which persons having different views of the world meet without anyone representing the 'objective' or 'authoritative' truth is, of course, quite common in modern literature, yet the concepts 'polysubjective' or 'polyphonic' (in the Bakhtinian sense) are not very often applied for these (cf. Biti 2001, 628–9; Malcuzynski 1984). Bakhtin himself says that 'polyphony', as used to characterize a new way of constructing a novel, is a mere metaphor taken from music: it is 'meant as a graphic analogy, nothing more' (1989, 22). I myself would say that in the manner in which he uses the term 'polyphony', the analogy to music is indeed quite remote, rather on the level of borrowing the term. In terms of content, on the other hand, the concept itself is not vague or casual at all; on the contrary, Bakhtin makes his understanding of the concept very clear.

The Romantic Idea of the Musical Composition of a Literary Work of Art: Friedrich Schlegel

While the concept of novelistic polyphony is generally considered to be a Bakhtinian concept, the idea of an analogy between a musical and a novelistic composition is, as Bakhtin must have known, much older and was especially cherished by the German Early Romantics (the term 'composition', of course, here lacks the connotation of 'merely mechanical' of Bakhtin's concept of 'compositional form'). The other concepts of novelistic polyphony I discuss in this chapter were conceived in connection with this tradition. It is therefore necessary to elucidate some basic tenets of the Romantic idea of the musical structure of a novel. The idea has been accused of being nebulous and non-analytical (cf. Christoffel 2009), but a closer look reveals the presence of certain distinctive features, which have formed the basis for further developments of the analogy.

The German Early Romantic thinkers and poets shared the view that there is a close affinity between different branches of arts, as well as between art, philosophy and religion. Friedrich Schlegel, the most important literary theoretician of the movement, writes in one of his famous *Athenäum* fragments that '[s]pirit is like music of thoughts' (Schlegel 1988a, 139).[2] 'Music of thoughts' implies a similarity between a musical composition and a philosophical one. The idea is further elucidated in another aphorism (or fragment), in which Schlegel writes that 'is not a theme developed, confirmed, varied and contrasted in it [the music] just like a subject of meditation in a philosophical line of ideas?' (Schlegel 1988a, 155).[3] Here a theme in a musical composition is assigned the same function of compositional unit as an idea in a philosophical one. The aphorism also shows that for Schlegel philosophy is not characterized by a systematic manner of dealing with a topic. Rather, ideas are dealt with in a manner similar to that which we usually associate with the themes in a musical composition, i.e. a theme is 'developed, confirmed [i.e. repeated?], varied and contrasted' with other themes. In the same sense, a literary text too is a composition of its basic units. The following aphorism has to be understood in this sense: 'All prose is poetic. – If prose must be juxtaposed with poetry, actually it is only logical prose that is prose proper' (Schlegel 1988b, 187).[4] In other words, only a text which follows completely the principles of (formal) logic is not poetic at all. What is poetic is a prose which deals with its materials similarly as a composer with musical themes. About the novel in particular, Schlegel says that '[t]he method of the novel is that of instrumental music. Even the characters in a novel may be dealt with as arbitrarily as themes are dealt with in a musical composition' (Schlegel 1988b, 234).[5] In a sense, music thus provides the model for the composition of a literary work of art, or, according to Schlegel, for any kind of art: '*Music* is among the fine arts what *religion* is in the world and algebra in mathematics. It is nothing and everything, the centre and the scope, the highest beauty and the arbitrariness' (Schlegel 1988b, 237; emphasis in the original).[6] That is to say, music presents the formal principles following which any art work is composed.

It remains to define the basic unit of a literary composition, corresponding to the theme in a musical and idea in a philosophical composition. This is not explicitly defined in the aphorisms cited above; the characters are mentioned as an example of the materials only with which the author is expected to deal as 'arbitrarily' as themes are dealt with in music. How Schlegel understands these units can be clarified by an analysis of a somewhat longer text, his review of Goethe's *Wilhelm Meisters Apprenticeship*, in which Schlegel frequently applies the vocabulary of musical analogy. According to Schlegel (1988c, 158), the end of Book I resembles 'intellectual music' (*geistige Musik*), while the beginning of

Book II 'repeats musically the results of Book I' (1988c, 159). Schlegel describes the atmosphere and events in this book: the wanderings of the hero, which are tuned by alternating melancholy and expectation, the temporal wavering between past, present and future, and in a few words the abstract 'content' of the characters ('Philine is the seductive symbol of the lightest sensuality', 'the fair-haired Friedrich represents sound and powerful unruliness'; Schlegel 1988c, 159).[7] In the end, 'merry and moving, furtive and alluring elements are in a wonderful manner interwoven in a finale, and the conflicting sounds reverberate shrilly side by side. This harmony of dissonances is still more beautiful than the music with which Book I ends' (Schlegel 1988c, 160).[8] We can conclude that the elementary units of the musical composition are here events or other elements of the fictive world, as far as they bear a certain meaning or a general quality, by which they contribute to the meaningful whole of the work. It would be an oversimplification to say that corresponding to the themes of a musical composition are those of a literary composition in the sense in which the term is used in literature, namely the abstract thematic content of a concrete event or object in the fictive world of the work of art, although that sometimes seems to be the case. Schlegel, however, is thinking more concretely: the material of which a literary work of art is made does not consist of abstract thoughts but of concrete events, persons and objects, which bear a specific meaning. The compositional units are thus both concrete and meaningful, i.e. not only things in the physical world; they oscillate between a concrete thing or event and the abstract meaning given to it in this particular work of art. Being both concrete entities in the fictional world and bearers of a meaning, the units of a literary composition differ from those of a musical composition, in which the units consist of 'mere' sound. We can now understand why Schlegel saw music as both nothing and everything in its relation to other branches of art: it is the form, all-pervasive but by the same token in itself empty, in which the elements of content are developed for example in a literary work of art.

The decisive difference between Schlegel's view of a literary work of art as a musical composition and Bakhtin's idea of the polyphonic novel, then, is that whereas for Bakhtin the basic unit in a polyphonic novel is a human voice, the 'word' in which a character's view of the world is revealed, in Schlegel's view the basic units of the musical composition of a literary work of art are themes or concrete pieces of the fictional world which carry a certain meaning. The author of a literary work of art is regarded as a composer, who deals with the material in the same manner as a musical composer deals with the sound material in a musical composition. Thus the author's role as the 'composer' of the whole of the work of art is emphasized, in contrast to Bakhtin's idea of the polyphonic novel, in which the author's role has been radically reduced compared to his early aesthetics. Bakhtin's idea of the polyphonic novel conforms with the self-understanding of literary realism, in the sense that in both the content of the fictive world – the characters, their interrelations, the events – seem to determine the structure of the whole of the work. In contrast, according to the Romantic idea of a novel as a musical composition, events, characters and objects in the fictive world do not determine the structure of the work of art; the author is free to compose the whole 'arbitrarily' out of these elements.

This understanding of the musical composition of a literary work of art is represented, in different variations, by several later authors, such as Novalis, Richard Wagner, Friedrich Nietzsche (who applied the idea in his philosophical writings as well), Thomas Mann, Hermann Broch and Milan Kundera. The continuity of the Romantic tradition can easily be shown up to Thomas Mann, while Broch, who generally detests Romanticism, considers Goethe as his predecessor in constructing a 'polyphonic' novel, and Kundera presents Broch as his model to follow. The metaphor of the musical structure of a novel (or, more generally, a literary work of art) is, of course, broader than the concept of the novelistic polyphony. The metaphor of polyphony as a construction principle of the novel, however, emerged in the framework of the broader tradition of thinking which saw a close affinity between musical and literary composition, a view not uncommon in the German literature of the nineteenth and even twentieth century.

The Polyphonic Composition of Thomas Mann's *Doctor Faustus*

As two examples of novelists who follow the Romantic idea of a novel as a musical composition of elements or themes I here discuss Thomas Mann and Milan Kundera. Mann speaks of the 'composing' (*komponieren*) of his literary works in the same sense as a musical composer creates his works.[9] I focus in particular on Mann's late novel, *Doctor Faustus* (1947), in which the musical method of composition is most completely developed. My second example, Milan Kundera, can be seen as a contemporary representative of this thinking. In spite of the fact that Mann and Kundera share the idea of the composition of a literary work of art in analogy with a musical composition, the concept of novelistic polyphony does not mean exactly the same thing when applied to the works of these two authors.

Thomas Mann's *Doctor Faustus* tells the life story of the (fictitious) ingenious German composer Adrian Leverkühn, from the beginning of the twentieth century. Mann (1990c, 187) himself has commented that the novel is in itself what it tells about, namely 'constructive music'. Leverkühn's new idea is that of a musical composition which is 'composed right through' (*durchkomponiert*), i.e. one in which every configuration of notes takes part of the development of the basic thematic material of the work: 'there is nothing unthematic left, nothing which could not show itself to derive from the same basic material' (Mann 1968, 186). Applied to the novel, this means that every detail in it bears a thematic meaning; Mann remarked already earlier that for him, 'every detail, which is not transparent for the idea behind it, is boring'.[10] To take just one example: the cold pond in the vicinity of Leverkühn's childhood home, and again of the place where he spends his last creative years, is not merely a geographical fact but bears a thematic meaning: it is connected with his being a new Faust, condemned to live without human warmth. The meaning of the whole of the novel emerges out of the complex interplay of such details in the fictive world bearing a thematic meaning. The themes are repeated, combined with each other and varied depending on the context in which they appear, just as in a musical composition. Thus the whole of the work is a composition of themes or ideas, as represented by the concrete details in the fictional world of the novels.

By stressing that a novel is a thematic composition, a composition of thought (*Gedankenkomposition*; Mann 1990a, 609), Thomas Mann actually – although not explicitly – denies that the sense of the whole of the work of art is created at the level of the story told in it. *Doctor Faustus* tells the story of Adrian Leverkühn, but the meaningful whole of the work is something much more and far more complex than just a (fictional) biography. In a sense, the whole is built analogous to a musical composition. However, the manner in which Mann describes his dealing with themes in such a thematic composition is only a partial truth about it.

In saying that *Doctor Faustus* is a thematic composition, Mann is emphasizing that it is themes that are at stake and not the incidents in the story as such. Thomas Mann actually understands a musical composition proper in analogy with this, too: in a composition, musical themes in the technical sense, as repeated sound figures, bear a meaning. Leverkühn says that Beethoven actually drafted his works as compositions of ideas: 'He usually sketched in words the course of ideas in a composition, at most putting in a few notes here and there' (Mann 1968, 159). On the other hand, Mann does not consider a philosophical work to be much else than a composition of ideas, or even a 'symphony of ideas' (*Ideensymphonie*; Mann 1990d, 530). This means that he does not consider a philosophical study to be a strict system, built purely rationally by following the irrefutable laws of logic; on the contrary, the philosopher too 'composes' his work by repeating and varying a number of themes and presenting them in ever new combinations. In this understanding of philosophy, Mann is of course following his great mentor, Friedrich Nietzsche.

We may now ask what significance Thomas Mann assigns to a specific mode of musical composition, namely musical polyphony, in characterizing

Doctor Faustus or any of his novels as musical compositions. Polyphony is among the musical terms which he applies for his novels. In his lecture on *The Magic Mountain* to Princeton students, he says that 'a novel was to me always a symphony, a work of counterpoint, a thematic weave, in which the ideas play the role of musical motifs' (1990b, 611). The composition based on counterpoint, i.e. polyphony, is here mentioned side by side with the symphony; moreover, Mann adds that in the composition of his novelistic works he follows the Wagnerian leitmotif technique. Walter Windisch-Laube contends that Thomas Mann's idea of his novels as 'good musical scores' (Mann 1990e, 319) actually conflates three different musical spheres: that of 'the classical symphony (prototype: sonata form), that of early polyphony, and that of the leitmotif technique of Wagner' (Windisch-Laube 1990, 338). In the case of *Doctor Faustus*, we have to add a fourth form of musical composition to these three: that of the twelve-tone technique of Arnold Schoenberg, which Mann, inspired by Theodor Adorno's writings on Schoenberg, lets Leverkühn invent. Like several other compositional forms applied by Leverkühn, Thomas Mann has the twelve-tone technique in mind as a model, when he composes his *Doctor Faustus*. The idea of the novel as *durchkomponiert* can be seen as an allusion not only to Wagner but also to the twelve-tone technique.

We can thus justifiably say that Thomas Mann, with his understanding of a literary work as a musical composition, follows the Schlegelian idea, in which a 'musical' composition refers to a composition of thematic elements, or elements in the fictive world bearing a certain meaning, which are dealt with in a music-like manner. But we still lack good reasons to maintain that it is precisely musical polyphony that forms the basis of Mann's understanding of the 'musical' composition of his novels. A closer scrutiny of *Doctor Faustus*, in terms of how its events are organized so as to form a meaningful whole, shows that actually not only one organizing principle is to be found in it, but a 'polyphony' of layers which follow different principles of organization.

In *Doctor Faustus*, Mann applies four fundamentally different ways of structuring his materials: the realistic, the mythical, the mythical-allegorical, and the musical.[11] The musical composition of themes is described above. Along with this basically Romantic manner of creating a meaningful whole out of the disparate materials in the fictive world, there are three others, of which two are actually announced in the title of the novel. The main title, 'Doctor Faustus', lets the reader understand that he is reading the story of a new Faust, one of the leading figures in modern European mythology, while the subtitle, 'The Life of the German Composer Adrian Leverkühn as Told by a Friend', informs us that the whole of the work is to be taken as belonging to the traditional genre of the (fictional) biography of an artist. In fact, Thomas Mann builds both of these structures into his novel. The fourth mode of structuring the material, the mythical-allegorical, is the level on which the question of Germany is dealt with in the novel; to this the title merely alludes in the word 'German' as an attribute of Leverkühn.[12]

The friend, Serenus Zeitblom, is an old school humanist, for whom the biography of an ingenious individual still has validity as a literary form. He is, however, not depicted without irony: the reader is supposed to recognize that Zeitblom's view of the world is old-fashioned and does not survive the catastrophes of the twentieth century. Mann wrote this novel, and lets his Zeitblom write Leverkühn's biography, during the final, catastrophic phase of World War II, with the collapse of the German culture which both Zeitblom and Leverkühn – in their different ways – represent. Zeitblom's narration of his friend's life follows closely the structuring of events in a realistic novel: events are causally connected, and the characters' actions are psychologically motivated. This is to say that in *Doctor Faustus* the way of structuring experience in the nineteenth-century realistic novel is preserved – on the surface. The reader, however, is able to read the novel against or 'behind' Zeitblom's intentions and perceive that for the protagonist – although not for Zeitblom – events are also organized as a replication of the Faust myth. Leverkühn identifies himself with Faust. He understands that he has bought 24 years of artistic productivity, or inspiration, with a pact with the Devil, actually a syphilis infection which affects in particular his brain, relieving his creativity of the mental crippling caused by his superior intellect. He thus understands his life and his relationships with other people from the perspective of his identity as a new Faust: love, for example, is forbidden to Faust, and he therefore considers himself guilty of the deaths of two persons whom he loves or who love him – even though at the realistic level of the biography he is in no way involved in the deaths of these persons. The reader is expected to read the novel both as a nineteenth-century style realistic biography and as a mythical story. Moreover, the novel also suggests that Leverkühn's story as a new Faust shall be read as an allegory of German 'destiny': of the Germans' pact with the 'devil', which ultimately destroyed them. Through this allegorical reading, the mythical layer of the novel is doubled. When the novel appeared in 1947, the reading public expected from Thomas Mann a judgement and coming to terms with recent German history; however, his mythical-allegorical way of dealing with the matter disappointed many.

Doctor Faustus is thus organized into a meaningful whole not just at one level, following a single logic, but fourfold, following four different logics of creating a meaningful whole out of the details of the fictive world. The simultaneous presence of four fundamentally different ways of organizing the materials – the realistic, the mythical, the mythical-allegorical and the musical – means that none of these modes is assigned the status of *the* truth about the events of the novel. There is no single, absolute 'truth' about what the events actually 'mean', but only several culturally mediated ways of making sense of human experience. By thus relativizing any culturally given modes of organizing the experience – the realistic one dominant in the nineteenth century and living on in the twentieth, the archaic, mythical one (in two different modes), and the Romantic, musical one – Thomas Mann clearly positions himself among the modernists, who question the absolute validity of any culturally given mode of making sense of disparate human experience.

Each of the four organizing forms, the realistic, the mythical, the mythical-allegorical and the musical, cover the whole range of the novel. This is why the term 'polyphony' is appropriate in describing the multi-layered structure of the novel: the four independent 'voices', structuring the elements in different manners, sound throughout the whole of the work. 'Polyphony' is thus a concept that refers to the total organization of the levels. The analogy with a polyphonic musical composition, which here is the reason for speaking of the polyphonic structure of the novel as a whole, is of course lacking in Bakhtin's polyphonic novel. Where Bakhtin's polyphony refers to the equality of the different subjective viewpoints or the 'voices' of the persons, in Mann's case polyphony refers to the manner of composing a novel by using simultaneously a number of (culturally given) authorial strategies for making sense of events in the fictive world and for constructing a whole out of them. Both polyphonies express the modern experience of a plurality of viewpoints, but this plurality manifests itself for Bakhtin and Mann in completely different formal structures of the novel. Thus 'polyphony' in the two cases refers to completely different things.

Polyphony as the Principle of Composition of a 'Novel in the Form of Variations': Milan Kundera

In his collection of essays entitled *The Art of the Novel* (2000), Milan Kundera describes his idea of a polyphonic novel. In so doing, he is not considering the Bakhtinian meaning of the term, nor is he thinking of Thomas Mann; in a later interview, however, he remarks that his concept of polyphony does not derive from Bakhtin (cf. Morello and Kundera 1996, 146–7). Actually, in *The Art of the Novel* he already indicates the source of his use of the term, or at least the idea: it is Hermann Broch, especially his novel trilogy *The Sleepwalkers* (cf. Kundera 2000).

Broch's *Sleepwalkers* consists of five 'lines' which 'differ radically in genre: novel, short story, reportage, poem, essay' (Kundera 2000, 75). Kundera comments that this 'integration of non-novelistic genres into the polyphony of the novel was Broch's revolutionary innovation':

> In Broch's work, the five lines evolve simultaneously, without meeting, united by one or several themes. I've described that sort of construction by a term borrowed from musicology: polyphony. You'll see that it's not so farfetched to compare the novel to music. Indeed, one of the fundamental principles of the great polyphonic composers was the equality of voices: no one voice should dominate, none should serve as mere accompaniment. (Kundera 2000, 75)

Here Kundera introduces the term 'polyphony', referring to Broch's novel, as his own, even though Broch himself actually used the term in this sense (Broch 1981, 117). Moreover, 'voices' do here not refer to human voices, but to the different 'lines' of the novelistic composition, which are considered analogous to different voices in a musical composition. Kundera continues: in Broch's *Sleepwalkers*, the five 'voices' are actually not equal – 'line number one', the main story of the novels, dominates the others by its far greater volume (Kundera 2000, 75). Kundera claims that in a truly polyphonic novel the 'lines', i.e. the different voices, have to be equal.

In his novel *The Book of Laughter and Forgetting* (1979), as well as – to a somewhat smaller extent – in *The Unbearable Lightness of Being* (1983), Kundera has already applied this idea of the novel in practice. In *The Book of Laughter and Forgetting* he calls it the 'novel in the form of variations' (Kundera 1996, 227); the 'polyphonic' novel can be regarded as a further development of this idea. In a 'polyphonic' novel or 'novel in the form of variations', the elements of the different 'lines' of the novel stand with each other in a relationship which he calls 'contrapuntal' (Kundera 2000, 65, 73, 75). The novel may consist of completely separate narrative and non-narrative, or essayistic, lines, in the sense of being about persons who never meet; they may also, as is the case in *The Book of Laughter and Forgetting*, belong to quite different types of discourse or genres. Two or more parts of the novel (Kundera's novels are divided into parts rather than chapters) may belong to the same 'line'. The coherence of the whole does not derive from the story told in any of its lines, but is thematic: unity of action, characteristic of the traditional novel, is replaced by unity of themes (Kundera 2000, 82). This means that the same themes are repeated and varied in different lines of the novel, together forming a thematic composition in analogy with a musical composition of themes.

Kundera comments on his novels that '[a] theme is an existential inquiry. And increasingly I realize that such an inquiry is, finally, the examination of certain words, theme-words' (2000, 84). In each novel, a number of basic themes are examined by varying them in different cases. Kundera elucidates his idea by drawing an analogy between the musical composition of a novel and Arnold Schoenberg's twelve-tone or 'row' technique – like Thomas Mann, omitting to point out that in strictly musical terms polyphony and the twelve-tone technique are mutually exclusive:

> In *The Book of Laughter and Forgetting*, the 'row' [of basic themes] goes: forgetting, laughter, angels, *litost*, border. Over the course of the novel, those five principal words are analysed, studied, defined, redefined, and thus transformed into categories of existence. The novel is built on those few categories the way a house is built on its pillars. (Kundera 2000, 84–5; emphasis in the original)

The musical treatment of the themes never exhausts them, on the contrary, they can be varied endlessly. Actually, Kundera's oeuvre as a whole shows that in his different novels he constantly returns to the same themes, which reappear in ever new variations and combinations (cf. Steinby 2013).

Thus for Kundera too the metaphor of polyphony refers to the way in which themes are dealt with in the novel. Like Thomas Mann, in his understanding of the novel as a musical composition of themes Kundera (probably without being aware of this) is following the Romantic ideas of Friedrich Schlegel. Unlike Mann, however, Kundera does not care to construct a surface narrative following the conventions of literary realism; his 'art of ellipsis' (Kundera 2000, 72) is rather based on the principle of leaving out any details that he does not consider essential in developing the 'row' of themes in the novel. The thematic level is thus much more explicit and pronounced in Kundera's polyphonic novelistic composition than in Mann's. The themes are also more conspicuous than in Dostoevsky's novels (as seen by Bakhtin), since it is not only through the consciousness and action of the characters that we come into contact with their 'life themes'; the author also continually comments on them and elaborates upon them in separate essayistic reflections.[13]

Another difference compared to Mann is, of course, that Kundera's novels actually lack the multilayered structure which forms the polyphony in the overall structure in Mann's novels. In contrast to a polyphonic piece of music, or to the construction of Mann's *Doctor Faustus* with the whole of the work following four different logics simultaneously, in a novel which is 'polyphonic' in the Kunderan sense the different 'voices' in the different lines are actually not 'heard' truly simultaneously. 'Polyphony' for Kundera merely means that the same themes are dealt with in different materials of the different lines of the novel. In claiming that this is 'polyphony', rather than a successive treatment of the same themes, Kundera is suggesting an 'architectonic' reading of a novel in which the different parts are seen as blocks contributing to the total composition of the works.[14] He assumes that in the reading experience of a polyphonic novelistic composition, the 'voice' of a particular part persists in the background as an echo (cf. Husserl's retention; Husserl 1980, 390–96) while the reader is engaged with the following parts. The impression of the simultaneity of 'voices' is enhanced by both Broch and Kundera by dividing a 'line' (a 'voice') into different parts of the novel separated by intervening text, thereby reinforcing the presence of the first 'voice' across the gap when another 'voice' is sounding. For Kundera, conceiving the work as a whole is essential in the reception of any work of art, thus emphasizing the simultaneity rather than the succession of the perception of the elements of the work.

In his concept of a polyphonic novelistic composition, Kundera represents the same experience of a plurality of viewpoints, typical of modernity, as Bakhtin and Thomas Mann. This sense of plurality, however, now does not appear as a plurality of subjective viewpoints, as in Bakhtin, or as a multi-layered structure of the whole of the work, as in Mann's *Doctor Faustus*, but rather as the inexhaustibility of certain basic questions or themes of human existence.

Notes

1. Bakhtin mentions several times (2008a, 10; 2008b, 41; 2008c, 392; cf. also Herrick 2004, 111) Blanckenburg and his *Versuch über den Roman* (1774, 'Essay on the Novel'), where Blanckenburg defines the novel of character (*Charakterroman*) as the most developed form of the novel (cf. Blanckenburg 1965).
2. 'Geist ist eine Musik von Gedanken [...]'.
3. '[W]ird das Thema in ihr nicht so entwickelt, bestätigt, variiert und kontrastiert, wie der Gegenstand der Meditation in einer philosophischen Ideenreihe?'
4. 'Alle Prosa ist poetisch. Sezt [sic] man Prosa der Poesie durchaus entgegen, so ist nur die logische eigentlich Prosa.'
5. 'Die Methode des Romanes ist die der Instrumentalmusik - Im Roman dürfen selbst die Charaktere so willkührlich behandelt werden, wie die Musik ihr Thema behandelt.'
6. 'Die *Musik* ist unter der Kunst was die *Religion* in der Welt, und die Algebra in der Mathematik. Sie ist nichts und Alles, Mittelpunkt und Umkreis; das höchste Schöne und die Willkühr.'
7. 'Philine ist das verführerische Symbol der leichtesten Sinnlichkeit; [...] repräsentiert der blonde Friedrich die gesunde kräftige Ungezogenheit.'
8. 'Das Lustige und das Ergreifende, das Geheime und das Lockende sind im Finale wunderbar verwebt, und die streitenden Stimmen tönen grell nebeneinander. Diese Harmonie von Dissonanzen ist noch schöner als die Musik, mit der das erste Buch endigte [...].'
9. Cf. letter to Agnes Meyer 1 July 1945 (Mann 1979, 409); Mann (1990b, 611).
10. 'Alles Detail ist langweilig, ohne ideelle Transparenz.'
11. The description of the polyphonic structure of *Doctor Faustus* given here draws on my study *Nietzsche als Roman: Über die Sinnkonstituierung in Thomas Manns Doktor Faustus* (see Saariluoma 1996).
12. The German title of the novel contains another allusion to the centrality of the problematic of Germany in the novel. Rather than referring to Leverkühn's profession

as 'Komponist', which is the normal word for 'composer' in modern German, the old-fashioned word 'Tonsetzer', of Germanic origin, is used. This hints – with irony and forewarning – at the ideology of 'truly German'.
13 Kundera has emphasized that it is he himself who speaks in his novels, not a constructed 'narrator' (cf. O'Brien 1992; Parnell 1996; Vibert 2003; Vibert 2005).
14 'Architectonic' in this sense has of course nothing to do with Bakhtin's 'architectonic form'.

References

Aczel, Richard. 2005. 'Polyphony'. In *Routledge Encyclopedia of Narrative Theory*. Edited by David Herman et al., 443–4. London and New York: Routledge.
Bakhtin, Mikhail. 1989 [1984]. *Problems of Dostoevsky's Poetics* (*Problemy poetiki Dostoevskogo*, 1963). Edited and translated by Caryl Emerson. Minneapolis: University of Minnesota Press.
_____. 1990. 'Author and Hero in Aesthetic Activity' ('Avtor i geroi v esteticheskoi deiatelnosti'). In *Art and Answerability: Early Philosophical Essays by M. M. Bakhtin*. Edited by Michael Holquist and Vadim Liapunov, translated by Vadim Liapunov, 4–256. Austin: University of Texas Press.
_____. 2008a [1981]. 'Epic and Novel: Toward a Methodology for the Study of the Novel' ('Epos i roman [O metodologii issledovaniia romana]'). In *The Dialogic Imagination*. Edited by Michael Holquist, translated by Caryl Emerson and Michael Holquist, 3–40. Austin: University of Texas Press.
_____. 2008b [1981]. 'From the Prehistory of the Novelistic Discourse' ('Iz predystorii romannogo slova'). In *The Dialogic Imagination*. Edited by Michael Holquist, translated by Caryl Emerson and Michael Holquist, 41–83. Austin: University of Texas Press.
_____. 2008c [1981]. 'Discourse in the Novel' ('Slovo v romane'). In *The Dialogic Imagination*. Edited by Michael Holquist, translated by Caryl Emerson and Michael Holquist, 259–422. Austin: University of Texas Press.
Biti, Vladimir. 2001. *Literatur- und Kulturtheorie: Ein Handbuch gegenwärtiger Begriffe*. Reinbek bei Hamburg: Rowohlt.
Blanckenburg, Friedrich von. 1965 [1774]. *Versuch über den Roman*. Stuttgart: Metzler.
Brandist, Craig. 2002. *The Bakhtin Circle: Philosophy, Culture and Politics*. London and Sterling, VA: Pluto Press.
Broch, Hermann. 1981. 'Das Weltbild des Romans'. In *Kommentierte Werkausgabe* 9, no. 2: *Schriften zur Literatur II*. Edited by Paul Michael Lützeler, 89–118. Frankfurt am Main: Suhrkamp.
Christoffel, David. 2009. '*Mélos*, roman et re*mélos*'. In *Désaccords parfaits: La réception paradoxale de l'œuvre de Milan Kundera*. Edited by Marie-Odile Thirouin and Martine Boyer-Weinmann, 279–89. Grenoble: Ellug, Université Stendhal.
Clark, Katerina and Michael Holquist. 1984. *Mikhail Bakhtin*. Cambridge, MA and London: Harvard University Press.
Cohen, Hermann. 1912. *Ästhetik des reinen Gefühls*, 2 vols. Berlin: Bruno Cassirer.
Herrick, Tim. 2004. *From Kant to Phenomenology: The Philosophical Affiliations of M. M. Bakhtin and Jacques Derrida*. PhD thesis. University of Sheffield.
Husserl, Edmund. 1980 [1928]. *Vorlesungen zur Phänomenologie des inneren Zeitbewußtseins*. Edited by Martin Heidegger. Darmstadt: Wissenschaftliche Buchgesellschaft.

Kundera, Milan. 1996 [1979]. *The Book of Laughter and Forgetting*. Translated by Aaron Asher. London: Faber & Faber.
———. 2000 [1988]. *The Art of the Novel* (*L'Art du roman*, 1986). Translated by Linda Asher. London: Faber & Faber.
Malcuzynski, M.-Pierrette. 1984. 'Polyphonic Theory and Contemporary Literary Practice'. *Studies in Twentieth-Century Literature* 9: 75–87.
Mann, Thomas. 1979. *Briefe*, vol. 3. Edited by Erika Mann. Frankfurt am Main: Fischer.
———. 1990a [1926]. 'Pariser Rechenschaft'. In *Gesammelte Werke*, vol. 11, 9–97. Frankfurt am Main: Fischer.
———. 1990b [1939]. 'Einführung in den "Zauberberg"'. In *Gesammelte Werke*, vol. 11, 602–17. Frankfurt am Main: Fischer.
———. 1990c [1949]. *Die Entstehung des Doktor Faustus*. In *Gesammelte Werke*, vol. 11, 145–301. Frankfurt am Main: Fischer.
———. 1990d [1938]. 'Schopenhauer'. In *Gesammelte Werke*, vol. 9, 528–80. Frankfurt am Main: Fischer.
———. 1990e [1918]. *Betrachtungen eines Unpolitischen*. In *Gesammelte Werke*, vol. 12, 7–589. Frankfurt am Main: Fischer.
———. 1968 [1949]. *Doctor Faustus: The Life of the German Composer Adrian Leverkühn as Told by a Friend*. Translated by H. T. Lowe-Porter. Harmondsworth: Penguin.
Morello, André-Alain and Milan Kundera. 1996. 'Questions et réponses échangées par écrit entrée André-Alain Morello et Milan Kundera'. *Dix-neuf/Vingt* 1: 145–9.
O'Brien, John. 1992. 'Milan Kundera: Meaning, Play, and the Role of the Author'. *Critiques: Studies in Contemporary Fiction* 34: 3–18.
Parnell, Tim. 1996. 'Sterne and Kundera: The Novel of Variations and the "Noisy Foolishness of Human Certainty"'. In *Laurence Sterne in Modernism and Postmodernism*. Edited by David Pierce and Peter de Voogd, 147–55. Amsterdam and Atlanta, GA: Rodopi.
Saariluoma [Steinby], Liisa. 1996. *Nietzsche als Roman. Über die Sinnkonstituierung in Thomas Manns 'Doktor Faustus'*. Tübingen: Niemeyer.
Schlegel, Friedrich. 1988a [1798]. 'Athenäums-Fragmente'. In *Kritisch Schriften und Fragmente*. Edited by Ernst Behler and Hans Eichner, vol. 2, 105–56. Paderborn: Schöningh.
———. 1988b [1796–1801]. 'Aus den Heften zur Poesie und Literatur'. In *Kritisch Schriften und Fragmente*, vol. 5, 163–268. Edited by Ernst Behler and Hans Eichner. Paderborn: Schöningh.
———. 1988c [1798]. 'Über Goethes Meister'. In *Kritisch Schriften und Fragmente*, vol. 2, 157–69. Edited by Ernst Behler and Hans Eichner. Paderborn: Schöningh.
Steinby, Liisa. 2011. 'Hermann Cohen and Bakhtin's early aesthetics'. *Studies in Eastern European Thought* 3: 227–49.
———. 2013. *Kundera and Modernity*. West Lafayette, IN: Purdue University Press.
Vibert, Bertrand. 2003. 'En finir avec le narrateur? Sur la pratique romanesque de Milan Kundera'. *La Voix narrative, vol. 2. Cahiers de narratologie no 10*, 3–18. Edited by Jean-Louis Brau. Nice: Université de Nice Sophia-Antipolis.
———. 2005. 'Milan Kundera: La fiction pensive'. *Temps Modernes* 629: 109–33.
Windisch-Laube, Walter. 1990. 'Thomas Mann und die Musik'. In *Thomas-Mann-Handbuch*. Edited by Helmut Koopmann. Stuttgart: Kröner.

Chapter 4

FAMILIAR OTHERNESS: PECULIARITIES OF DIALOGUE IN EZRA POUND'S POETICS OF INCLUSION

Mikhail Oshukov

Ezra Pound's long poem *The Cantos* (1970) seems to readily lend itself to Bakhtinian analysis: it provides ample evidence of literary and extraliterary heteroglossia, dialogization, irony, indeterminacy, and semantic openendedness. *The Cantos* may be especially instrumental in illustrating Bakhtin's idea of the development of the epic genre: comparing it with classic epic poems, one cannot but notice the disappearance of the absolute epic distance, the permeation of modernity in the text of this modern 'tale of the tribe', as well as dramatic changes in the way the author positions himself in the text.

Pound scholarship has long distanced itself from charges of fascism; nor did the ideas of militant monologism associated with it prove particularly productive in comparison with the dialogic approach, as represented by Line Henriksen's (2006) analysis of *The Cantos* as a heteroglossic model of lyric. References to the polyphonic nature of *The Cantos* have indeed become commonplace. The divide between the classic epic and the modern one is so obvious that a 'new' genre type has recently been suggested (Murphy 1989) for American long poems, the 'verse novel', with reference to Bakhtin's theory of the 'novelization' of genres and V. V. Ivanov's concept of 'prosaization' of twentieth-century poetry.

But however obvious Pound's polyphonism, it seems worthwhile to look into its mechanisms. Considering this probably most polyphonic text of the twentieth century in a Bakhtinian frame of reference provides an opportunity to discuss Bakhtin's concept of dialogue and highlight certain complexities in Bakhtin's approach, which is sometimes confused with politically correct multiculturalism. In this paper I therefore focus on the representation of the 'other' in *The Cantos*, on the nature of the poem's inclusiveness (thematic, linguistic and structural, according to Bakhtin's [1996, 159] genre criteria), the manner of orchestration of its polyphony, and the specifics of its dialogism. The analysis, which does not claim to be exhaustive, will be based on the early cantos (*Draft of XVI Cantos*, 1925), after which the revealed pattern will be elaborated with reference to Pound's prose reflections; finally, it will be tentatively extrapolated to certain larger contexts.

Hieratic Head

In 1914, shortly before his death, Henri Gaudier-Brzeska (1891–1915), Pound's friend and disciple, carved a famous marble figure, which came to be known as the 'hieratic head of Ezra Pound'. The epithet 'hieratic', obviously highlighting the sacral aspect of Pound's poetry, at the same time hints at the hieratic, i.e. simplified/reduced, Egyptian hieroglyphic writing system.

While working on the marble head, Brzeska was inspired by the ritual figures from Easter Island, particularly by the 2.5 metre high basalt figure of Hoa-haka-nana-ia, obvious traces of which are evident in Brzeska's work despite all the modifications he subjected the original to. Brzeska made a figure one third the size of the original and simplified its features to a minimum, emphasizing with laconic strokes a new message in the ancient form, for instance accentuating the phallic features of the figure, probably hinting thereby at the active character of Pound's creativity.

Pound treated Brzeska's project very seriously. He himself purchased the white marble for it, he enjoyed sitting for the figure and later referred to those hours as the happiest in his life. Pound liked the figure itself and its virile shape. James Laughlin, another disciple of Pound's and the future founder of the famous New Directions,[1] remembers the place the figure occupied in Pound's house and the impression it produced on visitors (Carpenter 1990, 528):

> And you accepted me to your 'Ezuversity' […]
> And the classes were held at meals in the dining room of what
>   you called the Albugerro Rapallo,
> Where Gaudier's head of you sat in the corner, an astonishment
>   to the tourists […]
> And you showed me with some relish that if one looked at the
>   back of the cranium it was clearly a scrotum.

The 'Head', so important for Pound, does not merely exemplify Brzeska's views on art and on Pound in particular; it is also an example of modernist culture dialogue, of a modernist interpretation of heteroglossia. Without any claims at verisimilitude, the 'Head' synthesizes various heterogeneous trends: the Rapa Nui cult, the phallic cult, elements of cubism, etc. All these constituents are subordinated to the will of the sculptor, whose implicit presence is manifest in the rough cuts intentionally left on the marble surface.

The Hieratic Head may be seen as a metaphor of Pound's own approach to culture dialogue and of his translation of 'culture' into the familiarized vernacular 'Kulchur': Pound's playful spelling, transforming the Latin root and highlighting the live phonetic nature of the word, both desacralizes and enlivens the concept.

Encountering Hades

In 1925, Pound published his first sixteen cantos, the ones he started working on at approximately the same time Gaudier-Brzeska was carving his white marble head. The motif of encountering 'the other' is manifest from the very first lines of the text, shaping the polyphony of the poem.

The first canto starts with the episode of Odysseus' descent to the realm of Hades and meeting Tiresias in search of a prophesy. Pound's own translation of Andreas Divus' (1538) Latin translation of the eleventh song of the *Odyssey* shows some characteristic strategies of textual manipulation which will persist throughout the whole poem: Pound cuts out a fragment of the original and impregnates it with his own message by slightly changing the accents.

The realm of Hades is described in a few very laconic strokes. Like Gaudier-Brzeska, Pound (1998, 3) cuts off everything 'superfluous', leaving just a few essential (even if obvious) features of the 'other'. The realm of dead souls looks the way it is supposed to look: it is surrounded by 'deepest waters', the land is covered by 'mist, unpierced ever with glitter of sun-rays nor with stars'. The image is foreign to Odysseus, though not exaggeratedly exotic.

However, having entered this land, Pound's Odysseus behaves as if at home. With his sword he digs a hole, which he calls by a word of his own, a 'pitkin' (Pound's neologism), offers a sacrifice 'as set in Ithaca', and drives off the approaching souls in a very matter-of-fact manner (Pound 1998, 3). Except for his mother, the only soul Odysseus talks to is Elpenor, a former companion of his, who broke his neck after getting drunk at Circe's feast. Having arrived in a foreign land, Pound's Odysseus chooses to talk to someone he knows rather than to a stranger.

The dialogue with Elpenor is much lengthier than even the conversation with Tiresias, which is supposedly Odysseus' only purpose in the Hades trip.

Moreover, Pound makes Tiresias sound like an old acquaintance of Odysseus'; his tone is casual and some words are humorously ambiguous:

> A second time? why? [...]
> Stand from the fosse, leave me my bloody bever
> For soothsay.
> (Pound 1998, 4)

Tiresias' prophecy, which Odysseus is supposedly seeking, is so brief and is pronounced so casually that it seems as though the message is not news to Odysseus:

> And he strong with the blood, said then: 'Odysseus
> Shalt return through spiteful Neptune, over dark seas,
> Lose all companions'.
> (Pound 1998, 4–5)

Thirty-seven lines of Andreas Divus' text are reduced to a mere three in Pound's canto. Pound cuts out all details of the prophecy, leaving only the core (safe return and loss of companions), and gets rid of all hesitancy in Tiresias' tone (conditionals, 'may' modality, etc.), leaving only firm unequivocal indicatives: 'shalt return', '(shalt) lose'.

In Canto I, Pound's character thus goes to the most remote and most foreign of the world's lands (the ultimate 'other') to acquire new knowledge, but what he in fact finds there is something (and someone) he already knows. From the very first lines, Pound's text foregrounds not the new, the strange, or the foreign, but the familiar in the 'other', even if in exotic disguise.

Pound's Odysseus is not transformed by his experiences in the Underworld: his interaction with the 'other' is minimal. The simultaneity of the Underworld is not disturbed by the linear development of Odysseus' quest. Equally, none of the 'events' occurring during the Hades quest will have any impact on the outcome of his trip. Even before arriving in Hades, Odysseus knows exactly what he is looking for: he needs the prophesy (the word) which will serve as a tool in dealing with 'spiteful Neptune' and the 'dark seas'. He is looking for the means of control, which he will need upon return to his 'own' world. This situation becomes archetypal in Pound's fictional world.

In Bakhtin's taxonomy, Tiresias' speech, rendered by Odysseus and 'translated' by Pound, exemplifies the third type of utterance, the dual-voice utterance in its bi-directional variant, as a rendering of the other's words with a shift of accents (Bakhtin 1994, 87). Tiresias' prophecy as rendered by Odysseus maintains its original 'object intention' (*predmetnaia intenciia*), but it also reveals Odysseus' voice and his intention. Moreover, positioned at the very beginning of Pound's epic, it obviously contains one additional voice, that of the author; this gives the words of the prophesy a metaphorical tone and relates them to his own text and his own quest. This last voice becomes even more audible towards the end of the canto.

A brief focalization shift at the end of the canto provides a new dimension to Pound's dialogical discourse. Pound goes even further than Brzeska: not only does he borrow a classical work as the basis for his own text, he also 'bares the device' (as Roman Jakobson would have put it) by providing a direct reference to the original. In the last lines of the canto, Pound's own voice suddenly interrupts the homodiegetic narrative of Odysseus, addressing Andreas Divus directly and giving a reference to the edition of Divus' translation he is using. Having done that, he proceeds with the narrative in a heterodiegetic manner:

> Lie quiet Divus. I mean, that is Andreas Divus,
> In officina Wecheli, 1538, out of Homer.
> And he sailed, by Sirens and thence outward and away
> And unto Circe
> (Pound 1998, 5)

Pound's montage, juxtaposing heterogeneous fragments of texts, accentuates the familiar in the 'other': name, year, place, book. Pound addresses Divus as his Odysseus addresses the dead souls in Hades. The metaphoric nature of the narrative shift also highlights the shared aspect in seemingly different forms: 'Lie quiet Divus' reminds us of Hades and of Elpenor, who, 'unwept, unburied', cannot 'lie quiet' in his death; Pound pays tribute to Divus as Odysseus does to Elpenor. Thus Pound's text starts as a complex dialogue of voices. While he speaks to Divus or shifts accents in the words of Odysseus or Tiresias, however, it is not with them that Pound is primarily building an argument. In Bakhtin's terms, the other's word in Pound's text is not bi- but tri-directional: recognized as the other's and revealing accent shifts, it is appropriated by the author and addressed to his contemporaries. Like Odysseus, Pound has his own 'spiteful Neptune' and 'dark seas' to fight against.

Walking with Kung

In the most general terms, the fictional space of Pound's epic is structured by two sacral poles of 'otherness': the quest proceeds 'between Kung and Eleusis', as Pound himself puts it (Pound 1998, 258). If the realm of Hades, which is related to the Eleusinian mysteries, is presented and familiarized in the first canto, Kung (Confucius) appears in Canto XIII. As in Canto I, we see the character *in medias res*:

> Kung walked
> by the dynastic temple
> and into the cedar grove,
> and then out by the lower river [...]
> (Pound 1998, 58)

Once again, describing the encounter with a foreign environment, Pound gives us but a few characteristically 'authentic' details, conforming with the sacral nature of the topos: the dynasty temple, cedar groves, apricot flowers, sounds of lute flying up like smoke. What starts with some resemblance of continuity, is followed by a collage of seemingly random quotes, fragments from the teaching of Confucius, retold by Pound from the French edition in Pauthier's translation, which do not follow any chronological or logical order but rather build up to a static image in its simultaneity:

> And 'we are unknown', said Kung,
> 'You will take up charioteering?'
> [...]
> And Kung said
> 'Respect a child's faculties
> 'From the moment it inhales the clear air,
> 'But a man of fifty who knows nothing
> Is worthy of no respect.'
> And 'When the prince has gathered about him
> 'All the savants and artists, his riches will be fully employed.'
> And Kung said, and wrote on the bo leaves:
> If a man have not order within him
> He can not spread order about him.
> [...]
> And he said
> 'Anyone can run to excesses,
> 'It is easy to shoot past the mark,
> 'It is hard to stand firm in the middle.'
> (Pound 1998, 59)

Pound reduces Confucianism to a minimum, leaving just a few phrases by Kung and his disciples. In Bakhtin's terms, Pound uses the other's word for his own ends, adding a new intention to that already present in the word. Cutting off the 'superfluous', Pound adds his own accentuation. However random and seemingly irrelevant some of the quoted lines may sound, one cannot but notice the repetition of one key word in the speeches of both the teacher and the disciples: the word 'order' (emphasis by M. O.):

> And Tseu-lou said, 'I would put the defences in *order*',
> And Khieu said, 'If I were lord of a province
> 'I would put it in better *order* than this is.'
> And Tchi said, 'I would prefer a small mountain temple,
> 'With *order* in the observances,
> with a suitable performance of the ritual',
> [...]
> And Kung said, and wrote on the bo leaves:
> If a man have not *order* within him
> He can not spread *order* about him;
> And if a man have not *order* within him
> His family will not act with due *order*;
> And if the prince have not *order* within him
> He can not put *order* in his dominions.
> And Kung gave the words '*order*'
> and 'brotherly deference'
> And said nothing of the 'life after death'.
> (Pound 1998, 58–9)

In this word, highlighted by the author, we distinctly hear several voices: the voice of Confucius, that of Pound interpreting and appreciating Confucius, and, finally, that of Pound pronouncing his judgement on modernity. Like Tiresias' brief prophecy in response to the Odysseus' unasked question, this word, repeated ten times throughout the seventy-eight-line canto, sounds like an answer to an implicit question by the narrator. The question will be explicitly articulated later, and in a different text.

As Bakhtin notes, the other's word incorporated in our speech inevitably acquires a new intention, *our own*, thus becoming biphonic (1994, 94). Reconstructing the image of Confucius, Pound creates a 'hieratic' portrait of the philosopher: he cuts off that which is 'superfluous' – the ambiguity and polysemanticism – and adds several very firm strokes of his own. The message of the other remains intact, but the shift in accent unmistakably reveals the presence of the second voice in the other's words. The language of Kung and his disciples, like that of Tiresias, sounds quite modern and recognizable, especially in such exclamations as 'You old fool, come out of it, get up and do something useful' (Pound 1998, 59). At times the second voice becomes more than audible and seems to modify not only the accent but the message of the original. Thus, in the sentence '[w]ithout character you will be unable to play on that instrument or execute the music fit for the Odes [...]'(1998, 60), instead of the original 'without human values', Pound uses the word 'character' (one of his favourite words); instead of the abstract term 'music', he makes Confucius say 'music fit for the Odes', i.e. music which fits Kung's own teaching, which (similar to Tiresias' prophesy in Canto I) sounds much more authoritarian than the original.

However, the Confucius of Canto XIII does not confine himself to quoting some of the author's favourite words and intonations; he proclaims a thesis which is seminal for Pound himself. If Tiresias, as the central figure in the realm of Hades, prophesizes that Pound's protagonist will be able to complete his quest, even if all his companions perish, Confucius too finishes his speech with a prophesy, though on a different scale:

> The blossoms of the apricot
> blow from the east to the west,
> and I have tried to keep them from falling
> (Pound 1998, 60)

Pound's Kung hints at his interest in spreading his teaching in the Western hemisphere, and hopes that the petals of Ta Hio, the Great Learning, will reach the other land intact. Like Tiresias, who pronounces the few words Odysseus wants him to say, Confucius in Canto XIII says exactly what Pound wants to hear from him. The word, while keeping its original message, takes on a new voice, a new direction and a new target listener: Pound's contemporaries. The dialogue proceeds on two levels: as Pound's reaction to Confucius and as his reaction to modernity.

Thus the China of the sixth century BC, while maintaining the attributes of the 'other', appears as a familiar land, close to us both historically and geographically. Its language sounds quite recognizable and modern, and the distance of two and a half thousand years becomes irrelevant: Confucius, in whose portrait we begin to recognize the reflection of Pound himself, promises us that the apricot petals of his teaching will overcome distance, bridging the chasm between Orient and Occident.

Certain characteristics of the fictional world in Canto XIII are similar to those of Canto I. The seemingly foreign, exotic and ancient is familiarized and modernized but the simultaneity of the 'other' world does not transform the narrator, who remains an observer and seems to have known all too well what message to expect from the other. Like Odysseus, the narrator comes to the foreign land in search of a tool. What that tool is, Pound will explain in his prose manifestos.

Guide to Otherness

Pound's manipulations with the 'other' and their role in structuring the polyphony of *The Cantos* become even more manifest if we look at another virtual quest towards otherness, that of *Guide to Kulchur* (1938) and *Confucius and Mencius* (1937), which, among other things, may be considered as an extended commentary on Pound's dialogue with Confucius, an attempt at a rationalization and legitimation of Pound's method.

In the preface to the *Guide*, Pound reveals the goal of his quest: '*Guide to Kulchur*: a mousing round for a word, for a shape, for an order, for a meaning' (1970b, 8). The word 'order', which reminds us of Canto XIII, shows what Pound was looking for in Confucianism. Pound's oriental quest appears to be a search not only for the word, but also for a shape and an order, i.e. a tool which might help provide a meaning for the word of ancient prophesy and for the modern world, as well as organize the latter.

The 'foreignness' of the other country is once again represented by a few characteristic strokes: in this case, it is the Chinese characters inserted into the text. The reader, who is defined as 'those who have not been able to afford a university education' (Pound 1970b, 6), is offered extracts from Confucius in the original. Even if we doubt Pound's sincerity and suspect that the target reader is someone much more involved in the system of higher education than Pound admits, still it remains unlikely that the average university professor was supposed to be proficient in Chinese. Apparently, Chinese characters serve not only as message carriers but also as a background legitimizing the message: they are not to be read but seen. Like the deepest waters and the absolute darkness of Canto I, or the bamboo plates, cedar groves and apricot petals of Canto XIII, Chinese characters here serve to provide the evidence of authenticity for the message they foreshadow. The other's word, inserted into the text in its pure foreign form, supports the voice of the author and a message addressed to his contemporaries.

Guide to Kulchur opens with the 'Digest of the Analects'. Through the scanty authentic details, we can see the edited, 'hieratic' portrait of Confucius. As in Canto XIII, Pound gives us a selection of Kung's sayings, and, like any selection, it becomes a reflection not only of its subject matter but also of the author of the digest and of his method. Similar to Odysseus in Canto I, driving off all the approaching souls so that he can talk to one of them, Tiresias, and then reducing Tiresias' speech two brief phrases, the narrator of *Guide to Kulchur* cuts off the 'superfluous' and offers us some of Confucius' 'main' ideas.

In the representation of Confucius, Pound emphasizes the familiar: 'Kung's life seems to be in conformity with the best modern views' (Pound 1970b, 272).

Seeing the Orient through the occidental optic and familiarizing China, he repeatedly draws parallels between East and West, using Western historical and cultural concepts in interpreting Chinese history, and vice versa: interpreting Western history through Chinese imagery. Emphasizing the familiar in the teaching of Confucianism, Pound includes Kung in a paradigm of his own, subordinating the image of the teacher to his own scheme, his own order. Thus Confucius appears to share company with those Western reformers who are especially dear to Pound, such as Clifford Douglas (author of the social credit theory) or Edmondo Rossoni (minister of agriculture in Mussolini's government).

Explaining Kung's methods, Pound refers to contemporary analogies: 'Kung's first public job was a Douglasite assessment of the productivity of the province set for his inspection' (1970b, 272). Pound tries to read Confucianism into Mussolini's economic practices: 'Of living men, Edmondo Rossoni, with his agricultural experts and his care for crops, is nearest the Confucian model' (1970b, 274). We learn what contemporary trends Kung would not have approved of: 'While interested in increasing agricultural production (as Cavour or Rossoni) he [Kung] was by analogy against the Bedaux and Stakhanov sweating and speeding-up systems' (1970b, 272). We learn that Kung would most probably have approved of Pound's interest in Oriental cultures: 'Kung is modern in his interest in folklore. All this Fraser-Frobenius research is Confucian' (1970b, 272). Thus Confucius becomes the archetype of a 'true' reformer.

On the other hand, in the portrait of Confucius, as in a mirror, we cannot but recognize certain features of Pound himself. Pound's voice, audible in Kung's quotations, is strengthened by several obvious parallels drawn by Pound: 'Kung was an anthologist and a shortener' (Pound 1973, 82) – this sounds like a justification of Pound's own method of reduction and montage. It appears that Pound appeals to Confucius as Odysseus did to Tiresias, seeking the word that he actually already knows.

The knowledge which Pound 'finds' in China not only reflects the best specimens of Western culture known to Pound, it is also a tool for transforming the West. The West is supposed to recognize itself in Pound's mirror and comply with the image. Pound speaks of 'the lessons of Confucius'. Pound wants 'to provide the average reader with a few tools for dealing with the heteroclite mass of undigested information hurled at him daily' (1970b, 23). Just as Gaudier-Brzeska reduces the sacred statue of Hoa-haka-nana-ia to a minimalist phallic image of Pound's creativity, so Pound himself reduces Confucianism to a minimum and turns it into a symbolic tool. This tool, carved by Pound, is not only necessary to the 'average reader' – it is vital, Pound claims, for the whole Western world: as 'hypodermic injection or strait-jacket' for some countries, and as a means of 'continuous hygiene' (1973, 79) to others.

The much-quoted Confucian word 'order', while keeping its 'otherness', its original message and addressed to the original target listener, in Pound's text becomes biphonic and bidirectional. By emphasizing the concept of order in Kung's teaching – 'at the centre of every movement for order or reconstruction in China you will find a Confucian' (1973, 79) – Pound implies the absence of order in the world around him. The world, 'the heteroclite mass of undigested information' needs an order: 'the whole of Western idealism is a jungle. Christian theology is a jungle. To think through it, to reduce it to some semblance of order, there is no better axe than the Ta Hio' (Pound 1973, 79). Confucianism is seen as a tool ('an axe') for shaping Western culture: reducing it to a meaningful form.

'In culture, exotopy is the most powerful tool of understanding', wrote Bakhtin (2002, 457). Bakhtin argues that it is to the outsider that a given culture reveals itself most fully, though never completely: the outsider (the 'other') makes it answer questions it would never ask itself. Pound was most certainly an outsider for the Chinese tradition (curiously, for European and American culture as well). Questioning the *other* culture with his *own* questions (as Bakhtin recommends), Pound was not proficient in Chinese; moreover, his knowledge of the East, as he admitted, was very approximate. There are numerous articles analysing Pound's errors in interpreting Chinese characters. However, the transformations of Oriental culture images in Pound's works are not merely the result of an inaccurate reading of the original, for they manifest an apparent system. There is a certain pattern (shape? order?) in Pound's method of familiarizing the 'other'. Pound creates an image of China as a hypodermic injection, a strait-jacket and an instrument of continuous hygiene for the West. However, the metaphorical treatment he designs for the occidental world appears to be a reflection of his own manipulations of the Orient: reducing the object to a minimum, injecting his own message into it, and ensuring the hygienic maintenance of certain essential characteristics of the original in their (supposedly) pure form.

The quest chronotope, to which these manipulations with 'the other' contribute, highlights the familiarity of the foreign topos despite the fact of its unquestionable otherness. The 'other' is void of markedly exotic or foreign features. However, the time of the 'other' world and that of the character/narrator are presented differently: the continuity of the quest emphasizes the simultaneity of the object of the quest. The encounter with the other does not transform the character, nor does the new knowledge the latter acquires appear entirely new. The purpose of this encounter is the word, which absorbs a new voice, a new message, and a new direction.

Analysing the representation of the 'other' in European Baroque culture, Gérard Genette notes the conflict between the acute awareness of the otherness and the inability of the era to perceive this otherness in a form other than disguised sameness. Genette explains this by the 'geographical giddiness' of Baroque culture caused by the discovery of the New World. Similarly, Pound's familiarization of China may be partly explained by the giddiness caused by Fenollosa's 'discovery' of Chinese poetry for the West. For Pound, China became a New World, like America for the European Baroque. 'It is possible', writes Pound 'that this century will find a new Greece in China' (1968, 215). This telescopic metaphor (Europe looking at/through China and seeing Greece, i.e. seeing itself in its pure original form, i.e. its own new beginning) illustrates Pound's chronotope of *The Cantos*, eliminating ages and thousands of miles in its ideogrammic simultaneity. Like Odysseus in Canto I, Pound seems to know all too well what he needs to find in the strange land: through the image of the 'other' he recognizes familiar archetypes, which promise to (re)shape his own world.

The Pattern Persists

If we define the nature of Pound's transformation of the 'other' in his early cantos as reducing the image while at the same time maintaining major characteristics of its pure otherness and accentuating the familiar in the 'other', we find that Pound does not apply this method to Chinese or Greek material alone. A similar pattern may be found in cantos devoted to American history, with their selection of names and episodes: including them in a certain paradigm, arranging them in a certain order, providing new accents and a new shape, and using the resulting picture as a tool for diagnosing and healing the modern world.

Pound considers historical facts, whether Chinese, European, or American, as discrete fragments, separate objects, which can be arranged and rearranged in different manners: he refers to them as 'slabs' and 'chunks'. These 'chunks' may be shuffled and split, they may be inserted into the text in a seemingly random order. In Pound's view, however, these fragments build up an ideogram, a complex picture, in which the signifier is adequate to the signified. History in Pound's interpretation appears not as a linear, continuous process but rather as a simultaneous collage made of 'slabs', 'chunks', or luminous details, as evidenced by both 'The China Cantos' (LII–LXI) and 'The Adams Cantos' (LXII–LXXI).

Pound modifies these 'slabs' not only by editing (reduction and familiarization) but also by montage, juxtaposing heterogeneous voices and fragments. Thus contextualized, quoted texts acquire new meanings and new significance. Montage destroys the linearity both of the text and of history: fragments representing different eras and cultures are placed next to each other as equal.

In order to better understand Pound's manipulations of the other's voice and his chronotope of encountering the other, we need to consider his texts in the context of the vorticist aesthetic. Vorticism as a literary movement was named and to a large extent shaped by Pound himself; even though it existed formally for only a few months in 1914, till the beginning of World War I, Pound nevertheless never stopped referring to vortex principles in his essays and letters, showing how important these concepts were for him.

In Pound's defence of vorticism, what is very important is the contrast between vorticism and symbolism. Although both symbolism and vorticism are based on the idea of a correspondence between an image and a certain spiritual state, Pound emphasizes the difference between the two approaches. 'The symbolists dealt in "association", that is, in a sort of allusion, almost of allegory. They degraded the symbol to the status of a word. They made it a form of metonomy' (Pound 1970a, 84). The last word gives a key to understanding vorticism and Pound's aesthetic. Consciously or subconsciously, Pound applies a frame of reference which will shape linguistic and literary studies in the first half of the twentieth century.

Roman Jakobson (1990) defines the dichotomy metaphor/metonymy not only as different poetic tropes, but as two opposite poles of language structure, as well as of any other semiotic structure. Moreover, considering the opposition in terms of paradigmatic/syntagmatic relations, Jakobson associates different aspects of linguistic behaviour and different literary traditions with either the metaphoric or the metonymic kind. Metonymy, the 'horizontal', syntagmatic type of relation, relies on the concepts of time, succession of events, and cause-and-effect relations, whereas metaphor, representing the 'vertical', paradigmatic axis of the message, is based on the concepts of space, simultaneity, and atemporal relations. Jakobson roughly links the metonymic approach with prose and the metaphoric one with poetry, but also shows that the prevalence of either metaphor or metonymy may be traced in various literary traditions, as well as in the visual arts; thus, Jakobson (1990, 128) refers to the metonymic aspects of cubism, the metaphoric nature of surrealism, Griffith's metonymic *mise-en-scènes* and Chaplin's metaphoric montage.

Pound seems to be thinking in similar terms. Analysing vorticism and contrasting it to symbolism, impressionism, and futurism, he bases his argument on two major oppositions: inward versus outward and temporal versus spatial. Opposing vorticism to impressionism, Pound calls the former intensive and the latter extensive. Thus impressionism is seen as a more superficial and temporal approach, as opposed to vorticism, which appears inwardly oriented and atemporal. Futurism is characterized as 'accelerated impressionism', with reference to 'outward' movement and to the temporal, and as 'spreading or surface art', which is an even more articulate accusation of the school as temporally developing, outwardly oriented and superficial.

Pound sees cinematography as the ultimate development of impressionism (the implicit reference is to the linear or temporal development of the image in cinema). Unlike futurism (as a descendant of impressionism), vorticism, according to Pound, does not have the 'curious tic for destroying past glories' (1970a, 90; a reference to its temporal development): it has a more complex view of the cultural context. The vorticist idea of the past, according to Pound, is not confined to four or five centuries or a single continent (a hint at the superficiality of futurism). It is interesting that in discussing the seemingly temporal issue, Pound brings up a spatial reference to 'continents' and dialogue with other cultures, which makes his concept of tradition more complex than that of his opponents.

Thus, the temporal aspect seems secondary to Pound – whether in the concept of art history or in the structure of a particular piece of art. 'Great works of art [are] lords over fact, over race-long recurrent moods and over to-morrow', proclaims Pound (1970a, 92). Art overcomes the temporal, as true art transcends both the past ('over race-long recurrent moods') and the future ('over to-morrow'). Pound's view of tradition (close to what T. S. Eliot would develop in his famous article, 'Tradition and the individual talent', in 1919) as a simultaneity suggests a metaphorical, 'spatial' arrangement of art works. As it turns out, a similar 'spatial' arrangement is what he seems to advocate in particular works of art. Vorticism, argues Pound, is about 'the organization of forms', i.e. the arrangement of spatial elements. Pound quotes Brzeska, who defines art in similar 'spatial' terms and discusses sculptural feeling as 'the appreciation of masses in relation' and the sculptor's work as 'the defining of these masses by planes' (1970a, 20). Obviously preferring the paradigmatic axis to the syntagmatic one, Pound praises the 'mathematics of harmony' over 'mimetic representation'. In a similar manner, favouring paradigmatic harmony over syntagmatic mimesis, he discusses the future of music: 'A new vorticist music would come from a new computation of the mathematics of harmony, not from a mimetic representation of dead cats in a fog-horn, alias noise-tuners' (Pound 1970a, 93).

'The organization of forms is a much more energetic and creative action than the copying or imitating of light on a haystack', believes Pound (Pound 1970a, 92). Thus, Pound (1970a, 92) organizes forms in his own texts: juxtaposes 'chunks' and 'slabs', voices and images, cutting linear narratives and arranging fragments in the simultaneity of an ideogram. This favouring of the spatial, paradigmatic, or metaphoric over the temporal, syntagmatic or metonymic in Jakobson's terms, explains the manner in which Pound treats the other in his dialogical text: the other is treated not metonymically but metaphorically. The Hades extract in Canto I is designed not to explain the nature of Homer's epic world but to reveal something about Pound's quest. The Kung episode of Canto XIII is not an attempt at a mimetic representation of China but a means of interpreting the West. The Chinese characters inserted into the text of Pound's epic are not meant to explain the Chinese writing system. Taken out of their original context and filled with new associations, they become tools for interpreting modernity.

The edited and familiarized voices of the other, images of history, 'chunks' of political economy or literature, are organized in Pound's text according to his understanding of the ideogram principle: an arrangement of concrete images contributing to an abstract idea. What is Pound looking for? He is trying to trace the origins, i.e. the essence and the 'pure' form of a phenomenon, which is always metaphorically linked to the present-day status quo. In Chinese history, he is looking for the roots of true philosophy and economic theory. In the European Renaissance, he is searching for the beginnings of the true dialogue between the power and culture in Europe; in Jefferson and Adams – the beginning of the new (true) America. Pound's 'ideogram', as a collage of self-sufficient 'chunks', tries to establish the simultaneous mode of representation of the continuous, a picture which capitalizes on its own origins.

Conclusion

There seems to be a common denominator in all of Pound's projects. Desperately looking for the originally pure and the essential, constantly trying to link the past and the present, the classical and the modern, the Oriental and the Occidental, American and European culture, Pound seems to be developing a complex 'ideogram'. Even his infamous fight against usury, in which he sees the intermediary as a 'superfluous' link between production and the consumer, seems to be part of a larger design.

Pound's utopia aims at bridging gaps. The gaps which Eliot (1994) wrote about:

> Between the idea
> And the reality
> Between the motion
> And the act
> Falls the Shadow [...]

Pound's project of imposing a new 'order' on reality may be seen as an attempt to return to the 'natural order of things'. That is why Pound is thrilled by Chinese characters: being aware of the arbitrariness of the connection between signifier and signified even in a pictogram, Pound still wants to see a natural link between referent and sign in Chinese writing; the more so, since 'the Occident lost the habit of verbal definition' (Pound 1973, 77). Pound's utopia, his hieratic writing, may be seen as an attempt to overcome the gap between signifier and signified and to present the image in its natural purity and simultaneity. Pound's polyphony aspires to unity, though it never achieves it; as the author admits in the last canto, Canto CXVI: 'I cannot make it cohere' (1998, 816).

Pound's case shows that when considering a text in a Bakhtinian frame of analysis one should not confuse polyphony with democracy. The cultural dialogue with the 'other' that Pound establishes in *The Cantos* is anything but democratic. Nor is it supposed to be. But even in this respect Pound's project is not too different from that of Bakhtin. As Craig Brandist (2006) has shown in his analysis of Bakhtin's concept of carnivalization, Bakhtin's liberation of voices means but a system of filtering and confining them within the frame of the novel genre. Pound, who writes openly in *Guide to Kulchur* of the 'totalitarian poetics of inclusion' and 'taking totalitarian hold on our history', may be credited for not even claiming to be democratic, for being quite aware of the nature of his dialogue with 'the other' and for exposing the mechanisms of inclusion of 'other' voices in his ideogram.

Note

1 New Directions Publishing Corp., established in 1936 and dedicated to experimental literature.

References

Bakhtin, M. M. 1994. *Problemy tvorchestva Dostoevskogo*. Kiev: Next.

———. 1996. 'Problema rechevykh zhanrov'. In *Sobranie sochinenii*, vol. 5, 159–206. Moscow: Russkie slovari.

———. 2002. 'Otvet na vopros redakcii "Novogo mira"'. In *Sobranie sochinenii*, vol. 6, 451–7. Moscow: Russkie slovari – Iazyki slavianskoi kultury.

Brandist, Craig. 2006. 'Neobkhodimost intellektualnoi istorii'. *NLO* 79. http://magazines.russ.ru/nlo/2006/79/bra4-pr.html (accessed 25 October 2012).

Carpenter, Humphrey. 1990. *A Serious Character: The Life of Ezra Pound*. New York: Delta.

Eliot, T. S. 1994 [1922]. *The Waste Land: A Facsimile and Transcript of the Original Drafts Including the Annotations of Ezra Pound*. New York: Harcourt Brace & Company.

Genette, Gérard. 1966. *Figures I*. Paris: Seuil.

Henriksen, Line. 2006. *Ambition and Anxiety: Ezra Pound's Cantos and Derek Walcott's Omeros as Twentieth-Century Epics*. Amsterdam and New York: Rodopi.

Homer. 1994–2009. *Odyssey*. http://classics.mit.edu/Homer/odyssey.11.xi.html (accessed 25 October 2012).

Jakobson, Roman. 1990. 'Dva aspekta iazyka i dva tipa afaticheskikh narushenii'. In *Teoriia metafory*, 110–32. Moscow: Progress.

Murphy, Patrick D. 1989. 'The Verse Novel: A Modern American Poetic Genre'. *College English* 51, no. 1: 57–72. Online: http://www.jstor.org/stable/378185 (accessed 25 October 2012).

Pound, Ezra. 1970a. *Gaudier-Brzeska: A Memoir*. New York: New Directions.

———. 1970b. *Guide to Kulchur*. New York: New Directions.

———. 1973. *Selected Prose 1909–1965*. New York: New Directions.

———. 1998 [1970]. *The Cantos*. New York: New Directions.

Chapter 5

AUTHOR AND OTHER IN DIALOGUE: BAKHTINIAN POLYPHONY IN THE POETRY OF PETER READING

Christian Pauls

The Problem of Bakhtinian Terminology and Poetry

Much of the terminology developed by Bakhtin seems eminently suitable for the analysis of poetry; yet, due to his valorization of novelistic over poetic discourse, we might well hesitate to do so, at least if we follow Bakhtin's insistence on the novel's social relevance and meaning, as opposed to poetry's – alleged – inherently monologic and authoritative tendencies.

His concept of the novel as being allied with the centrifugal forces of culture, associated with the anti-canonical, the anarchic, with dialogic discourse, contrasts starkly with his conception of poetry as monologic. He *de facto* accuses poetry of tending toward the authoritarian or at least towards the solipsistic recreation of a single consciousness:

> The language of poetic genres, when they approach their stylistic limit, often becomes authoritarian, dogmatic and conservative, sealing itself off from the influence of extraliterary social dialects. Therefore such ideas as a special 'poetic language', a 'language of the gods', a 'priestly language of poetry' and so forth could flourish on poetic soil. (Bakhtin 1981, 273)

He thus declares poetry to be free of language's natural dialogism, or to be at least suppressing it, limiting the purview of the poet to his own consciousness and language. The unsettling political implications contained in this statement aside, we may agree with it as far as the poetic styles of, say, the symbolists, or similarly hermetic or esoteric poetic movements, are concerned.

Yet Bakhtin's drawing of a generic line of demarcation congruent with the dialogic-monologic dichotomy seems questionable at best – especially in view of the development of poetry in modern and postmodern times. For all that, however, Bakhtin's pronouncements on this matter are still all too often taken for granted. As Mara Scanlon has summed up this paradoxical situation: 'On its face Bakhtin's limiting claim about poetry seems to fall somewhere between naïve and outrageous and yet, as several Bakhtinian literary critics have noted, it has in practice become a working truism' (2007, 2).

Yet, Bakhtin seems to be not only inconsistent but downright self-contradictory, in that he elsewhere declares *all* language to be dialogic by nature, although he undercuts his own assertions when it comes to the generic distinction: 'In fact most of Bakhtin's attempts to distinguish between the characteristics of poetry and prose [...] seem less to be examples of the "authoritative word" than of the "word with a loophole", the "word with a sidelong glance"' (Richter 1990, 12).[1] At his most forceful, Bakhtin seems to deny the word's capacity to retain traces of dialogism when it is incorporated into authentic poetic discourse, and this injunction against poetry as socially bounded is as powerful as it is mystifying and anachronistic in the eyes of anyone even slightly familiar with modern and postmodern poetry.[2]

Martin Eskin points out the theoretical aporia in Bakhtin's work created by this ill-defined connection between genres and modes of discourse:

> Bakhtin's apparently negative attitude toward poetry is informed by his overt subscription to the traditional notion of poetic speech as highly tropical, that is, to the very concept of poetry propagated by the symbolists: in poetry, Bakhtin contends, words are functionalized as direct, intentional symbols or metaphors and as such tend to be ambiguous or polysemous but not double-voiced or dialogic. The implicit contradiction in Bakhtin's oscillation between a strictly monologic conception of poetry and the simultaneous acknowledgement of the possibility and undeniable facticity of dialogic, prosaicized poetry remains [...] unresolved in Bakhtin's oeuvre. (Eskin 2000, 385)

Eskin, using one of Bakhtin's own examples, illustrates the possibility of a 'prosaicized poetry' by means of Pushkin's *Eugene Onegin*, showing that the intense interplay between poetic rhythm and prosaicized voices creates a text that can be no longer reduced to Bakhtin's simplifying dichotomy of monologue and dialogue. Eskin (2000, 386–8) concludes that 'polyphony in poetry is always somewhat precarious and not as "easy" to achieve as in novelistic discourse, since dialogue in poetry must permanently counteract homogenizing forces', yet that it is possible nevertheless. Eskin consequently continues by positing the poetic text as a site where monologism and dialogism can be brought into intense interaction, where, in short, the poet has to make the words his own, while being at the same time aware of their intense and inescapable social markedness.

While such a reading offers a possible solution for poetry's devaluation in Bakhtin's thought, it raises new questions if we wish to retain the connection between dialogue and ethics, arguably a condition for assuming that polyphony can be the structuring element of poetic texts. Scanlon seems to point to a way out in her article 'Ethics and the Lyric' (2007), resolving many of the problems arising from the view of poetry as being – at its core – monologic. Scanlon argues that the problem at hand is not grounded in a genre-bound essentialism, as Bakhtin would have us believe, and that this can be demonstrated by the historical development that has led to a new, truly prosaicized poetry. Offering the example of Pound's *The Cantos* or Eliot's *The Waste Land*, texts that 'admit at least the possibility of dialogic illumination within the poem', Scanlon shows that poetry has indeed securely established itself in the realm of the novel, using genuine dialogism as its basis. (2007, 8)

Polyphony and the Poetic Text

Gary Saul Morson and Caryl Emerson stress that polyphony is not only '*not* an attribute of all novels' but that it cannot possibly be read as being synonymous with 'heteroglossia' (1990, 232; emphasis in the original). The former is a structural device organizing a whole text or utterance; the latter merely indicates the presence of various sub-languages deviating from the 'official' or 'high' language. Nor does it indicate a 'lack of unity' on the part of the text, or the absence of an 'authorial point of view'. Bakhtin himself, drawing on the image of cosmological conceptualizations of the world, pointed out that

> the tasks that confront the author and his consciousness in a polyphonic novel are considerably more complex and profound than in a homophonic (monologic) novel. The unity of the Einsteinian world is more complex and profound than that of the Newtonian world, it is a unity of a higher order. (Bakhtin 1984, 298)

This higher order finds its expression in 'a dialogic sense of truth and a special position of the author necessary for visualizing and conveying that sense of truth' (Morson and Emerson 1990, 234). The sense of truth Bakhtin has in mind here is different from any monologic conception insofar as it actually requires more than one voice to be expressed. Such a truth would be not only inexpressible but even incomprehensible in a monologic frame of mind, depending on polyphony to organize itself into a multiplicity of independent voices:

> It is quite possible to imagine and postulate a unified truth that requires a plurality of consciousnesses, one that cannot in principle be fitted into the bounds of a single consciousness, one that is, so to speak, by its very nature *full of event potential* and is born at a point of contact among various consciousnesses. (Bakhtin 1984, 82; emphasis in the original)

And, indeed, Bakhtin finds this in Dostoevsky's works, where

> the principle of construction is everywhere the same. Everywhere there is an *intersection, consonance, or interruption of rejoinders in the open dialogue by rejoinders in the heroes' internal dialogue.* Everywhere *a specific sum total of ideas, thoughts, and words is passed through several unmerged voices, sounding differently in each.* (Bakhtin 1984, 265; emphasis in the original)

This also illustrates why, in Bakhtin's view, poetry could not actually achieve polyphony: poetry understood as monologic and expressive of only one consciousness has no structural possibility of developing an 'open dialogue'. Nor could the monologic conception of poetry make room for a poetic voice that allows itself to become relativized by other voices, that does acknowledge other ways of speaking beside its own. That such a position is hardly tenable in the light of contemporary poetry is also central to Mikhail Oshukov's argument in the current volume. He demonstrates this point convincingly for yet another conceptualization of the monologic-dialogic dichotomy, one that stands as another alternative I argue for, between the Bakhtinian understanding of poetry as necessarily monologic and the possibility of a polyphonic poetry. As suggested by Oshukov's apt reference to Pound's hieratic head as a metaphor for Pound's own *modus operandi*, i.e. his appropriation and incorporation of other voices into the *The Cantos*, this dichotomy needs to be understood not as a binary either–or, but rather as a spectrum of possible attitudes that can be assumed by the authorial role in relation to the voices it incorporates into the text.

As Scanlon rightly observes: '[in] the last century, poetic forms […] have emerged that boldly challenge the novel's proprietary hold on heteroglossia' (2007, 6). This trend is perhaps nowhere as pronounced as in the case of British post-war poetry, whose trajectory seems to suggest a radical turn towards the representation of voices previously not heard in poetry. Ian Gregson even suggests that this shift towards heteroglot voices must be understood as the defining moment in the development of contemporary poetry. He points out that poets as diverse as for example the Irish Seamus Heaney and Paul Muldoon, or the English poets Tony Harrison, Douglass Dunn, James Fenton, Craig Raine, Fleur Adcock and Carol Ann Duffy, are all writing poetry that is based on 'the dialogic rather than the dialectic, on the juxtaposition of worlds rather than the refining of a single world. In their poems synthesis is avoided in favour of an open-ended argument which preserves a vivid and untidy lack of reconciliation' (Gregson 1996, viii).[3] It is this trend that, I argue, is clearly visible in the works of the late Peter Reading.

Reading (1946–2011) must have been among the most prolific and inventive of his peers. It is for this very reason that it seems both necessary and worthwhile to find a critical approach that allows for the analysis of a poet who 'cannot be simply placed', since he 'generates his own context' (O'Brien 2001, 573). His generative poetic powers have given rise to a variety of critical and scholarly responses, but thus far, I suggest, not to an approach that would do justice to the underlying unity of his wide-ranging oeuvre. In an effort to rectify this situation, I suggest in the following that Reading's work can best be approached in its totality through the concept of Bakhtinian polyphony. Due to restrictions of space, I can only do so by means of examples.

Peter Reading's Polyphonic Poetry

From the beginning of his career as a poet, Peter Reading showed an interest in experimentation with regard to poetic forms and also to the voices he would use in his poetry. While early works contained a poet-persona identifiable with the author himself, he soon turned to writing poetic texts that not only blurred the line between single poems by way of typographical organization of the text on the page, but also by way of expressly carnivalizing the relation of the (implied and actual) author to his own creation.[4] Besides employing increasing numbers of personae, Reading has also managed to incorporate a large number of 'found' texts as well as inserted genres, such as letters, diaries, medieval medical prescriptions, etc.[5] The use of different voices early on alerted critics to the inherently Bakhtinian qualities espoused by Reading's poetry.[6]

His use of dialogized heteroglossia, however, is not merely an end in itself but has to be read as a means, along with the treatment of authorial discourse, toward achieving polyphony. He creates a structure that effectively goes beyond Bakhtin's notion of 'novelized poetry', showing the way to a socially relevant and engaged poetry that incorporates novelistic as well as poetic means, exposing Bakhtin's essentializing concept of the prose/poetry distinction as all too simplistic.[7] The volume I have chosen to exemplify this claim is *Ukulele Music*, first published by Secker and Warburg in 1985 and reprinted in the second volume of Reading's *Collected Poems* by Bloodaxe Books in 1996.

Ukulele Music is subdivided into three parts of roughly equal length, each part characterized by different voices. The first part is given over to the charlady Viv, who, as we gather from the notes she writes to communicate with one of her two employers, works for a poet and retired captain. She produces a kind of 'parodistic *skaz*', i.e. a written text that bears all the hallmarks of orality and that is reprinted with all spelling-errors and erased passages intact.[8] She writes, as can be expected from a semi-literate charlady, in prose, and her notes alternate with poems written by the poet-persona. The quotidian horrors Viv relates are in fact the poet's main subject matter since – as he declares in the motto that opens his first poem: '*Few atrocities / of which* H. sap. *can conceive / remain unfulfilled*' (Reading 1996, 11; emphasis in the original). In the following twelve pages Viv and the poet take turns and, while she addresses the poet directly, he answers indirectly, by turning her idiosyncratic prose into elegiac distiches. Before he starts to react to Viv's voice, however, he already remarks on his obsession with 'atrocities', turning to self-reflexivity:

> Stubbornly, Taffs, at their damn-fool anachronistic eisteddfods,
> still, with this breach in the hull, twang (ineffectual lyres).
> [...]
> [When] blood-swilling (Allah is wonderful) Middle-East Yahoos had purchased
> nuclear hardware, he found distich the only form apt.
> (Reading 1996, 13)

Thus he begins his demolition of the current poetry scene, taking the Welsh tradition of the poetry festival as a metonym for a larger tradition of escapist, romantic poetry. Such poetry, he implies, is merely striking the lyre while the ship, a metaphor introduced here and expanded throughout the book, is sinking. He not only mocks any inherent connection between form and content in poetry, but also seems to question the project of poetry in general, especially in the face of the modern world and its particular horrors.[9] The poet's passage ends with another reference to music, another motif that, as the book's title suggests, is a returning metaphor: '**Sing in Your Bath if You want to Seem Sexy and Blood-Bath in Jordan** / vie for the front page in the tabs. Doh ray me fah soh lah te' (Reading 1996; emphasis in the original).

While the poet is thus established as the world-weary, cynical voice of the disillusioned, Viv's notes characterize her as perhaps uneducated – and somewhat dyslexic perhaps – but also as far from being ignorant, as her note regarding the rumoured existence of a fallout shelter under the local civic centre reveals: '*he* [the captain] *has seen it with OWN eyes so knows it is true. where I thought it was just Underground Car Park etc. under* ~~Civic~~ *Civet Centre is not just Car Park but bunk for FALL if there is trouble, that sometimes seems likely with uSA and russiens with there bomb warfair*' (Reading 1996, 13; emphasis in the original). While Viv is established as the concerned voice of human reason and sanity, the poet continues his observations on a world gone mad and the futility of poetry in the face of it: 'Lieder's no art against these sorry times' (Reading 1996, 15). That Viv is not only telling stories but is also being told them by the captain becomes evident from her ominous proleptic remark: '*worse things happen at SEA!*' (Reading 1996, 18; emphasis in the original). Before the passage ends the reader is confronted with a poem that explicitly discusses the reception of Peter Reading's poetry by critics and can be read as his *apologia*:

> Life is too black as he paints it' and 'Reading's nastiness sometimes
> seems a bit over the top' thinks a review – so does *he*.
>
> Too black and over the top, though, is what the Actual often
> happens to be, I'm afraid. He don't *invent* it, you know.
> (Reading 1996, 19; emphasis in the original)

The poem continues with a list of atrocities the poet has gleaned from the newspaper, which he reports in his laconic elegiac distich. This list is meant not only to serve as a validation and justification for Reading's choice of subject matter, but also plants his poetological flag firmly in the realm of the 'actual', i.e. the real, social world. Even so, he evidently feels compelled to defend this choice explicitly, in the face of criticism that seems to be grounded in the expectation that poetry has to blind itself to a range of 'un-poetic' subjects – an idea related, no doubt, to Bakhtin's contention of the monologic nature of 'poetry in the narrow sense'. Yet the poem ends not only on an angry note towards critics who would have poetry as un-social as possible, but paradoxically also on the certainty that poetry indeed 'makes nothing happen': 'Clearly we no longer hold *H. sapiens* in great reverence / (which situation, alas, no elegiacs can fix)' (Reading 1996, 20).

Meter and vocabulary change markedly after the first part firmly establishes the registers of two of the volume's voices, thus introducing in the following the captain, Viv's other employer. He is retelling his adventures at sea, yet the reader is cautioned from the beginning that something else might be afoot here, since his diction is unexpectedly archaic and lyrical. The relation between the captain, his yarns, Viv and the poet is established on the narrative level by the fact that Viv is also the captain's charlady, as well as on the structural and metaphorical level, as pointed out by Isabel Martin:

> Apart from their function as a counterpoint to the mundane horrors back home [...] the maritime poems also indirectly corroborate both the positive

principle of the book, Viv's 'resilience' [...] and the poet's compulsion to versify. Another function is the allegory of the Ship of State going down [...] which on this level links up with the past glory of England's naval power. (Martin 2000, 138)

The captain may prove to share Viv's resilience, but his adventures also seem to share in the poet's pessimistic outlook: what he has to tell are stories of various catastrophes he lived through at sea, all to some degree recognizable as parables for historical events. At the same time they also function as allegories for the human condition in a more global sense. The archaic, nautical register he employs works as a defamiliarizing device that turns the sea into a *mare incognitum*, holding unknown wonders and terrors, infusing the poet's 'actual' with an air of the fantastic (and thus marking the captain as a distant relative of Coleridge's *The Rime of the Ancient Mariner*).

Among other things, he relates how once, aboard a ship sailing a 'hundred miles off Bikini', one of the sailors reported that the 'sun rises in the West'. He and the crew see a fireball appearing on the horizon in eerie silence, followed by a massive uproar, concluding with 'weird white ashes / as *swirled*, d'ye see?, / down onto decks, men, rigging… / That ash made us ill (*later*)' (Reading 1996, 29; emphasis in the original). The reader, unlike the yarn's narrator, can easily identify the event described as the test of a nuclear weapon, and the white ashes as nuclear fallout, connecting this tale to the portentous existence of a fallout shelter under the local civic centre. The captain closes with some reflections on poetry of his own. His first poetological assumption is that the production of poetry is not entirely a matter of choice but rather of custom or reflex: 'I am impelled to convey / salt observations, a tar's / chantey habit, d'ye see?' thus demonstrating a fatalistic attitude, its bleakness somewhat alleviated by the supposition that this habit can probably

> be counted
> as ye dignified defiance
> [...]
> that e'en in pitching Gulphward,
> our salt kind brings forth chanteys.
> (Reading 1996, 32–3)

Translating experience into poetry, then, is an idealistic endeavour for the captain, who thereby stands in opposition to the poet – the only other voice that has spoken in (and on) poetry so far. The final part of the volume, however, affords one more voice the opportunity to weigh in on the question of the adequacy of poetry as a medium: Viv has by now mastered the poet's own mode of discourse, and begins the third and final part of the book by articulating herself in elegiac distich:

> *Who would have thought it Sir, actually putting ME in a WRITING!*
> *me and the Capting and ALL. What a turn up for the books.*
>
> *Only, I must say I do not know HOW them people in poems*
> *manage to say what they want – you know, in funny short lines,*
>
> *or like what YOU do with them ones of yours sir, made of two lines like.*
> *Still, when you're USED to it like, then you can speak natural.*
> (Reading 1996, 36; emphasis in the original)

Viv begins to occupy the poet's mode of speaking and comments on the critical voices that the poet responded to at the end of the first part. The reader thus learns that his predilection for violent subject matter and the incorporation of demotic registers into his poetry have been criticized. Viv, however, consoles him that he has actually achieved authenticity: '*this is JUST how we speaks like, / me and the Capting and all (only not just in two lines*' (Reading 1996, 34; emphasis in the original). Viv evidently has not only become a poet in her own right but a literary critic as well – judging the poet's writing in which she herself is supposed to be a mere character, her discourse attaining here, at least temporarily, autonomy from the poet's voice.

The voices in the final part now start to alternate in ever faster succession. Viv continues her own narrative in verse, reporting, amongst other things, on a TV program about '*"Narrow" which plays on a fiddle, all the time Roam burnd*', adding another stroke to the question of the function of poetry in the face of catastrophe. Yet she seems to be the only one who accords poetry any meaningful role, seeing in it an actual chance for survival, likening it to the claustrophobic safety of the fallout shelter:

> *Maybe we're better off under the Civic Centre than up here*
> *what with the LUTEing and that – them inner-cities is BAD,*
>
> *maybe we're better off here in his WRITINGS, orrible though they*
> *often is sometimes, then HERE – out in that awful real-life.*
> (Reading 1996, 39; emphasis in the original)

Meanwhile, the poet is heaping one apocalyptic urban crime upon another, and introduces *en passant* the final voice to join the text: 'Meanwhile, I've gotten the 5-Minute Uke Course (Guaranteed Foolproof) – / plinkplinka plinkplinka plonk plinkplinka plinkplinka plonk' (Reading 1996, 38). It adds a note of hysteria to the subsequent cacophony, extolling the virtues of the Ukulele, declaring boldly that too 'much mystery and confusion have shrouded Uke playing! The Uke is an instrument for the best accompanying of happytime songs!' At the same time the poet and Viv engage in one of their answer-response passages; the poet bemoans the ill favour of his critics, parroting their verdicts ('"This is not Poetry, this is reality, untreated, nasty", / "This is demotic and cheap", "This is mere caricature"') while Viv tries to console him. The captain's voice also changes: not only does he now speak in elegiac distich as well, but his tales have grown even stranger, incorporating the other voices' discourse:

> tighten the B string and place finger at the back of the second
> fret of the A string and keep spondees and dactyls close-clewed,
>
> trim yr heroic hexameter (or it may be dactylic),
> splice the pentameter aft, finger yr frets as ye go.
> (Reading 1996, 42–3)

The barriers, and with them by necessity all hierarchies, between the individual voices disappear, all the characters of the volume are now united semantically as well as geographically – they are together in the fallout shelter mentioned, weathering some unnamed catastrophe.[10] The only one able to salvage her own discourse under these circumstances is Viv, who correctly diagnoses the situation they all find themselves in:

> *mind you the Powertree Bloke and the Capting doesn't arf GABBLE –*
> *what with the Capting and his YARNS: tother keeps chaingin is VOICE*
>
> *anyone'd think they was Everyone All Times Everywhere, way they*
> *gabbles and rambles and that: still, they can't help it poor souls.*
> (Reading 1996, 46; emphasis in the original)

Yet, Viv's indignation and confusion caused by the confabulations of 'poetry bloke' and the captain lead her to the accurate assumption that their identities and voices have become mutually permeable; the two have effectively merged their textual horizons into one, making it impossible for her, as well as the reader, to distinguish them any longer. This is the final carnivalizing act of the book, in which the poet's authority is irrevocably eradicated, his voice dethroned, and the charlady, who began in prose, is given the (pen-)ultimate word. The book's ultimate lines, however, belong to the sound of someone strumming the Ukulele – its inane 'plinkplinka plonk' is printed with metrical notations: the Ukulele is playing a last elegiac distich.

Polyphony as Macroscopic Structure

The volume's last pages bring its polyphonic nature into even sharper focus, breaking down, at least in part, the respective individuality of the voices, stripping especially the poet, as the metonymic voice of poetic authority, of any distance or control. The end is not a mere synthesis of voices but a carnivalistic restructuring in the spirit of polyphony, bearing out Bakhtin's dictum that the 'important thing in [...] polyphony is precisely what happens *between various consciousnesses*, that is, their interaction and interdependence' (Bakhtin 1984, 36; emphasis in the original). What sets *Ukulele Music* off against Bakhtin's notion is its self-reflexivity, which may owe something to postmodern self-referentiality, but should, I suggest, be read as Reading's attempt to dialogize the traditional conceptualization of poetry itself, especially vis-à-vis decidedly prosaic realities. The poet, who operates as a voice among voices and as a placeholder for the author, enacts the very role Bakhtin named as a precondition for polyphony, while of course the actual author remains in control of his creation: 'The characters' freedom we speak of here exists within the limits of the artistic design, and in that sense is just as much a created thing as is the unfreedom of the objectivised hero' (Bakhtin 1984, 64).

The voices present in *Ukulele Music* unfold their own discourse, often informed by ideologies different from those of their creator, as well as that of the implied author. At the same time, the polyphonic structure is the framework that organizes these freedoms in a way determined by the author, being therefore neither arbitrary nor random since the author is at all times ultimately in charge of his creation:

> Every creative act is determined by its object and by the structure of its object, and therefore permits no arbitrariness; in essence it invents nothing, but only reveals what has been present in the object itself [...] Once he has chosen a hero and the dominant of his hero's representation, the author is already bound by the inner logic of what he has chosen, and he must reveal it in his representation [...] A character's discourse is created by the author, but created in such a way that it can develop to the full its inner logic and independence as *someone else's discourse*, the word of the *character himself*. (Bakhtin 1984, 64–5; emphasis in the original)

The discourses developed in Reading's texts are not only those of individual voices reacting to each other, questioning and answering each other. Concurrently they also develop a discourse on (and in) poetry itself, evaluating it at times harshly, yet proving unable to escape it as a medium of expression. Poetry is forced into familiar contact with itself, thereby losing any aspiration of being 'a language of the Gods'. The text thus reveals a true polyphony of consciousnesses, enacting polyphony as poetry and poetry as polyphony. And it does so at the cost of any monologic certainties or authority that Bakhtin had postulated for this genre. The poetry that emerges here is in this sense thoroughly dialogized, and its polyphony demands a rigorous re-evaluation of Bakhtin's pronouncements on the matter.

What sets Reading apart from, say, Craig Raine's Martian defamiliarizations or Tony Harrison's appropriations of traditional forms to contemporary contexts (for example in *V*) is his insistence on the uncertainties of the poetic project itself and a deep mistrust of its ability to actually communicate in a meaningful way. That this mistrust of the medium is expressed within the medium of poetry itself is a paradox that fills his writing with a nervous, pessimistic energy that is certainly unique to himself. This kind of polyphonic poetry, then, not only forces a re-negotiation of the prose/poetry dichotomy, revealing it in Bakhtin to be something 'posited' rather than 'given', but it also points to a third option between the poles of poetry and the novel, dialogizing poetry as well as any simplifying conceptualization thereof.

Notes

1 For examples of Bakhtin's evasiveness on this matter see the chapter 'Discourse in Poetry and Discourse in the Novel' in 'Discourse in the Novel', 275–300.
2 Bakhtin himself admits elsewhere the possibility of a dialogic incorporation of heteroglot languages into poetic texts, yet he does not see this as an opportunity to revise his notion of poetry: 'Of course, even in poetic speech works are possible that do not reduce their entire verbal material to a single common denominator, but in the nineteenth century such instances were rare and rather specific. To this group belong, for example, the "prosaic" lyric of Heine, Barbier, some works of Nekrasov, and others (not until the twentieth century is there a drastic "prosification" of the lyric). The possibility of employing on the plane of a single work discourses of various types, with all their expressive capacities intact, without reducing them to a common denominator – this is one of the most fundamental characteristic features of prose. Herein lies the profound distinction between prose style and poetic style' (Bakhtin 1984, 200). That Bakhtin's assertion can actually be reversed has been suggested by Dana Polan (1989, 8), who claims that Bakhtin effectively deconstructs the prose/poetry dichotomy, leading thus to a new way to read poetry. A similar idea is expressed in Clare Cavanagh's contribution to the problem. She suggests that 'not the novel, but lyric poetry is, in certain of its incarnations, the ideal genre to articulate the vision of the world that Morson, following Bakhtin, calls "prosaic"' (Cavanagh 1997, 8).
3 Gregson makes the political dimension of the shift in British poetry even more explicit elsewhere in his introduction. He argues that British poetry, although incorporating

the strategies of postmodernism, has always accorded 'the real a residual respect and allow[ed] it a residual place'. Even more incisive is his diagnosis of the shift from Movement to postmodern poetry: '[w]here the Movement poetic assumed that writers and readers were white, English middle-class males, contemporary poetry is acutely aware of voices that insist on their differences from that model and draw attention to their class, gender, nationality or race' (Gregson 1996, v).

4 A classic postmodern example of such a subversive treatment of the author-persona and the reader's expectations, formed no doubt by an understanding of poetry similar to Bakhtin's, can be found in the volume *Fiction* (1979, republished in *Collected Poems 1* in 1995), where an author named 'Donald' invents another character named 'Donald' who writes under the nom de plume 'Peter Reading'. The ensuing farcical, interpersonal, inter-diegetic confusion ends with Donald, who 'sues a man whose *real* / name is "Peter Reading"' (emphasis in the original). As Donald's lawyer ('Donald, QC') helpfully remarks at the poem's end: 'Even one's self is wholly fictitious' (1995, 137–8). This carnivalization holds sway not only in single poems but soon turns the organization of whole later volumes upside-down.

5 Dennis O'Driscoll remarked *apropos* the sheer number of inserted genre: 'If [Reading] has not yet made poetry from the telephone directory, he has at any rate proved his ability to draw on crossword puzzle clues and wedding gift lists for inspiration' (1994, 210).

6 Neil Roberts is certainly correct when he points out that 'some of these poets [discussed in his book] could be described as "Bakhtinian" in a strong sense, in that they exemplify or even articulate ideas about language that closely resemble Bakhtin's. The most obvious case is perhaps Peter Reading, whose work [...] is unimaginable without what Bakhtin calls "dialogised heteroglossia": the creation of meaning by the interaction of the social varieties of language' (Roberts 1999, 4).

7 That Reading's poetry makes use of Bakhtinian polyphony was also pointed out by Roberts, who writes of Peter Reading's volume *C* (1984) that the '[w]hole text might be seen as the multi-voiced outcry of a supra-individual protagonist, a kind of suffering carnival monster whose bodily protuberances are devouring tumours, and whose orifices emit repellent fluid uncontrollably' (Roberts 1999, 137). *C* deals with a number of personae suffering from cancer. The text is another example of polyphony at work in Reading, and suggests a truly post-Renaissance form of carnival, one, as it were, with opposite signs: while structurally and formally comparable to the Bakhtinian notion of carnival, the carnival idea in *C* is anti-utopian; not life affirming but life threatening. Carnival here is more closely related to its horrible 'other': the medieval notion of the *danse macabre*.

8 For a discussion of the term see Bakhtin (1984, 194).

9 This strategy can be found in the majority of Reading's texts, where there usually is a poet-persona who is mocked and/or where the formal qualities of poetry are ridiculed, especially the idea of any inherent connection between form and content. As Roberts noted in regard to the volume *C*: 'This jeering against verse is a repeated [...] element [...] and one of its function's [...] is to dethrone the monologic author, and establish the text as an arena in which different voices compete' (Roberts 1999, 170).

10 That the nature of this event has to do with a nuclear accident is briefly alluded to in a list of 'questions that Councillors mean to raise at the Meeting', for example: 'What was the level of contamination? Where had it come from? / What is a "low level" leak? Why was the public not told?' (Reading 1996, 41).

References

Bakhtin, Mikhail. 1981. 'Discourse in the Novel' ('Slovo v romane'). In *The Dialogic Imagination: Four Essays*. Edited by Michael Holquist, translated by Caryl Emerson and Michael Holquist, 259–422. Austin: University of Texas Press.

———. 1984. *Problems of Dostoevsky's Poetics* (*Problemy poetiki Dostoevskogo*, 1963). Edited by Caryl Emerson. Minneapolis: University of Minnesota Press.

Cavanagh, Clare. 1997. 'The Forms of the Ordinary: Bakhtin, Prosaics and the Lyric'. *Slavic and East European Journal* 41, no. 1: 40–56.

Eskin, Martin. 2000. 'Bakhtin on Poetry'. *Poetics Today* 21, no. 2: 379–91.

Gregson, Ian. 1996. *Contemporary Poetry and Postmodernism: Dialogue and Estrangement*. Basingstoke: Macmillan.

Martin, Isabel. 2000. *Reading Peter Reading*. Newcastle upon Tyne: Bloodaxe Books.

Morson, Gary Saul and Caryl Emerson. 1990. *Mikhail Bakhtin: Creation of a Prosaics*. Stanford: Stanford University Press.

O'Brien, Sean. 2001. 'Contemporary British Poetry'. In *A Companion to Twentieth-Century Poetry*. Edited by Neil Roberts, 571–84. Oxford: Blackwell.

O'Driscoll, Dennis. 1994. '"No-God and Species Decline Stuff": The Poetry of Peter Reading'. In *In Black and Gold: Contiguous Traditions in Post-War British and Irish Poetry*. Edited by C. C. Barfoot, 201–18. Amsterdam: Rodopi.

Polan, Dana. 1989. 'Bakhtin, Benjamin, Sartre: Toward a Typology of the Intellectual Cultural Critic'. In *Discontinuous Discourses in Modern Russian Literature*. Edited by Catriona Kelly et al., 3–18. New York: St. Martin's Press.

Reading, Peter. 1995. *Collected Poems 1: 1970–1984*. Newcastle upon Tyne: Bloodaxe Books.

Reading, Peter. 1996. *Collected Poems 2: 1985–1996*. Newcastle upon Tyne: Bloodaxe Books.

Richter, David H. 1990. 'Dialogism and Poetry'. *Studies in the Literary Imagination* 23, no. 1: 9–27.

Roberts, Neil. 1999. *Narrative and Voice in Postwar Poetry*. New York: Longman.

Scanlon, Mara. 2007. 'Ethics and the Lyric: Form, Dialogue, Answerability'. *College Literature* 34, no. 1: 1–22.

Chapter 6

TRADITION AND GENRE: THOMAS KYD'S *THE SPANISH TRAGEDY*

Edward Gieskes

At the close of Thomas Kyd's play *The Spanish Tragedy* (c. 1590), the problem of speech is located in the context of a social interaction between hero, actor and audience. The dialogue between the characters Balthazar and Hieronimo suggests that the language is oriented towards the audience, whose understanding is an important consideration in the construction of an utterance. Balthazar feels anxious about the audience's inability to understand Hieronimo's play: 'This will be a mere confusion, / And hardly shall we all be understood' (Kyd 1989, 4.1.179–180).[1] Hieronimo comforts Balthazar by pointing out that 'the conclusion / Shall prove the intention, and all was good' (Kyd 1989, 4.1.181–2). Thus both Balthazar and Hieronimo recognize the orientation of speech towards response.

A similar concern with the social nature of discourse pervades all of the Bakhtin Circle's thinking about language. Whether in Bakhtin's extended investigations of dialogic interactions in the book on Dostoevsky, in the essays collected in *The Dialogic Imagination* (1981) or in Voloshinov's *Marxism and the Philosophy of Language* (1986), their thoughts stress the irremediably social nature of any kind of verbal communication. Voloshinov writes that

> utterance, as we know, is constructed between two socially organized persons, and in the absence of a real addressee, an addressee is presupposed in the person, so to speak, of a normal representative of the social group to which the speaker belongs. *The word is oriented toward an addressee.* (Voloshinov 1986, 85; emphasis in the original)[2]

All utterances presuppose the social existence of a real or notional audience. Here as elsewhere in his book, Voloshinov argues against an abstract notion of language, instead constructing an account that is profoundly historical and material. Utterance has to be understood historically – partly by understanding the social formations that give rise to it – and any account of change has to be situated in terms of these kinds of verbal interactions between 'socially organized persons', actual or hypothetical. He goes on to argue that the orientation of the word to the addressee has important consequences:

> Orientation of the word toward the addressee has an extremely high significance. In point of fact, *word is a two-sided act*. It is determined equally by *whose* word it is and *for whom* it is meant. As word, it is precisely *the product of the reciprocal relationship between speaker and listener, addresser and addressee* [...] A word is territory shared by both addresser and addressee, by the speaker and his interlocutor. (Voloshinov 1986, 86; emphasis in the original)

Word, to adopt his phrasing, is not only socially organized, but is also the product and mechanism of a relation between addresser and addressee. This reciprocity means that the word is oriented not only towards the hearer, but toward the hearer's potential response. It anticipates reactions from its hearers and that anticipation structures the utterance. Part of what I will be arguing here is that literary history can usefully be seen as a part of the shared territory Voloshinov describes.

In the same chapter of *Marxism and the Philosophy of Language*, Voloshinov explicitly includes books among the forms of verbal communication that share territory and that inevitably have a kind of reciprocal relationship with potential responses:

> A book, i.e., a verbal performance in print, is also an element of verbal communication. It is something discussable in actual, real-life, dialogue, but aside from that, it is calculated for active perception [...] Thus the printed verbal performance engages, as it were, in ideological colloquy of large scale: it responds to something, objects to something, anticipates responses and objections, seeks support, and so on. (Voloshinov 1986, 95)

A book is something that can enter into communication as an object of discussion, as in the critical conversation about literature; equally significantly, it expects 'active perception' by its immediate audience as well as the larger one of history. When Voloshinov writes that a book (and I think it reasonable to extend this to include theatrical performance) 'inevitably orients itself with respect to previous performances' (1986, 95) and to succeeding ones he is arguing that the work is taking part in a literary or scientific metadialogue. I am not going to be engaging in the longstanding debate about whether drama is or is not monological; rather, I wish to investigate some of the implications of treating whole works as utterances in dialogue with their predecessors, contemporaries, and followers.³ This conception of literary works as part of an enormous dialogue of utterance and rejoinder, I argue, suggests alternative ways to conceptualize relations between works and between writers.

Works, then, are inevitably oriented towards other works (not to mention audiences), and that orientation, like that of the rejoinder in spoken dialogue, comprehends in various ways the utterance to which it is responding. This idea is a consistent feature of the Bakhtin Circle's theoretical writing, from early texts like *Marxism and the Philosophy of Language* all the way to later works like the essay 'The Problem of Speech Genres'. As Bakhtin writes in that essay:

> Utterances are not indifferent to one another, and are not self-sufficient; they are aware of and mutually reflect one another. These mutual reflections determine their character. Each utterance is filled with echoes and reverberations of other utterances to which it is related by the communality of the sphere of speech communication […] each utterance is filled with various kinds of responsive reactions to other utterances of the given sphere of speech communication. (Bakhtin 1986, 91)

Utterances' mutual awareness and reflection of each other operates at the level both of the individual word and of the work as a whole. The refutations, affirmations, and supplements Bakhtin refers to here are one of the primary engines of generic change, not least because they represent the taking of a position in a specific field of discourse.⁴

Part of the project of this chapter is to determine some of the responsive positions taken by early modern drama with regard to both classical and Neo-Latin drama. While the kinds of reflections and reactions that Bakhtin writes of here operate across generic boundaries as much as within them, I will be focusing on the drama. I would emend Bakhtin's (or the translator's) 'reflection' to 'refraction' in order to better characterize the transformation of style or form across generic boundaries and to stress the ways that these responsive reactions are active rather than passive responses. In what follows, I consider Kyd's play as a responsive reaction to Neo-Latin Senecan drama through the lens of Bakhtin's theory of genre.

The Tradition of Neo-Latin Drama in Kyd's Time

Many early modern playwrights were exposed to the tradition of Neo-Latin drama at the universities or in the Inns of Court and drew on that exposure in their dramatic careers. Thus this chapter considers interactions between the tradition of Neo-Latin drama at Oxford and Cambridge and the professional stage in London in the late sixteenth century. There was a long and vigorous tradition of Latin drama at the universities, and early educators looked to classical drama for teaching materials. Professional playwrights also looked to classical antecedents for subject matter and technique. Shakespeare, for example, makes extensive use of Latin comedy in plays like *Comedy of Errors*, which draws on two plays by Plautus – the *Menaechmi* and *Amphitrio*, which themselves draw on Greek originals – for both structure and incident. Shakespeare returns to Ovid repeatedly throughout his career – whether in tragedy, as in *Titus Andronicus*, or in comedy, as in *Midsummer Night's Dream*.[5] Less direct appropriations of classical drama abound as well. Thomas Kyd's *The Spanish Tragedy* is often described as the first Senecan tragedy on the early modern stage; and this is because of style, not content.

Thomas Kyd was born in 1558 and was educated at the Merchant Taylors' School in London; the school had been recently founded by Richard Mulcaster, one of the most prominent Tudor educators. Here Kyd would have become very familiar with Latin, and would also have learned some Greek. As with many educational institutions of the period, the Merchant Taylors' School put on plays, both as part of its pedagogical program and for performance before the Queen. By 1585 Kyd was writing plays for the Queen's Men – one of the leading acting companies of the time – and was close to other writers, such as Christopher Marlowe and Thomas Lodge. *The Spanish Tragedy*, the play he is best known for, dates to around 1590 and was an immediate and enduring success on the early modern stage.[6] The play remained a consistent part of the repertory throughout the period, and is referred to constantly by other playwrights.[7] It has no single major source; using Senecan tools, Kyd develops a story about justice and revenge, without reference to any specific antecedent. In this, I would argue, lies his response to the practice of performing classical drama in early modern England: his is a creative response to the resources made available by these plays. Kyd's response in *The Spanish Tragedy*, it is often said, inaugurates the tradition of revenge tragedy on the public stage in England, a tradition that becomes one of the more important components of early modern drama more generally. Here I characterize some of what Kyd appears to have been responding to.[8]

Source Study and 'Ideological Colloquy'

Source study has a long history in English studies and has recently begun to be reconsidered by such scholars as Robert Miola, among others. Bullough's invaluable *Narrative and Dramatic Sources of Shakespeare* (1957–1975) can serve as an exemplar of the field. It focuses on the sources of event, character, language, and plot more than on those of technique or form, in part simply because it is far easier to identify these kinds of sources than the more subtle and debatable matters of technique. Source study thus allows scholars to perceive how Shakespeare worked with the given materials of his cultural milieu and to determine the kinds of transformation effected as, say, prose romance moved to the stage. This model, however, tends to emphasize the content of the source over its form, and by virtue of this emphasis perhaps overlooks sources of technique. Writing about relations between Shakespeare's *Othello* and Seneca's *Hercules Furens*, Miola describes source study as moving between the traditional notion of a source, as 'an imitated text that manifests its presence in verbal or stylistic echo or adaptation' – a concept, despite its power and usefulness, limited 'by a tendency to rely almost exclusively on verbal iteration as proof of influence' – and that of a source as 'an intermediated text (i.e. tradition)' manifesting its presence in the same way (Miola 1990, 49). As Miola argues, this model, while plural and wider-ranging than the iteration model, is itself limited by a tendency to 'succumb to a vague impressionism that timorously avoids committing itself to any single text as source' (1990, 49). Miola advocates a synthetic, eclectic approach that uses both notions strategically.

Bakhtin's notion of works as utterances engaged in a kind of literary dialogue is a productive way to avoid the impasses of the iteration and tradition models of source study, and allows for a more dynamic account of generic change. In the late essay on speech genres, Bakhtin argues that all utterances are necessarily responsive reactions to other utterances; they therefore contain, in various ways, the utterances to which they are responding. Furthermore, these reactions do not always take the form of citations or importations:

> One's responsive reaction to them can be reflected only in the expression of one's own speech [...] in the selection of language means and intonations that are determined not by the topic of one's own speech but by the other's utterances concerning the same topic [...] [V]ery frequently the expression of our utterance is determined not only – and sometimes not so much – by the referentially semantic content of this utterance, but also by others' utterances on the same topic to which we are responding or with which we are polemicizing. (Bakhtin 1986, 91)

Plays often engage directly in such polemicizing – making claims for the value of the work-utterance at hand, denigrating other works, or pointing to the inadequacies of others' appropriations of a particular genre or topic. The early seventeenth century Poet's War between Ben Jonson, John Marston, and Thomas Dekker is only the most obvious example of this kind of contention. Any period appropriation of Senecan material is necessarily engaged in the kind of dialogue Bakhtin is describing here, and Kyd's is no exception.

If Bakhtin is right that works are engaged in an enormous literary metadialogue – an 'ideological colloquy', in Voloshinov's terms – and that the contributions of all participants are actively oriented towards the response of others (readers or works), then understanding the shape and contours of this colloquy can provide a particularly useful way to characterize literary history generally and generic change more specifically. In what follows, I intend to trace the part of this metadialogue that Thomas Kyd engaged in with his responsive reaction to the tradition of classical and neoclassical drama that was an important part of early modern England's educational and dramatic traditions. His reaction is as much discursive as it is thematic. Kyd appropriates structures from the tradition of Latin drama, repurposes them and fills them with other kinds of language. At the same time *The Spanish Tragedy* embraces the ethical problems of justice and revenge, problems that are explored in Seneca's plays and that at least some Neo-Latin adaptations paper over or simply ignore.[9] Later plays, like Shakespeare's *Titus Andronicus* or the revenge tragedy that takes at least some of its inspiration from *The Spanish Tragedy*, are among the texts that respond to Kyd's innovation and expand on it in what Bakhtin calls the chain of speech communion.

Kyd, Speech Genres and Literary History

In the 'Speech Genres' essay, Bakhtin argues that speech genres, and by extension genres more generally, develop over a long history and that literary genres represent an especially complicated example of this process:

> Historical changes in language styles are inseparably linked to changes in speech genres. Literary language is a complex, dynamic system of linguistic styles. The proportions and interrelations of these styles in the system of literary language are constantly changing. Literary language, which also includes nonliterary styles, is an even more complex system, and it is organized on different bases. In order to puzzle out the complex historical dynamics of these systems and move from a simple (and, in the majority of cases, superficial) description of styles, which are always in evidence and alternating with one another, to a historical explanation of these changes, one must develop a special history of speech genres (and not only secondary, but also primary ones) that reflects more directly, clearly, and flexibly all the changes taking place in social life. (Bakhtin 1986, 65)

These changes include for example educational developments, increasing (or alternative) access to literary traditions, developments in audiences, and changes in sites of production.[10] Moving beyond 'simple description' entails, in addition to that description, an extensive investigation into a far wider array of changes. Part of this effort must be to characterize the stylistic context and available resources at a given moment in the development of a specific variety of literary language, and that is the project of this chapter. In the following section, I offer a brief characterization of some of the styles and modes – both vernacular and Neo-Latin – available to playwrights of Kyd's generation; Kyd's innovations, to adopt Bakhtin's language are part of a complex historical dynamic and a survey of the field is necessary for a more adequate characterization of his work.

As noted above, throughout the sixteenth century Latin drama was an important part of the cultural and educational life of both universities as well as the Inns of Court in London. A glance at Harbage's *Annals of English Drama 975–1700* (1964) demonstrates the frequency of performances of classical and Neo-Latin plays at Oxford and Cambridge. Both institutions mandated that Latin plays be performed each year, and many critics and historians have noted the importance of Latin dramatic texts in humanist pedagogy. Bruce Smith's book *Ancient Scripts and Modern Experience on the English Stage* (1988) discusses performances of classical plays between 1500 and 1700 and very usefully documents the prevalence of such performances. Gordon Braden's 1985 book *Renaissance Tragedy and the Senecan Tradition* remains the landmark study of the influence of Seneca on English drama, and in the sections on English tragedy focuses on the legacy of what Braden terms a Senecan selfhood for conceptions of character in such plays as Marlowe's *Tamburlaine* and Kyd's *The Spanish Tragedy*.[11] More recently, Howard B. Norland's *Neoclassical Tragedy in Elizabethan England* (2009) has offered a thorough examination of the neoclassical dramatic tradition at Oxford, Cambridge, and the Inns of Court in an effort to demonstrate the importance of this tradition to the vernacular drama of the 1580s and later.

A great deal of critical attention has understandably been given to particular 'Senecan' elements of later tragedy – especially revenge tragedy – such as the presence of ghosts, a declamatory mode on the part of the revenger, long speeches of lament, and in some cases (though not in all, and not as much in Shakespeare as in others) the use of stichomythia to construct stage dialogue.[12] These elements do have a clear connection to the tradition of Latin tragedy, and early modern English playwrights are clearly adapting those elements. What I want to suggest here is that the responsive reaction a play like Kyd's *The Spanish Tragedy* is making to classical tragedy operates at the level of technique and intellectual content as much as it does by way of direct reference.

Seneca was available to early modern readers in Latin, though a collection of English translations appeared in print in 1581. *Seneca: His Tenne Tragedies* contains English translations of *Hercules Furens*, *Thyestes*, *Thebais*, *Hippolytus*, *Oedipus*, *Troas*, *Medea*, *Agamemnon*, *Octavia* and *Hercules Oetaeus*. Three of the plays were translated by Jasper Heywood, the son of John Heywood who was himself an important playwright in the 1530s and 1540s. Heywood's translations put Seneca's plays into common early modern English dramatic form; as Norland argues, his translations 'established the model for Senecan translation that his younger contemporaries emulated and adapted but never bettered' (2009, 46).[13] They also add and alter parts of the plays to 'perfect' them for the English stage; this free disposition towards the classical text is an important feature of early modern dramatic practice. An example of this mode of translation can be found in *Hercules Furens* (translated in 1561). Here Juno describes her plans:

> Let now Megara bring to sight, and with her mournful hand
> For burning rage bring out of hell a huge and direful brand.
> Do this, require your vengeance due, and pains of hell his spoil.
> Strike through his breast, let fiercer flame, with his bosom boil
> Than which in Aetna furnace beats, so furiously to see.
> That mad of mind and witless may Alcides driven be
> With fury great through pierced quite, myself must first of all
> Be mad. Wherefore doth Juno yet not into raging fall?

The verse here is in the conventional rhymed couplets characteristic of many plays of the period. Plays of the 1560s and 1570s characteristically use this mode – Thomas Preston's *Cambyses*, an oft-performed play printed in 1569, uses precisely the same form of rhymed fourteeners to alternately comic and tragic effect – and this is the mode later caricatured by the classically learned poet-playwright Ben Jonson in his 1616 play *The Devil Is An Ass*. No effort is made to echo the prosody or structure of the Latin verse; instead the play deploys the rhyming couplets of Tudor interludes. The syntax of the lines is distorted in the interest of meter and rhyme, and sounds highly artificial to an ear more accustomed to plays from the 1580s and later. Technical features like stichomythia do appear in the play, but the verse is assimilated to the model of the early drama, and the play is Senecan only in the sense that it presents an accurate translation of the content of Seneca's play – in an already established native form.

Other writers in the period treat this Senecan legacy differently and write original plays in Latin on classical subjects rather than translating or adapting the plays into vernacular drama. William Gager (1555–1622) was a canon lawyer, poet and playwright whose Latin plays were produced at Oxford in the 1580s and 1590s. His 1583 play, *Meleager*, was performed in 1585 for an audience including Sir Philip Sidney and the Earls of Leicester and Pembroke (both of whom were patrons of acting companies), and his plays were among those performed for the Queen when she visited Oxford in 1592. He was widely praised in contemporary commentary including Francis Meres' *Palladis Tamia* (London, 1598):[14]

> [T]he best for comedy amongst us be *Edward* Earl of Oxford, Doctor *Gager* of Oxford, Master *Rowley*, once a rare scholar of learned Pembroke Hall in Cambridge, Master *Edwards*, one of her Majesty's Chapel, eloquent and witty *John Lilly, Lodge, Gascoyne, Greene, Shakespeare, Thomas Nash, Thomas Heywood, Anthony Mundye*, our best plotter, *Chapman, Porter, Wilson, Hathway*, and *Henry Chettle*. (Oo3v)

Meres begins his listings by stating who were the best writers in each genre in Greek and Latin and then lists English writers who follow those classical precedents. As Norland notes, Meres clearly had a preference for academic drama and it is the writers of Oxford and Cambridge who receive praise first. However, Gager's name appears in a list that includes non-academic writers like Shakespeare, suggesting that in Meres' eyes there was a fair amount of literary (for lack of a better term) contact among these writers. From references such as this, it is clear that Gager's work exerted an influence over academic drama (and that professional dramatists were involved in bringing some of his plays to press). *Meleager* takes up the story of Meleager as chronicled in Ovid's *Metamorphoses* but converts the Ovidian narrative into a Senecan tragedy and is Gager's invention. The play opens with a lengthy speech delivered by Megaera and setting out the plot, which chronicles the destruction of Meleager, his mother Althaea, and his father Oeneus to satisfy Diana's anger over Oeneus' failure to sacrifice to her; this echoes the opening of Seneca's *Thyestes*. As Frederick Boas writes of the play:

> He uses, as a matter of course, the Senecan machinery and technique, and he observes the unities strictly. But it is only a superficial view that would dismiss the play as merely imitative and unoriginal. Gager [...] shows genuine inventiveness and dexterity in his management of the plot, fusing into an attractive whole episodes of his own devising with those of which Ovid was the direct source. (Boas 1966, 175)

Gager wrote other original plays – his comedy *Rivales* and the 'tragoedia nova' of *Ulysses Redux* – that display this 'inventiveness and dexterity' and that demonstrate the usefulness and power of Senecan dramaturgy for non-Senecan plays. According to Howard Norland, Gager's drama 'reduced the static qualities and elevated style of Seneca and his sixteenth-century imitators in order to accommodate the stage practice of the popular theater' (2009, 192). It is this innovation that Kyd's drama builds on.

Meres' description of tragedy in England is equally illuminating for my purposes here, as it mentions Kyd specifically. Just before he turns to listing the best for comedy, he offers a list of tragic writers:

> [T]hese are our best for tragedy, the Lord *Buckhurst*, Doctor *Leg* of Cambridge, Doctor *Edes* of Oxford, Master *Edward Ferris*, the author of the *Mirrour for Magistrates*, *Marlow*, *Peele*, *Watson*, *Kid*, *Shakespeare*, *Drayton*, *Chapman*, *Decker*, and *Beniamin Iohnson* [...] As M. *Anneus Lucanus* writ two excellent tragedies, one called *Medea*, the other *de Incendio Troiae cum Priami calamitate*, so Doctor *Leg* hath penned two famous tragedies, the one of *Richard the 3*. the other of the destruction of *Jerusalem*. (Oo3r)

The list, as with that for comedy, begins with academic writers like Thomas Legge, whose *Ricardus Tertius* was an influential play, but turns to professional playwrights like Christopher Marlowe, Shakespeare and Thomas Kyd. Kyd's work then figures as part of a perceived group of those English writers 'best for tragedy' (vernacular or not). These listings point towards Kyd's participation in the metadialogue which is the subject of the next section.

The Spanish Tragedy and Conversation

Kyd's play participates in a broad dialogue with other plays – a dialogue that might usefully be considered to be more collaborative than contentious – and is responding as much to the content of earlier texts as to their reception. Writing about an early stage version of Seneca's *Oedipus*, Bruce Smith argues that the additions and revisions to Seneca's text 'tell us a great deal about how university audiences listened to tragedy. From the speech they heard declaimed onstage they expected not just revelations of character and emotion but moral wisdom, formulated with epigrammatic precision' (1988, 216). This mode of hearing plays was structured by a humanist mode of reading. Playwrights, as Smith goes on to suggest, added material to their classical originals that spoke to that mode of reading and to what he terms an academic delight in speechmaking even when such additions work against the argument of the play: 'the only difficulty is that Seneca's ethical assumptions and Gager's polemical program work at cross purposes. Gager evinces [the] assumption that one can make a simple moral judgment about the tragic protagonists and the complicated situations in which those characters find themselves' (Smith 1988, 216). This is the assumption that Kyd does not seem to make and that constitutes one of the most distinctive features of his response to the deployment of Senecan practices in early modern drama. Kyd's play depends crucially on the ambiguities and problems of revenge, of a stoic response to injustice, and makes no effort to ignore or sidestep them. By refusing to offer a singular moral gloss on the events on stage, Kyd's play denies the possibility of simple moral judgments. That denial is an important part of many later English tragedies.

Kyd, then, does not translate the matter of Senecan tragedy so much as he adopts its forms and structures in producing what is often described as the first English revenge tragedy. His response is not a rejection or a criticism so much as a deployment and development of earlier work-utterances. Rather than choosing classical matter like Gager's plays that draw on stories in Ovid or Homer, Kyd's play chronicles a series of interlocking revenges that derive from the unchivalrous killing of Don Andrea, a Spanish gentleman, by Balthazar, Prince of Portugal, and ends with the deaths of most of the Spanish court as well as the Portuguese Prince. The play begins with the ghost of Don Andrea describing his death at the hands of Balthazar and his desire for revenge, which is promised to him by Revenge. Andrea and Revenge remain onstage throughout the play to watch the eventual satisfaction of that desire. The primary revenger is Hieronimo, a court official, whose son has been murdered by Balthazar and Lorenzo, a Spanish nobleman. That murder drives a proliferation of revenge plots that culminate in a murderous play-within-the-play and Hieronimo's suicide in the final act. Andrea is only avenged as a side-effect of Hieronimo's revenge. I do not intend to provide a reading here, but rather to indicate ways in which specific moments in the play appear to be responding to English neo-Senecan drama.

In the play, Kyd adopts something of the philosophical disposition of Seneca's plays in his use of what Braden terms 'Senecan selfhood' in characterizing his main avenger. Influences in terms of style are an elusive object of study – especially in translation or adaptation – but the tone of Kyd's play clearly owes a great deal to Seneca and his English inheritors. Kyd translated the French playwright Robert Garnier's *Cornelie* (printed in 1595, probably translated earlier) and his work demonstrates an engagement with this dramatic tradition. In the first scene of the play, the ghost of Don Andrea and Revenge enter (they never leave the stage) and Andrea reports his condition to the audience. The declamatory mode of this speech and, more accurately, the whole of the play make it difficult to excerpt only brief quotations, so I quote the speech at length:

> When this eternal substance of my soul
> Did live imprisoned in my wanton flesh,
> Each in their function serving other's need,
> I was a courtier in the Spanish court.
> My name was Don Andrea; my descent,

> Though not ignoble, yet inferior far
> To gracious fortunes of my tender youth.
> In secret I possessed a worthy dame
> Which hight Bel-Imperia by name.
> But in the harvest of my summer joys
> Death nipped the blossoms of my bliss,
> Forcing divorce between my love and me.
> For in the late conflict with the Portingale
> My valor drew me into danger's mouth,
> Till life to death made passage through my wounds.
> When I was slain, my soul descended straight
> To pass the flowing stream of Acheron;
> But churlish Charon, only boatman there,
> Said my rights of burial not performed,
> I might not sit amongst his passengers.
> (Kyd 1989, 1.1.1–22)

The speech goes on for a total of some 85 lines. Andrea goes on to describe his passage through the underworld – which is purely classical – chronicling the various deferrals of judgment of where he should be lodged until Proserpine asks to be given the right to decide. She whispers instructions to Revenge, who conveys Andrea to the stage; there they watch the action of the play, which will show 'the author of [his] death, / Don Balthazar, the prince of Portingale, / Deprived of life by Bel-Imperia' (Kyd 1989, Ind. 87–9). The choric induction here has clearly been deeply influenced by Seneca, while at the same time Kyd transforms this material in a response to plays which either follow the pattern very closely, as in Heywood's translation, or treat Senecan technique as a resource but only in Latin. Kyd's specific intervention in the dialogue is to use these technical resources in the vernacular and for an audience not composed of scholars or students; this represents what Bakhtin terms a responsive reaction to the tradition within which the play takes shape.

Kyd uses patterns of construction from Senecan drama to build his play, and later in the play he stages a stichomythic courtship scene between Horatio, Andrea's friend, and Bel-Imperia that is overheard by Balthazar (who desires her) and Lorenzo (her brother):

> BEL-IMPERIA. Why stands Horatio speechless all this while?
> HORATIO. The less I speak, the more I meditate.
> BEL-IMPERIA. But whereon dost thou chiefly meditate?
> HORATIO. On dangers past, and pleasures to ensue.
> BALTHAZAR. On pleasures past, and dangers to ensue.

BEL-IMPERIA. What dangers and what pleasures dost thou mean?
HORATIO. Dangers of war, and pleasures of our love.
LORENZO. Dangers of death, but pleasures none at all.
(Kyd 1989, 2.2.24–31)

Instead of a conversation between two people, Kyd gives us a conversation overheard and commented on by two other interlocutors, but in terms familiar from more standard forms of stichomythic dialogue. The lovers turn each other's phrases playfully – playing on dangers and pleasures – while the eavesdropping villains play on the same phrases in a dialogue of threat that only they can hear. The dialogue here is not deliberative or directly confrontational (as in many other uses of this mode), but instead is simultaneously both playful and threatening. The effect derives from the overlaid dialogue: multiple voices speak at the same time, but are not heard at the same time. The overlaid and competing dialogues here represent an example of the kind of heteroglot, many-voiced, language that Bakhtin sees as characteristic of literary language (and language more generally). Moreover, this doubling and overlaying represents a response to and deployment of elements of classical drama that Kyd uses here to remarkable dramatic effect.

Elsewhere in the play, he uses this same structure in a conversation between Lorenzo and Balthazar in which they trade lines of sonnets in order to lament the woes of the lover. The exchange combines classical technique and contemporary verse forms:

LORENZO.   My lord, though Bel-Imperia seem thus coy,
           Let reason hold you in your wonted joy:
           'In time the savage bull sustains the yoke,
           In time all haggard hawks stoop to lure,
           In time small wedges cleave the hardest oak,
           In time the flint is pierced with softest shower' –
           And she in time will fall from her disdain,
           And rue the sufferance of your friendly pain.
BALTHAZAR. No, she is wilder, and more hard withal,
           Than beast, or bird, or tree or stony wall.
           (Kyd 1989, 2.1.1–10)

The lines marked with quotation marks here are quotations from a collection of sonnets by Thomas Watson called *Hekatompathia, or Passionate Century of Love, Divided into two parts: whereof, the first expresseth the Authours sufferance in Love: the latter, his long farewell to Love and all his tyrannie*; the book was published in London in 1582. All of the sonnets are prefaced with extensive headnotes explaining the rhetorical situation, the condition of the speaker, the source for the poem, etc. The lines, not perfectly recalled, are from Watson's sonnet 58. This particular sonnet has a lengthy preface, worth quoting more or less in full:

> This passion conteineth a relation through out from line to line; as, from every line of the first staffe as it standeth in order, unto every line of the second staffe: and from the second staffe unto the third. The oftener it is read of him that is no great Clarke, the more pleasure he shall have in it. And this posie a scholler set down over this Sonnet, when he had well considered of it: *Tam causa, quam arte et industria*. (F4v)[15]

The two characters here demonstrate their cultural capital and familiarity with recent lyric poetry (Balthazar continues in the same mode in his own words, but – perhaps due to a lesser cause – with less art and zeal). Here they are behaving in accord with the prescriptions of courtesy handbooks, such as Castiglione's *Book of the Courtier*, which require the courtier to demonstrate a familiarity and (more importantly) a facility with the work of the best wits of the period. Lorenzo shows his ability to repurpose literary language from one mode into another. The irony here, at least for an audience familiar with Watson's text, is that this poem is said to require repeated reading by 'him that is no great Clarke' in order to gain the full measure of enjoyment from the complicated repetitions of motifs from stanza to stanza. Such artfulness is lost on Balthazar, who proceeds to offer more poetry in his own words, but poetry that merely repeats itself without the structural articulation of the sonnet. Kyd draws on the stichomythic dialogue of Senecan tragedy and at the same time on the discourse of lyric poetry to stage this exchange, and combines them to characterize his speakers. This innovation is applied, more famously, by Shakespeare in *Romeo and Juliet*, where sonnet language is used throughout the play to heighten the tragic affect of the plot.

Hieronimo, the central character of Kyd's play, speaks in a declamatory mode that also responds to the Senecan tradition; he even appears onstage carrying a book of Seneca's tragedies. He cites three plays – *Agamemnon*, *Troades* and *Oedipus*. The speech quotes lines from those plays in what looks like an effort to convince himself to pursue private revenge in the face of the failure of more sanctioned forms of justice. However, as Scott McMillin (1974, 207) has noted, he chooses passages that do not have anything specific to do with revenge. For example, the passage from *Agamemnon* that Hieronimo quotes is 'per scelera semper sceleribus tutum est iter' ('the safe way through crime is by [further] crimes'), which he takes as justification for seeking revenge. In the context of Seneca's play, however, those lines do not refer to revenge; they come from a speech in which Clytemnestra is deciding that after ten years of crime she can only secure her 'safety' by killing Agamemnon. The other citations are similarly distant from thoughts of revenge. McMillin concludes that Hieronimo's reading of Seneca here 'finds significance in the situations of language rather than in the literalism of words', and sees this as a pattern in Hieronimo's speech and action through the rest of the play. I would add that this disposition to Senecan inspiration is precisely Kyd's in composing the whole of the play. In other words, it is not just Hieronimo who looks at the book of Seneca (and by extension at books influenced by Seneca), and finds more significance in situations of language than in literal meanings. Kyd looks to Seneca in the same way. This mode of response represents a dialogue with playwrights who focus more on the literal meaning of the Senecan 'original'. Kyd's intervention in the broad ideological colloquy of the literary field is to contribute to the development of a disposition toward the Senecan legacy that enables creative adaptations instead of varieties of duplication. Where Gager translates and writes new plays that hew fairly closely to the Senecan material, Kyd treats that material as a resource in a way unlike even other appropriators of Seneca.

Kyd's play explores problems of justice, the state, and private revenge, and uses elements and techniques from Senecan and neo-Senecan drama to conduct this exploration. The declamatory mode of lament, the stichomythic dialogue of complaint and courtship, and the spectacular violence of the play all draw on earlier plays; thus Kyd's deployment of these elements in his revenge tragedy constitutes a response to earlier drama – a response that in turn exerts a profound influence over later works. Moreover, he synthesizes other modes into a particularly English version of Senecan tragedy: citing the language of the sonnet, paralleling the main plot with an almost parodic subplot but one that keeps the language of Senecan tragedy, etc. This synthesis appears to have been quite productive and can be seen as an influence on other transformations of the genre in plays such as Shakespeare's *Titus Andronicus* or *Romeo and Juliet*. *The Spanish Tragedy*'s responsive reaction to an earlier tradition changed the shape of what Bakhtin and Voloshinov term the large ideological colloquy of utterance; in so doing it changed the shape and purview not only of revenge tragedy as such, but of the tragic genre in general.

Notes

1 All further citations of the play will be to this edition.
2 I will not address the vexed question of the authorship of this text here as it is not strictly relevant to my argument. For my purposes the close association of Bakhtin and Voloshinov's thought is sufficient. That closeness of thought is particularly clear when reading *Marxism and the Philosophy of Language* alongside 'The Problem of Speech Genres'.
3 In many cases, it seems to me that such debates miss the point that Bakhtin seems to be referring to a pretty specific kind of drama, not drama as such and certainly not the

drama of early modern England. For a more developed argument about Bakhtin and drama see Siemon (2002), and for another perspective see Wise (1989).
4 Pierre Bourdieu picks up on these insights and develops them further in works like *The Rules of Art* (1996) and *The Field of Cultural Production* (1993).
5 These facts have been commented on and extensively documented in such magisterial works as Bullough's *Narrative and Dramatic Sources of Shakespeare* (1957–1975).
6 Repeated references (under various versions of the title) appear in Henslowe's *Diary* and the play was consistently profitable.
7 The best example of this is Ben Jonson who makes remarkably frequent reference to the play – often to critique what he wants to characterize as a particular kind of theatrical bad taste. See *Every Man In His Humour* and *Bartholomew Fair* for examples.
8 Kyd, of course, was only one of a number of playwrights working with this material. This chapter will look narrowly at Kyd, but I do not intend to suggest that Kyd is some kind of solitary innovator. A larger version of this argument will explore the work of these writers as well as offering deeper accounts of playing at the universities. Franco Moretti's recent *Graphs, Maps, and Trees* (2005) provides some of the methodological frame for this larger project of literary history.
9 See Howard B. Norland's *Neoclassical Tragedy in Elizabethan England* (2009) for an extended discussion of early modern efforts to simplify and reduce the complexities of Seneca's plot to fit various kinds of didactic purposes.
10 See Pierre Bourdieu, *The Rules of Art* (1996) for an extensive account of the French literary field in the nineteenth century that operates along these lines. My purpose here is more limited in that I am describing one element in this much more general and complex process.
11 Braden does discuss style, but curiously passes over the Latin Senecan drama performed at Cambridge and Oxford, except for some passing references to Thomas Legge's *Ricardus Tertius*. He discusses continental Senecanism far more fully.
12 There remains some debate about how directly such elements come from Seneca's plays – many later plays seem to get their Senecan elements at second or third hand, constituting an English Senecan tradition that is at some remove from the classical 'source'. Stichomythia, the exchange of single lines between two characters, has long been remarked on as an important technical legacy of classical drama.
13 Norland (2009, 47) characterizes Gager as one of the most accurate of Seneca's early translators into English but at the same time, it is striking how much he relies on native dramatic traditions.
14 Gager's name is mentioned in a list of those who are 'best for comedy' even though the majority of his works (and the only ones that survive) are neo-Senecan tragedies like *Meleager*. This may be a result of the early modern use of comedy to mean drama more generally.
15 *Tam causa, quam arte et industria*. The Latin translates to 'from so great a cause, as much art and zeal'. Each of the poems in Watson's collection is prefaced with this kind of headnote. They offer a kind of pre-emptive gloss of the content of the poems as well as a guide to reading (and using them).

References

Bakhtin, M. M. 1986. 'The Problem of Speech Genres' ('Problema rechevykh zhanrov'). In *Speech Genres and Other Late Essays*. Edited by Caryl Emerson and Michael Holquist, translated by Vern W. McGee, 60–102. Austin: University of Texas Press.

Boas, Frederick S. 1966 [1914]. *University Drama in the Tudor Age*. Oxford: Oxford University Press.
Bourdieu, Pierre. 1993. *The Field of Cultural Production*. New York: Columbia University Press.
———. 1996. *The Rules of Art*. Stanford: Stanford University Press.
Braden, Gordon. 1985. *Renaissance Tragedy and the Senecan Tradition*. New Haven: Yale University Press.
Bullough, Geoffrey. 1957–1975. *Narrative and Dramatic Sources of Shakespeare*. 8 vols. New York: Columbia University Press.
Harbage, Alfred. 1964. *Annals of English Drama 975–1700*. London: Methuen.
Kyd, Thomas. 1989. *The Spanish Tragedy*. Edited by J. R. Mulryne. London: A. C. and Black.
McMillin, Scott. 1974. 'The Book of Seneca in *The Spanish Tragedy*'. *Studies in English Literature, 1500–1900* 14, no. 2: 201–8.
Miola, Robert S. 1990.'Othello Furens'. *Shakespeare Quarterly* 41: 49–64.
Moretti, Franco. 2005. *Graphs, Maps, and Trees*. New York: Verso.
Norland, Howard B. 2009. *Neoclassical Tragedy in Elizabethan England*. Newark, DE: University of Delaware Press.
Siemon, James R. 2002. *Word Against Word: Shakespearean Utterance*. Amherst: University of Massachusetts Press.
Smith, Bruce R. 1988. *Ancient Scripts and Modern Experience on the English Stage*. Princeton: Princeton University Press.
Voloshinov, V. N. 1986. *Marxism and the Philosophy of Language* (*Marksizm i filosofiia iazyka*, 1929). Cambridge, MA: Harvard University Press.
Wise, Jennifer. 1989. 'Marginalizing Drama: Bakhtin's Theory of Genre'. *Essays in Theatre* 8, no. 1: 15–22.

Chapter 7

BAKHTIN'S CONCEPT OF THE CHRONOTOPE: THE VIEWPOINT OF AN ACTING SUBJECT

Liisa Steinby

Bakhtin's Concept of Chronotope: An Epistemological Category?

Bakhtin's concept of the chronotope has been received by literary scholars probably with more enthusiasm than any other of his concepts, and has been widely applied in different fields of study and to literature from different periods. In the essay 'Forms of Time and of the Chronotope in the Novel', which is the main source for his chronotopic thinking, Bakhtin emphasizes that chronotopes function as the basis of the historical development of genres of the novel.[1] By now, his ideas about the chronotope have not only been drawn upon in historical poetics and the genre theory of the novel; for example reception theorists and narratologists have been able to include this Bakhtinian element in their thinking. The chronotope has proved to be a valuable tool of literary analysis, despite the fact that it is far from clear what Bakhtin actually meant by the concept, and that consequently it has been understood and used in a wide range of different ways.

Bakhtin does not use the term 'chronotope' before the mid-1930s. From this period we have two long essays in which 'chronotope' is used. The first, on the *Bildungsroman*, 'The Novel of Education and its Significance in the History of Realism', was probably written during 1936–38;[2] 'Forms of Time and of the Chronotope in the Novel' was written at almost the same time, during 1937–38, except for the 'Concluding Remarks', an addition from 1973. The terms 'chronotope' and 'chronotopic' are used in the *Bildungsroman* essay, but are not defined there. It is true that Bakhtin is not a theoretician who proceeds systematically from the definition of a concept to its use, and his use of a term can often be confusingly inconsistent (cf. Hirschkop 1986, 73; Scholz 1998). The chronotope essay, however, begins with the following definition: 'We will give the name chronotope (literally, "time space") to the intrinsic connectedness of temporal and spatial relationships that are artistically expressed in literature' (Bakhtin 2008, 84). With regard to the term, Bakhtin mentions his debt to Einstein's theory of relativity, in which time and space are presented as interconnected, even though the term is borrowed 'almost as a metaphor (almost, but not entirely)' (Bakhtin 2008, 84). Compared to this, he describes the literary chronotope as a 'concrete whole', in which '[t]ime, as it were, thickens, takes on flesh, becomes artistically visible; likewise, space becomes charged and responsive to the movements of time, plot and history' (Bakhtin 2008, 84). Somewhat later, Bakhtin in a footnote comments on the relationship between his chronotope and Kant's concepts of time and space:

> In his 'Transcendental Aesthetics' (one of the main sections of his *Critique of Pure Reason*) Kant defines space and time as indispensable forms of any cognition. Here we employ the Kantian evaluation of the importance of these forms in the cognitive process, but differ from Kant in taking them not as 'transcendental' but as forms of the most immediate reality. We shall attempt to show the role these forms play in the process of concrete artistic cognition (artistic visualization) under conditions obtaining in the genre of the novel. (Bakhtin 2008, 85)

Kant's notions of time and space as transcendental *a priori* preconditions of perception (cf. Kant 1975a, 69–86) are here acknowledged as a source of the chronotope; however, in difference to these Kantian ideas, 'chronotope' is said to refer to time-space as 'forms of the most immediate reality' which also play a role in artistic cognition, or 'artistic visualization', in the novel. How Bakhtin here understands 'the most immediate reality' is in need of further clarification, since Kant's time and space of course also refer to the 'immediate reality' of perception. The two definitions, however, have provided scholars with a foundation for understanding Bakhtin's concept of the chronotope.

Despite considerable differences in views, scholars generally understand the 'chronotope' as a concept referring first of all to temporal-spatial forms of cognition, secondly to the representation of this cognition or experience in literature (in the novel). The two are of course interconnected, and are seldom spoken of separately. For example, the entry concerning the chronotope in Holquist's 'Glossary' for Bakhtin's *Dialogic Imagination* stresses the literary representation of experience in chronotopes:

> Literally, 'time-space'. A unit of analysis for studying texts according to the ratio and nature of the temporal and spatial categories represented. The distinctiveness

of this concept as opposed to most other uses of time and space in literary analysis lies in the fact that neither category is privileged; they are utterly interdependent. The chronotope is an optic for reading texts as x-rays of the forces at work in the culture system from which they spring. (Holquist 2008, 425–6)

In his *Dialogism: Bakhtin and His World* (2002), Holquist speaks of the chronotope, following the Russian Formalists' view of how literary 'devices' function, as a means of 'deforming' the temporal sequence of the story (Holquist 2002, 114).[3] Later on, however, he stresses that the chronotope is an 'epistemological category' (cf. Holquist 2010, 20); according to him, there is 'no perception, no thinking or understanding of the self or the world' without them (Holquist 2010, 28). In the *Routledge Encyclopedia of Narrative Theory*, Bakhtin is said to insist with this concept on the 'intrinsic connectedness' of space and time in literature: '*A way of understanding experience*, of modelling the world, chronotopes provide a "ground" for *representation* out of which narrative events emerge, a series of temporal markers conjoined with spatial features which, together, define specific historical, biographical, and social relations' (Pier 2005, 64; emphasis by L. S.). Here both aspects of the chronotope, its being a form of experience and of representation, are mentioned separately but as being interconnected. For example Roderick Beaton emphasizes the previous aspect: '[T]he chronotope is to be understood as the distinctive configuration of time and space that defines "reality" within the world of the text, *as conceptualized within that world itself*' (Beaton 2010, 62; emphasis in the original). In the introduction to a recent volume of articles on Bakhtin's chronotope (Bemong et al. 2010), which includes Beaton's article, Nele Bemong and Pieter Borghart similarly contend that time and space for Bakhtin constitute a fundamental unity, 'as in the human perception of everyday reality' (Bemong and Borghart 2010, 3).

Despite considerable differences in understanding and applying the concept (e.g. Bemong et al. 2010), the basic view shared by theoreticians is that the chronotope is a category of perceiving or understanding things; in other words, it is epistemological in character. Chronotopes are forms of cognition, or/and categories for representing these. Moreover, scholars unanimously follow Bakhtin in emphasizing that there is not just one chronotope, or spatio-temporal form of experience, but a plurality of them: there are different chronotopes for different views of the world and different social situations. Gary Saul Morson and Caryl Emerson, for example, contend that 'Bakhtin's crucial point is that time and space vary in *qualities*; different social activities and representations of those activities presume different kinds of time and space' (Morson and Emerson 1990, 367; emphasis in the original). Scholars have also adopted the Bakhtinian view, as presented in 'Forms of

Time and of the Chronotope in the Novel', that chronotopes vary historically and that a novel can contain several chronotopes, thus being 'heterochronic' (cf. Falconer 2010). Graham Pechey goes so far as to suggest that a plurality of chronotopes, and 'the actuality of choice between them' are characteristic of the novel in general, in contrast to the epic, in which a single chronotope prevails (1998, 174).

The interpretation of the chronotope as an epistemological category draws of course on Bakhtin's own definitions of the concept, in which it is defined in relation to Einstein's concept of time-space (as a single category) and to Kant's idea of time and space as forms of perception. What may prompt some hesitation concerning the epistemological interpretation of the chronotope, however, is that Bakhtin's concept – or non-concept – of 'most immediate reality' may have another but purely epistemological content. If it is true that Bakhtin never abandoned his ethical viewpoint of human existence, but on the contrary based on it his exploration of the phenomena of art and the novel, then we should rather think of his 'most immediate reality' in terms of the real 'events' of human life, the 'once-occurrent Being in its concrete actuality' (Bakhtin 1993, 2) in which we are involved as ethical subjects. By this reading, we would tie the chronotope to Bakhtin's early ethics in *Toward a Philosophy of the Act* and the ensuing works on aesthetics and the poetics of the novel, namely 'Art and Hero in Aesthetic Activity' and *Problems of Dostoevsky's Poetics*.

There are some scholars who have emphasized the ethical – or 'axiological' – relevance of the category of the chronotope. Holquist contends that 'time and space are never merely temporal and spatial, but *axiological* as well (i.e. they also have *values* attached to them) [...] Perception is never pure; it is always accomplished in terms of evaluation of what is perceived' (Holquist 2002, 152; emphasis in the original). The axiological aspect thus appears for Holquist as something that is added or attached to the perception of time and space; moreover, he considers that this always necessarily is the case. According to him, even Aristotle's and Einstein's categories of time and place are inherently connected with value: there is for them no 'purity of time/space, that is time or space in themselves (without an attendant value)' (Holquist 2002, 157). I think that here is a profound misunderstanding concerning the categories of time and space in Aristotle and Einstein; however, more important from the viewpoint of Bakhtin is that the idea of space and time as categories necessarily bound to values is unacceptable in Kantian and Neo-Kantian thinking, in which categories of cognition (or 'pure reason'), among them space and time, and of ethics ('practical reason') are strictly separate. Moreover, Holquist does not distinguish between action as an ethical category and change in the sense of a natural event; in other words, he does not distinguish between 'event' as a category of natural science and the Bakhtinian concept of 'event'.

He contends that Einstein's relativity theory and Bakhtin's 'dialogism' (the term he uses for Bakhtin's thinking) 'begin by assuming that time is knowable only in terms of action, that is of changes in the natural world: temporal relations are first constituted by physical relations that obtain not among static things but among *events*' (Holquist 2002, 159; emphasis in the original). Thus what is essential in Bakhtin's chronotope for Holquist is its being about change in time and place.

In their discussion of the chronotope, which they consider as 'a way of understanding experience', Morson and Emerson, in *Mikhail Bakhtin: Creation of a Prosaics* (1990), quote approvingly Bakhtin's words that his chronotopes, like Kant's time and space, are 'indispensable forms of cognition' (Morson and Emerson 1990, 367). However, they conclude that since a chronotope is 'a specific form-shaping ideology for understanding the nature of events and actions', 'the chronotope essay may be understood as a further development of Bakhtin's early concern with the "act"' (Morson and Emerson 1990, 367). This of course contradicts their view, expressed earlier in the book, that 'the early manuscripts are very much the product of influences Bakhtin soon outgrew' (Morson and Emerson 1990, 7). They continue: 'Actions are necessarily performed in a specific context; chronotopes differ by the ways in which they understand context and the relation of actions and events to it' (Morson and Emerson 1990, 367). For Morson and Emerson, 'action' here seems to imply an ethically responsible subject; however, they do not consequently differentiate the ethical act from a natural process. They emphasize Bakhtin's debt to the biologist A. A. Ukhtomskii, from whom he borrowed the term 'chronotope', and they assume that the latter's concept of 'activity' in biological organisms coincides with Bakhtin's concept of action and how time-space is related to them:

> Bodies must organize their own external activities and internal processes in time and space. Organisms operate by means of, and must coordinate, a variety of rhythms differing from each other and from those of other organisms. Furthermore, different social activities are also defined by various kinds of fused time and space: the rhythms and special organization of the assembly line, agricultural labor, sexual intercourse, and parlor conversation differ markedly. (Morson and Emerson 1990, 268)

When Morson, in an article from 2010, takes up once again the concept of the chronotope, it appears in connection with human action, but rather than as an ethical category Morson discusses the chronotope in terms of change (Morson 2010). This seems similar to Holquist; Morson, however, stresses not the change as such but the unpredictability of the change which does not follow any necessary (natural) laws. In this sense, he now redefines the concept of the event:

> Not all events have eventness. An event has 'eventness' if and only if presentness matters, only if the present moment is something more than the automatic result of prior moments [...] The possibility of more than one outcome makes an event not just something that happens but something that happens even though it might not have. It is that quality – the might-not-have-been – that constitutes eventness. (Morson 2010, 94)

Here 'event' is used in two different meanings, neither of which is identical with Bakhtin's understanding of event as a co-being between two or more ethically responsible subjects. The first meaning coincides with the common understanding of the word: this appears in the first sentence 'Not all events have [...]'. These events in the common sense of the word are distinguished from events 'proper', characterized by 'eventness': those that are unpredictable. The unpredictability of events presumes that human action based on freedom of choice can have an effect on what happens. The emphasis in this understanding of the chronotope is not on the ethical act of the individual but on the dynamic aspect of the chronotope, implying change. What is essential for Morson is not the change as such but the unpredictability of change and the ensuing representation of the world in the novel as 'unfinalizable' (cf. also Morson and Emerson 1990, 419).

Neither Holquist nor Morson and Emerson provide us with a satisfactory answer to the question of what it would mean to interpret Bakhtin's concept of the chronotope in the context of his ethical thinking. As indicated in the Introduction and in Chapters 1 and 3, a continuity can be traced from Bakhtin's early *Toward a Philosophy of the Act*, through the early aesthetics in 'Author and Hero in Aesthetic Activity', to *Problems of Dostoevsky's Poetics*. This continuity consists of the persistence of the question of how the individual, as an ethically responsible subject involved in a concrete event, i.e. in an encounter with other individuals, is conceived of as the foundation of our understanding of ourselves and the world, and/or as the subject matter of literature (the novel). Here I ask whether this line can be followed up to Bakhtin's concept of chronotope, and how the concept of chronotope is in that case to be understood.

The founding of the new 'first philosophy' in *Toward a Philosophy of the Act* was meant to be an answer to the question of how to find a way out of the contemporary crisis of culture (Bakhtin 1993, 54), which was felt so intensely on the German intellectual scene in the 1920s, i.e. after the catastrophe of World War I (cf. e.g. Natorp 1923). According to Bakhtin, what had been forgotten was that an individual human being is an autonomous ethical subject responsible for his or her acts in real 'events' in his or her life. Theories of philosophical ethics which deal with ethical principles abstractly are to be abandoned. Bakhtin's commitment to the human individual, involved in the real 'events' of life, can be understood as an indication of his attachment to the 'philosophy of life' of, e.g. Dilthey, Bergson and Scheler.[4] 'Philosophy of life', however, does not for Bakhtin mean irrationality: it is not that the 'unitary and once-occurrent Being-as-event' (Bakhtin 1993, 19) cannot be dealt with in language,[5] and it is Bakhtin's intention to present such a philosophy of the act involved in real 'events'. In 'Author and Hero in Aesthetic Activity', ethical theory was transformed into an aesthetic theory of the 'hero' as an ethically acting concrete individual and of the author as the one who is able to bestow upon the hero a 'consummating', 'finalized' form (Bakhtin 1990, 12, 87, 101), which is the aesthetic form of the work of art. Here Bakhtin follows the idea, common in German thought, that while philosophy and science deal with abstract concepts, art preserves the concreteness of the object. Art thus appears for Bakhtin as the medium in which the concrete individual, the subject of ethical acts, can be presented. However, in *Problems of Dostoevsky's Poetics*, or actually in its predecessor *Problems of Dostoevsky's Art* (1929), the concept of aesthetic activity in 'Art and Hero' was abandoned. Here Bakhtin criticizes the author-centred novel, precisely in terms of how author-centeredness is presented in 'Author and Hero', as 'monologic', contrasting it with Dostoevsky's 'polyphonic' or dialogic novel. In the polyphonic novel, the characters are represented independently of the form-giving, or 'consummating', activity of the author. They appear just as they conceive themselves, as ethically acting individuals in the real 'events' of life, i.e. in encounters with other individuals. Individuals as ethically acting subjects involved in the 'events' of life are thus what the novel (or art) is about for Bakhtin, from his early aesthetics down to the polyphonic novel as presented in the Dostoevsky book. The fact that the first version of the Dostoevsky book, from 1929, preceded the writings on the chronotope, while the second version appeared well after them, in 1963, indicates that the ideas of novelistic polyphony and of the chronotopic view of the novel co-existed in Bakhtin's thinking, further encouraging us to enquire into the latter's connections with his philosophy of the act.

The suggestion that the chronotope should be understood in relation to Bakhtin's ethical thinking means challenging the prevailing epistemological view of the chonotope. We might think that the notion of 'the most immediate reality' in Bakhtin's definition of the chronotope opens up the possibility of an ethical understanding of the concept; however, in enquiring into the possible connection between the concept of the chronotope and Bakhtin's previous philosophy of the act we cannot limit the analysis merely to

Bakhtin's own – very preliminary – definitions of the concept, but have to examine how he actually uses it. In the following analysis, my purpose is to show how the concept of the chronotope arose out of Bakhtin's understanding of Goethe's insight into historical subjectivity; to describe in what sense the acting subject, as presented in the early philosophy, is at the heart of Bakhtin's account of different kinds of chronotopes; and to elucidate the role of chronotopes in the formation of genres.

The *Bildungsroman*: Seeing the Acting Subject in History

The *Bildungsroman* essay begins with a classification of novels 'according to how the image of the main hero is constructed', resulting in the subgenres of 'the travel novel, the novel of ordeal, the biographical (autobiographical) novel, the *Bildungsroman*' (Bakhtin 2007a, 10). Bakhtin discusses the first three types only briefly, but the discussion is illuminating for our purposes because it reveals to what extent the novel as a genre, in Bakhtin's view, is determined by the hero's (or heroes') position in it. In this classification, it is precisely the hero's relation to events that determines the type of the novel. In a travel novel, for instance, the hero 'is a point moving in space', and he himself 'has no essential distinguishing characteristics' (Bakhtin 2007a, 10), whereas a novel of ordeal 'is constructed as a series of tests of the main heroes' (Bakhtin 2007a, 11). That the hero's position in the whole of the work is the decisive criterion of the (sub)genre accords with Bakhtin's views both in 'Author and Hero' and in *Problems of Dostoevsky's Poetics*; in the former the most important constitutive element of a novel, or even of a work of art in general, is its author's relation to its hero, whereas in the latter the polyphonic novel is distinguished from the monologic on the basis of the heroes' independent position in the novel.

The fourth type of novel, the *Bildungsroman*, is presented in the essay as the most significant. Here 'man's individual emergence is inseparably linked to historical emergence. Man's emergence is accomplished in real historical time, with all of its necessity, its fullness, its future, and its profoundly chronotopic nature' (Bakhtin 2007a, 23). It is here that the term 'chronotopic' occurs for the first time in Bakhtin's writings, unfortunately in a context that leaves its meaning obscure: What is meant by the 'profoundly chronotopic nature' of historical time? For clarification, we have to search further in Bakhtin's discussion of the *Bildungsroman*, or rather of Goethe's 'seeing time in space'.

A striking feature of the introductory sentences of the discussion on the *Bildungsroman* is the connection Bakhtin sees between the 'emergence' of an individual human being, that is, the hero of the novel, and the emergence of a historical world. In all earlier novels, '[t]he world, existing and stable in this existence, required that man adapt to it, that he recognize and submit to the existing laws of life. Man emerged, but the world itself did not' (Bakhtin 2007a, 23). In contrast, in a *Bildungsroman*, such as Goethe's *Wilhelm Meister's Apprenticeship*,

> human emergence is of a different nature. It is no longer man's own private affair. He emerges *along with the world* and he reflects the historical emergence of the world itself. He is no longer within an epoch, but on the border between two epochs, at the transition point from one to the other. This transition is accomplished in him and through him. What is happening here is precisely the emergence of a new man. (Bakhtin 2007a, 23; emphasis in the original)

In what follows, Bakhtin focuses on Goethe's ability to 'see' the past in its remnants and signs in the present, a gift which for Goethe (1982, 32) himself appeared curious and to which Cassirer (1932, esp. 10–11) has dedicated a book-length study. The main part of Bakhtin's essay is actually not, as one might expect, about the developing hero in a *Bildungsroman*, but about how the most important of the *Bildungsroman* authors, Goethe, included in his perception of the present its historical past.

Bakhtin contends that Goethe introduced into the novel a new manner of seeing things: he never described a locality 'as an immobile background, a given that is completed once and for all, but as an emerging whole, an event' (Bakhtin 2007a, 25):

> His eyes did not recognize simple spatial contiguities or the simple coexistence of things and phenomena. Behind each static multiformity he saw multitemporality: as remnants or relics of various stages and formations of the past and as rudiments of stages in the more or less distant future. (Bakhtin 2007a, 28)

Goethe had a 'startling ability to see time in space' (Bakhtin 2007a, 30): 'His seeing eye saturates landscape with time – creative, historically productive time' (Bakhtin 2007a, 36). According to Bakhtin, Goethe's interest in topography was never an interest merely in a geological and geographical landscape per se, but something revealing a 'potential for historical life':

> This is an arena of historical events, a firmly delineated boundary of that spatial riverbed along which the current of historical time flows. Historically active man is placed in this living, graphic, visual system of waterways, mountains, valleys, boundaries, and routes. He builds, drains marshes, lays routes across mountains and rivers, develops the minerals, cultivates the irrigated valleys, and so on. One sees the *essential* and *necessary* character of man's historical activity. (Bakhtin 2007a, 37–8; emphasis in the original)

Thus 'all criteria for evaluation, all measures, and the entire living human scale of the locality can be understood only from the standpoint of *man the builder*' (Bakhtin 2007a, 35; emphasis in the original).

Bakhtin characterizes Goethe's specific manner of seeing time in the locality as chronotopic seeing, a 'chronotopic visualizing of locality' (Bakhtin 2007a, 36). It is in his discussion of Goethe's *Italian Journey*, in which Bakhtin detects numerous examples of seeing historical time in localities, that he first uses the term 'chronotope': 'It is in Rome that Goethe experiences especially keenly this impressive condensation of historical time, its fusion with terrestrial space [...] Rome is a great chronotope of human history' (Bakhtin 2007a, 40). In concluding his account of Goethe's Italian plans for some literary works with a local and historical topic, he describes all of these 'unrealized creative projects as "profoundly chronotopic"' (Bakhtin 2007a, 49).

How can we interpret Bakhtin's concepts of the chronotope, and of the chronotopic seeing and presenting of things, in view of his disquisition on Goethe? To begin with, it is clear that in this essay chronotopic seeing and the chronotopic description of localities in literature is a quality of only certain specific authors, such as Goethe. In contrast to his later views, here Bakhtin does not regard the chronotope as something that always inevitably structures one's seeing of things, or at least how they are represented in literature (or in the novel). Furthermore, chronotopic perception appears here as only possible after a certain point in history, after which man's natural and social living conditions are no longer taken for granted but are regarded as shaped by man's historical work. Accordingly, time that is included in the idea of the chronotope is historical time, as clearly demonstrated by the example he gives of Rome as 'a great chronotope of human history'.

What is most important is that historical time, which Bakhtin is here talking about, is not the historical past in the sense of past centuries and historical remnants as such; it is the past of 'creative historical time', time as the dimension of man's historical activity that shapes the natural and human world. Bakhtin stresses this difference when he describes Goethe as actually loathing not only the artificial ruins of the Romantics but also genuine remnants of the past, when they were cut off from human significance and historical continuity. The existence of relics of the past as merely petrified or objectified pieces of a foreign reality Bakhtin calls the 'estranged' past (Bakhtin 2007a, 33). Goethe's seeing time in place means seeing localities and remnants of the past in relation to past human actions, perceiving in them the results of man's creative activity; in the configuration of a landscape Goethe sees 'a *vestige of a single human will acting in a planned way*' (Bakhtin 2007a, 32; emphasis in the original). The difference resembles the contrast between encountering someone as an object or as a subject, which is vital for Bakhtin and which he primarily discusses in the Dostoevsky book, but not only there. The 'estranged' past is past cut off from human subjectivity, whereas chronotopic seeing means perceiving the past activity of human subjects.

The observation that for Bakhtin the chronotope and chronotopic seeing refer to time in relation to *human action* is most important, because it challenges the usual understanding of time (and space) in Bakhtin's chronotope as a mode of *perceiving objects*. As we have seen, Bakhtin himself is partly to blame for this misunderstanding, because in neither of his definitions of the concept is creative and practical-ethical human action mentioned; instead, he refers to Kant, for whom time and space are *a priori* forms of perception in the phenomenal world. On the basis of the *Bildungsroman* essay, however, it is evident that chronotopic seeing pertains to the realm of human action and does not refer to our manner of perceiving objects. Thus, where for Kant time and space are modes of perception in the realm of phenomena only, which are the consideration in the (natural) sciences following pure theoretical reason, Bakhtin's chronotopic seeing belongs to the realm of practical reason in the Kantian sense of the term: it has to do with human action considered as a matter of individual free will and ethical responsibility.[6]

This means that Bakhtin's chronotope in fact is fundamentally different from Kant's time and space. Time is a measurable dimension of events only in the phenomenal world of objects, whereas the time of human action is not measurable. Bakhtin must have been aware of the distinction, which was discussed in Neo-Kantian philosophy because he was familiar with Max Scheler's *Formalism in the Ethics and Material Ethics of Values: A New Attempt of Founding Ethical Personalism* (*Der Formalismus in der Ethik und die materiale Wertethik: Neuer Versuch der Grundlegung eines ethischen Personalismus*, 1913–16). Here Scheler elaborates upon the difference between a person's actions as a free subject and psychic functions regarded as naturally determined. Measurable time belongs only to the latter regarded as natural phenomena, whereas ethical human action is not measurable in time: 'Acts spring from a person into time: functions are facts in the phenomenal realm of time [in the Kantian sense] and indirectly, on the basis of their phenomenal temporal relations to phenomena with a measurable temporal duration, themselves measurable' (Scheler 1927, 403).[7] To Scheler's formulation that acts spring into time, we could add that time is a dimension within which creative human action becomes visible. Time is thus in a sense what is available for human action. Thus 'chairological' time, in the Heideggerian (Heidegger 2001, 102–4) – as well as early Greek – sense of the word may be relevant to an understanding of Bakhtin's chronotope: *kairos* is the right point in time, the right time of action.

Heidegger analyses 'chairological' time in the context of Aristotle's practical philosophy, where he sees it as connected with the concept of *phronēsis*, i.e. practical wisdom or prudence. *Phronēsis* is the wisdom to know how to act at the moment at hand (cf. Heidegger 2002, 55). The idea that human life is guided by the practical orientation of concern or care (*Sorge*) is of course all-important in Heidegger's own thinking, especially in his *Being and Time*. He therefore employs the concept of 'chairological time' or '*Augenblick*' (moment, instant), in referring to the time of human action in which the perspective is concern (cf. Heidegger 1979, 338; 1989, 408–9; 2001, 102–4), in contrast to measurable chronological time. I suggest that the most adequate way to understand Bakhtin's chronotope is to consider it as a 'chairological' time or moment, i.e. as time and place not in the physical sense but in the sense of the (right) moment for certain kinds of human action.

If we understand the chronotope in this manner, we can also explain why Bakhtin (2008, 85) says that time is the more important component of a chronotope. A chronotope provides the right moment of time and place for human action, but the action itself 'makes use of' time to become reality. A human subject can perform an act only by 'using' time. This is in accordance with the *Bildungsroman* essay, in which time appears as the medium for performing human action.

If chronotopic time means, as I suggest, a time and place for human action, the ideas of the chronotope and of chronotopic seeing indeed form a continuum with Bakhtin's early philosophy of the act. The early philosophy of the act would thus be (once again) concretized in the idea of the chronotope and of chronotopic seeing, if this means 'seeing' human action in historical remnants or – as further developed in the chronotope essay – observing how certain forms of potential action are connected with certain kinds of localities.

Chronotopes: Forms of the Time of Human Action as Conditioned by Concrete Circumstances

Considering that 'Forms of Time and of the Chronotope in the Novel' was probably written only slightly later than the *Bildungsroman* essay, the differences between the two in their understanding of the chronotope are quite remarkable. First of all, in the chronotope essay Bakhtin no longer distinguishes between authors who think chronotopically and those who do not: all novels are now considered to be organized according to the various chronotopes used in them. Chronotopic thinking is no longer restricted to the period following the rise of historical consciousness at the end of the eighteenth century; now novels from all periods, starting with the emergence of the novel in Greek antiquity, are chronotopically organized. Novelistic structure is organized by chronotopes even in those novels in which the temporal development of matters is minimized: Dostoevsky's novels, which according to Bakhtin are built – unlike those of Goethe – following principles of simultaneity and contiguity rather than development over time (Bakhtin 1989, 28), are now considered to be characterized by the use of certain kinds of chronotopes (cf. Bakhtin 2008, 248–9). At issue in the chronotope essay is the definition and description of different chronotopes, which form the basis of different subgenres of the novel (Bakhtin 2008, 84–5).

A further difference is that rather than speaking of chronotopic seeing as a way of seeing things in the world (locations, landscapes, buildings etc.), chronotopes are now discussed only insofar as they organize time and space in novels. Bakhtin says explicitly that he is not going to deal with chronotopes in other areas of culture, and that he also intends to bypass all questions concerning the origin of literary chronotopes (Bakhtin 2008, 84, 86). It is, however, clear that Bakhtin believes that chronotopes do not exist in literature alone: otherwise it would not make sense to speak of 'assimilating an actual historical chronotope in literature' or 'assimilating real historical time and space in literature' (Bakhtin 2008, 85, 84). Indeed, later in the chronotope essay he remarks that language outside of literature as well 'is fundamentally chronotopic' (Bakhtin 2008, 251). However, some of Bakhtin's characterizations of the chronotope might lead one to believe that chronotopes as discussed here are first and foremost a matter of artistic expression, for instance when Bakhtin speaks of them as 'methods for artistically fixing time and space' (Bakhtin 2008, 86) in the novel, or when he defines the chronotope as a way in which time and space are 'artistically expressed in literature' (Bakhtin 2008, 84). These formulations recall the ideas in 'Author and Hero', where Bakhtin considered that the content of a work of art consists of the hero and his world, while the artistic form, which transgresses the horizon of the hero but 'consummates' his 'content', derives from the author. In *Problems of Dostoevsky's Poetics*, the author is no longer assigned this role; the artistic whole is thought to emerge from the configurations occurring between individuals in the world of the novel itself, each of whom has their own view of the world. Is the chronotope, then, to be understood as a form given to the content by the novelist, or is it a constituent of the fictive world itself and significant for the persons acting within it?

At the end of the chronotope essay, Bakhtin speaks of the 'tangential' relation of the author-creator to the chronotopes in a novel (Bakhtin 2008, 254, 256). Chronotopes are part of the representation of the world in the novel (Bakhtin 2008, 254–5). However, it seems to me quite clear that chronotopes are not merely forms given to the materials by the author, or even 'consummating' forms of the experienced content; rather, they also crucially define the space-time of experience and action *in* the represented world of a novel.

To illustrate this, let us examine the best known of Bakhtin's chronotopes, the adventure-time chronotope of the Greek novel (or romance). Bakhtin describes the kinds of adventures that take place in a Greek novel, the typical plot, how the characters appear, how they face the obstacles confronting them in their pursuit of happiness, what changes the characters undergo (none), and the depiction of the world as immutable, while the fate of the individual is full of unpredictable twists and turns. In this genre, 'initiative is handed over to chance, which controls meetings and failures to meet' (Bakhtin 2008, 95). 'The adventuristic events of Greek romance have no essential ties with any particular details of individual countries that might figure in the novel, with their social or political structure, with their culture or history. None of these distinctive details contribute in any way to the event as a determining factor' (Bakhtin 2008, 100). The world of the Greek romance is an 'abstract-alien' world (Bakhtin 2008, 108): '[E]verything in it is indefinite, unknown, foreign. Its heroes are there for the first time; they have no organic ties or relationships with it; [...] in this world, therefore, they can experience only random contingency' (Bakhtin 2008, 100–101). I believe that these examples suffice to show that Bakhtin continuously speaks of how the world appears to a person confined to the world as presented in a Greek romance. He does not suggest that this was how the world actually appeared to individuals living in late antiquity; but nor does he speak of chronotopes as aesthetic forms created by the author to give form to the experiences of the hero from an artistic distance. Rather, he describes what the possibilities of action for a person were in the world of a Greek romance. The adventure-time chronotope determines precisely this: what one can and cannot experience or do. In spite of the adventurousness, the hero's action space in a Greek romance is quite restricted: he can only bravely withstand anything that he encounters.

The manner with which Bakhtin describes the chronotope of the Greek romance corroborates the assumption that chronotopes are about time and space in relation to human action. In the *Bildungsroman* essay, past action was detected in remnants of the past; in the chronotope essay, the world in a novel appears temporally and spatially structured in a specific way in relation to the possibilities of human action. In both cases, a chronotope shows the world *sub specie* human action.

Nevertheless, the adventure-time chronotope also shows that human action does not arise from human will alone, understood abstractly as totally free. On the contrary, what a hero can actually do is strictly limited by the chronotope in which the events take place. Of course, he still has to make choices – and he is ethically judged accordingly – but the spectrum of his choices is chronotopically restricted. This is the same as saying that a human being is always conditioned by his surroundings in his action, although he never loses his ethical autonomy.

A chronotope that determines a whole subgenre of a novel – as the adventure-time chronotope determines the ancient Greek adventure novel – thus defines the genre in terms of the possibilities of action available to the individuals in the world of the novel. This can be compared to Bakhtin's previous grounds for distinguishing different types of the novel. As already noted, Bakhtin defined the polyphonic novel in opposition to the monologic one in terms of a difference in the hero(es)' relation to the author, and at the beginning of the *Bildungsroman* essay he distinguishes between different subgenres of the novel – the travel novel, the novel of ordeal, the biographical novel and the *Bildungsroman* – according to the hero's position in the world of the novel. Here differences in the hero's autonomy or in his possible choices of action serve as the basis for distinguishing between different types of novel. We observe a similarity to the chronotope: chronotopes, too, define possible action spaces for the characters in the world of a novel, and they are likewise assigned the function of determining the subgenre of the novel.

We now have to ask whether what has above been said about the adventure-time chronotope holds true for other chronotopes as well. As test cases, we might choose some of the chronotopes described, or only briefly mentioned, in the last section of the chronotope essay, entitled 'Concluding Remarks'. Here Bakhtin briefly discusses a number of chronotopes typical of the nineteenth-century realistic novel.

It is characteristic of the chronotopes outlined in 'Concluding Remarks' that none of them is, like adventure-time, a chronotope that prevails throughout an entire novel; instead, each individual novel is now supposed to be composed of numerous different chronotopes. The adventure-time chronotope was of course not a simple chronotope either; Bakhtin (2008, 97–100) describes chronotopes or chronotopical motifs, such as the motif of meeting, which are subordinated to the adventure-time chronotope and included in it. The chronotopes of the nineteenth-century novel discussed in the 'Concluding Remarks' are all of this non-inclusive type. One such chronotope is the ('Flaubertian type of') provincial town chronotope. Such 'petty-bourgeois provincial towns' are 'the locus of cyclical everyday time':

> Here there are no events, only 'doings' that constantly repeat themselves. Time here has no advancing historical movement; it moves rather in narrow circles: the circle of the day, of the week, of the month, of a person's entire life [...] Day in, day out the same round of activities are repeated [...] This is commonplace, philistine cyclical everyday time [...] Time here is without event and therefore almost seems to stand still [...] It is a viscous and sticky time that drags itself slowly through space. (Bakhtin 2008, 247–8)

Here Bakhtin describes in a lively and partly metaphorical manner the time experience of a certain social milieu. In his description, the milieu as such determines what can happen and how life is experienced. This indicates very clearly that for Bakhtin a chronotope in a novel determines what the persons 'belonging' to that chronotope can experience and how they can act.

Some of the examples of chronotopes in the nineteenth-century realistic novel refer to a concrete space which is part of the milieu, such as a parlour, salon or threshold. The parlour and salon are places

> where encounters occur (no longer emphasizing their specifically random nature as did meetings 'on the road' or 'in an alien world' [of the Greek novel]). In salons and parlors the webs of intrigue are spun, denouements occur and finally – this is where *dialogues* happen, something that acquires extraordinary importance in the novel, revealing the character, 'ideas' and 'passions' of the heroes. (Bakhtin 2008, 246; emphasis in the original)

Furthermore, the salon is described as the place where 'the weaving of historical and socio-public events together with the personal and even deeply private side of life' takes place; here 'political, business, social, literary reputations are made and destroyed, careers are begun and wrecked' (Bakhtin 2008, 247). The threshold and 'related chronotopes' are typical of Dostoevsky's novels, being 'places where crisis events occur, the falls, resurrections, renewals, epiphanies, decisions that determine the whole life of a man. In this chronotope, time is essentially instantaneous' (Bakhtin 2008, 248).

In all these cases, a concrete place is endowed with crucial importance with regard to what can actually happen: certain kinds of actions take place in certain localities. Social localities are not a neutral, passive background of action but on the contrary determine its chronotopic form. What a person can do is conditioned by the setting and the locality. Here temporality is a temporality of experience and action: for instance, the actions that can be performed in a provincial town cannot generate any historical change or even any change in one's own life. The salon in a realistic novel is a place where decisions are made, and the threshold appears as a place of sudden but profound turning points in life. Thus localities have to do with 'chairological' time, the right moment of action. They present a concrete situation where certain kinds of action are possible; by the same token, however, they also restrict the possibilities of action. In this respect, the function which localities – social milieus and more concrete localities – have for the persons in a novel is comparable to the function that localities have for man's historical action in Goethe's vision: for him too, human creative action is both made possible and conditioned by local circumstances. Goethe, however, seems to place more stress on man's creative activity compared to what is possible for the heroes in many nineteenth-century realistic novels.

This emphasis on social determination could be interpreted as proof that the later Bakhtin's view of man was more 'sociologically' oriented, compared to his early, more 'idealistic' thinking (cf. Morson and Emerson 1990, 206; Hirschkop 1999, 58, 167). Just like the variety of speech genres in 'Problems of Speech Genres' (Bakhtin 2007b), chronotopes let man appear as essentially social in his character: they do not deal with individual modes of human action, but with socially conditioned action. However, since already in *Toward a Philosophy of the Act* Bakhtin is interested in ethically responsible action by real individuals involved in real life 'events' and not in abstract ethical subjects, the idea of the individual being influenced by his or her concrete surroundings, both natural and social, is not foreign to Bakhtin from the very beginning. The idea of chronotopic determination of the possible time-space of action in no way diminishes for Bakhtin the characters' responsibility for their acts. This is exemplarily demonstrated by the hero of Greek romance, who has very few options to choose from but who is still judged according to his action as an ethically responsible subject. In fact, in chronotopes Bakhtin presents a version of how a work of art brings together two aspects of an individual's existence which are theoretically irreconcilable: his or her being determined by natural and social circumstances and simultaneously free as an ethically acting subject.

Of course we have to remind ourselves that chronotopes are not discussed as actual social formations but only as constitutive forms in a novel. Thus we can only say that a chronotope conditions how acting persons are represented in a novel, without making any claims as to man's behaviour outside of it. After the *Bildungsroman* essay, Bakhtin no longer thematizes the relationship between the chronotopic view of man's behaviour in the novel and outside of it; he deals with chronotopes as forms of representation, not as claims about the unavoidable influence of certain kinds of circumstances in the real world. Nevertheless, the fact that the chronotopes used in the Greek novel are completely different from, say, those occurring in a realistic novel of the nineteenth century indicates a connection between novelistic chronotopes on the one hand and social practices and ways of thinking in the real historical world on the other. It is worth adding that Bakhtin mentions the social character of chronotopic thinking *in* the tradition of literature: like other cultural and literary traditions, they are 'preserved and continue to live not in the individual subjective memory or a single individual [...] but rather in the objective forms that culture itself assumes (including the forms of language and spoken speech), and in this sense they are inter-subjective and inter-individual (and consequently social)' (Bakhtin 2008, 249).

We may add that some of the topics which Bakhtin discusses under the heading of 'Form of Time and the Chronotope in the Novel' seem rather odd, if the chronotope is understood in terms of epistemology, such as the whole chapter dedicated to the rogue, clown and fool in the novel, or the 'series' of eating, defecating and other bodily functions in the 'Rabelaisian chronotope'. However, these chronotopes appear less strange when we understand the chronotope as the specific spatio-temporal form of a certain possibility of human action, and see in playing the role of a rogue, a clown or a fool, as well as in displaying bodily functions, possibilities of human action – possibilities that are important in Bakhtin's 'Menippea' and in the work of Rabelais as he understands it, respectively.

At the end of the chronotope essay, along with everything he has said about chronotopes, Bakhtin adds: '[A]ny and every literary image is chronotopic. Language, as a treasure-house of images, is fundamentally chronotopic. Also chronotopic is the internal form of a word'; furthermore, 'any motif may have a special chronotope of its own' (Bakhtin 2008, 251, 252). This implies that a novel is a complex whole, consisting of a vast number of chronotopic elements in various relations to one another; as Bakhtin puts it, '[c]hronotopes [in a novel] are mutually inclusive, they co-exist, they may be interwoven with, replace or oppose one another, contradict one another or find themselves in ever more complex interrelationships' (Bakhtin 2008, 252). This extension of the concept to comprise a vast, indefinite number of different minor chronotopes which are in various relations to each other is reasonable if by 'chronotope' we understand a manner of conceiving human action with its temporal determinants as attached to certain physical, social and cultural localities.

To conclude: Bakhtin's view of the construction of the aesthetic whole of a novel (or a work of art more generally) underwent considerable changes between the beginning of his career and his essays on the chronotope, but it also shows considerable continuity. While in 'Author and Hero in Aesthetic Activity' the ethically autonomous hero provides the content of the work of art whom the author endows with an aesthetic form, in *Problems of Dostoevsky's Poetics*, the aesthetic form arises directly from encounters between the different worlds (or 'words') of the characters, who are represented as autonomous subjects of cognition and ethical action. In Bakhtin's concept of the chronotope, human action in the novel appears in the frame of temporal-spatially determined possibilities. Chronotopes open up to the characters a certain time-space of possible action, which is conditioned by a locality or a social situation but still leaves the individual the freedom of ethical choice. Thus chronotopes are primarily not categories of cognition but of the possibilities of human action.

Notes

1 'The chronotope in literature has an intrinsic *generic* significance. It can even be said that it is precisely the chronotope that defines genre and generic distinctions [...] These generic forms, at first productive, were then reinforced by tradition [of literature]; in their subsequent development they continued stubbornly to exist, up to and beyond the point at which they had lost any meaning that was productive in actuality or adequate to later historical situations. This explains the simultaneous existence in literature of phenomena taken from widely separate periods of time, which greatly complicates the historico-literary process.' (Bakhtin 2008, 84–5)
2 For the history of the manuscript, cf. Hirschkop (1999, 113, 176).
3 'Stated in its most basic terms, a particular chronotope will be defined by the specific way in which the sequentiality of events is "deformed" (always involving a segmentation, a spatialization) in any given account of those events.'
4 Cf. Tihanov (2000, 7, 21); Holquist (2002, 153); Hirschkop (1999, 132); Freise (1993, 143); Bakhtin (1993, 56, 13).
5 'It would be a mistake to assume that this concrete truth [*pravda*] of the event that the performer of the act sees and hears and experiences and understands in the single act of an answerable deed is something ineffable, i.e. that it can only be livingly experienced in some way at the moment of performing the act, but cannot be uttered clearly and distinctly. I think that language is much more adapted to giving utterance precisely to that truth, and not to the abstract moment of the logical in its purity [...] Historically language grew up in the service of participative thinking and performed acts, and it begins to serve abstract thinking only in the present day of its history.' (Bakhtin 1993, 31)
6 The practical reason assumes the concept of freedom as its regulative principle; see Kant (1975b, 163).
7 'Akte entspringen aus der Person in die Zeit hinein; Funktionen sind Tatsachen in der phänomenalen Zeitsphäre und indirekt durch Zuordnung ihrer phänomenalen Zeitverhältnisse auf die meßbaren Zeitdauern der in ihnen gegebenen Erscheinungen selbst meßbar' (Scheler 1927, 403).

References

Bakhtin, M. M. 1989 [1984]. *Problems of Dostoevsky's Poetics* (*Problemy poetiki Dostoevskogo*, 1963). Edited and translated by Caryl Emerson. Minneapolis: University of Minnesota Press.

———. 1990. 'Author and Hero in Aesthetic Activity' ('Avtor i geroi v esteticheskoi deiatelnosti'). In *Art and Answerability: Early Philosophical Essays by M. M. Bakhtin*. Edited by Michael Holquist and Vadim Liapunov, translated by Vadim Liapunov, 4–256. Austin: University of Texas Press.

———. 1993. *Toward a Philosophy of the Act* ('K filosofii postupka'). Edited by Michael Holquist and Vadim Liapunov, translated by Vadim Liapunov. Austin: University of Texas Press.

———. 2007a. 'The *Bildungsroman* and Its Significance in the History of Realism (Toward a Historical Typology of the Novel)' ('Roman vospitaniia i ego znachenie v istorii realizma'). In *Speech Genres and Other Late Essays*. Edited by Caryl Emerson and Michael Holquist, translated by Vern W. McGee, 10–59. Austin: University of Texas Press.

———. 2007b. 'The Problem of Speech Genres' ('Problema rechevykh zhanrov'). In *Speech Genres and Other Late Essays*. Edited by Caryl Emerson and Michael Holquist, translated by Vern W. McGee, 60–102. Austin: University of Texas Press.

———. 2008 [1981]. 'Forms of Time and of the Chronotope in the Novel: Towards a Historical Poetics' ('Formy vremeni i khronotopa v romane: Ocherki po istoricheskoi poetike'). In *The Dialogic Imagination*. Edited by Michael Holquist, translated by Caryl Emerson and Michael Holquist, 84–258. Austin: University of Texas Press.

Beaton, Roderick. 2010. 'Historical Poetics: Chronotopes in *Leucippe and Clitophon* and *Tom Jones*'. In *Bakhtin's Theory of the Literary Chronotope: Reflections, Applications, Perspectives*. Edited by Nele Bemong et al., 59–76. Gent: Academia Press.

Bemong, Nele et al. (eds). 2010. *Bakhtin's Theory of the Literary Chronotope: Reflections, Applications, Perspectives*. Gent: Academia Press.

Bemong, Nele and Pieter Borghart. 2010. 'Bakhtin's Theory of the Literary Chronotope: Reflections, Applications, Perspectives'. In *Bakhtin's Theory of the Literary Chronotope: Reflections, Applications, Perspectives*. Edited by Nele Bemong et al., 3–16. Gent: Academia Press.

Cassirer, Ernst. 1932. *Goethe und die geschichtliche Welt*. Berlin: Bruno Cassirer.

Falconer, Rachel. 2010. 'Heterochronic Representations of the Fall: Bakhtin, Milton, DeLillo'. In *Bakhtin's Theory of the Literary Chronotope: Reflections, Applications, Perspectives*. Edited by Nele Bemong et al., 111–29. Gent: Academia Press.

Freise, Matthias. 1993. *Michail Bachtins philosophische Ästhetik der Literatur*. Frankfurt am Main: Peter Lang.

Goethe, Johann Wolfgang von. 1982 [1811–33]. *Aus meinem Leben: Dichtung und Wahrheit [vierzehntes bis zwanzigstes Buch]*. In *Werke*, Hamburger Ausgabe, vol. 10, 8–187. Hamburg: Deutscher Taschenbuch Verlag.

Heidegger, Martin. 1979 [1927]. *Sein und Zeit*. Tübingen: Niemeyer.

———. 1989. *Die Grundprobleme der Phänomenologie*. Gesamtausgabe, vol. 24. Frankfurt am Main: Vittorio Klostermann.

———. 2001 [1985]. *Phenomenological Interpretations of Aristotle: Initiation into Phenomenological Research* (*Phänomenologische Interpretationen zu Aristoteles: Einführung in die phänomenologische Forschung*). Gesamtausgabe, vol. 61. Edited by Walter Bröcker and Käte Bröcker-Oltmanns, translated by Richard Rojcewicz, 102–4. Bloomington: Indiana University Press.

———. 2002 [1922]. *Phänomenologische Interpretationen zu Aristoteles*. Edited by Günther Neumann. Stuttgart: Reclam.

Hirschkop, Ken. 1986. 'A Response to the Forum on Mikhail Bakhtin'. In *Bakhtin: Essays and Dialogues on His Work*. Edited by G. S. Morson. Chicago and London: University of Chicago Press.

———. 1999. *Mikhail Bakhtin: An Aesthetic for Democracy*. Oxford: Oxford University Press.

Holquist, Michael. 2002 [1990]. *Dialogism: Bakhtin and His World*. London and New York: Routledge.

———. 2008. 'Glossary'. In *The Dialogic Imagination*. Edited by Michael Holquist, translated by Caryl Emerson and Michael Holquist, 423–34. Austin: University of Texas Press.

———. 2010. 'The Fugue of Chronotope'. In *Bakhtin's Theory of the Literary Chronotope: Reflections, Applications, Perspectives*. Edited by Nele Bemong et al., 19–33. Gent: Academia Press.

Kant, Immanuel. 1975a [1781]. *Kritik der reinen Vernunft*. In *Werke*, vol. 3. Darmstadt: Wissenschaftliche Buchgesellschaft.

_____. 1975b [1788]. *Kritik der praktischen Vernunft*. In *Werke*, vol. 6, 103–302. Darmstadt: Wissenschaftliche Buchgesellschaft.

Morson, Gary Saul. 2010. 'The Chronotope of Humanness: Bakhtin and Dostoevsky'. In *Bakhtin's Theory of the Literary Chronotope: Reflections, Applications, Perspectives*. Edited by Nele Bemong et al., 93–110. Gent: Academia Press.

Morson, Gary Saul and Caryl Emerson. 1990. *Mikhail Bakhtin: Creation of a Prosaics*. Stanford: Stanford University Press.

Natorp, Paul. 1923. *Fjedor Dostojewskis Bedeutung für die gegenwärtige Kulturkrise: Mit einem Anhang zur geistigen Krisis der Gegenwart*. Jena: Eugen Diederichs.

Pechey, Graham. 1998. 'Modernity and Chronotopicity in Bakhtin'. In *The Contexts of Bakhtin: Philosophy, Authorship, Aesthetics*. Edited by David Shepherd, 173–82. Amsterdam: Marwood.

Pier, John. 2005. 'Chronotope'. In *Routledge Encyclopedia of Narrative Theory*. Edited by David Herman et al., 64–5. London – New York: Routledge.

Scheler, Max. 1927 [1913–16]. *Der Formalismus in der Ethik und die materiale Wertethik: Neuer Versuch der Grundlegung eines ethischen Personalismus*. Halle a. d. S.: Niemeyer.

Scholz, Bernhard F. 1998. 'Bakhtin's Concept of "Chronotope": The Kantian Connection'. In *The Contexts of Bakhtin: Philosophy, Authorship, Aesthetics*. Edited by David Shepherd, 141–72. Amsterdam: Marwood.

Shepherd, David (ed.) 1998. *The Contexts of Bakhtin: Philosophy, Authorship, Aesthetics*. Amsterdam: Marwood.

Tihanov, Galin. 2000. *The Master and the Slave: Lukács, Bakhtin, and the Ideas of Their Time*. Oxford: Clarendon.

Chapter 8

THE PROVINCIAL CHRONOTOPE AND MODERNITY IN CHEKHOV'S SHORT FICTION

Tintti Klapuri

The concept of the chronotope, which Bakhtin launches in the essay 'Forms of Time and Chronotope in the Novel' ('Formy vremeni i khronotopa v romane'), pertains to historically developing spatio-temporal forms in the novel.[1] Bakhtin describes the chronotope as expressing the inseparability of space and time (time being the fourth dimension of space):

> In the literary artistic chronotope, spatial and temporal indicators are fused into one carefully thought-out, concrete whole. Time, as it were, thickens, takes on flesh, becomes artistically visible; likewise, space becomes charged and responsive to the movements of time, plot and history. (Bakhtin 2008, 84)

In what follows, I explore and develop further the concept of the chronotope of the provincial town, which Bakhtin mentions in passing in the concluding remarks to his lengthy essay. Here Bakhtin takes up three of the most important spatio-temporal forms and their main representatives in nineteenth-century realistic literature: the chronotope of the provincial town (Flaubert), that of the threshold (Dostoevsky), and that of biographical time (Tolstoy) (Bakhtin 2008, 247–50). The provincial chronotope is characterized by themes of repetition and unchangeability; according to Bakhtin, provincial towns are the realms of cyclical everyday time, since '[h]ere there are no events, only "beings" that constantly repeat themselves' (Bakhtin 2012, 493).[2] Here I follow the interpretation suggested by Liisa Steinby in Chapter 7, that the chronotope and the chronotopic way of seeing, elaborated by Bakhtin in his essay 'The *Bildungsroman* and its Significance in the History of Realism'

('Roman vospitaniia i ego znachenie v istorii realizma', probably written 1936–38), can actually be seen as continuing Bakhtin's early philosophy of act when approached from the viewpoint of the acting subject. I understand the chronotope – in its peculiar provincial form – as an aesthetic means of observing how certain forms of potential action are connected with certain kinds of localities and temporalities.

Anton Chekhov (1860–1904) is famous for his descriptions of Russian provincial longing: a yearning away from provincial stagnation for another kind of life somewhere else, a nostalgia for the past, and the characters' sense of life constantly passing by almost without noticing. These profoundly spatio-temporal themes dominate both the writer's dramatic work and his short fiction, and are also prominent in his documentary travelogue *Sakhalin Island* (*Ostrov Sakhalin*, 1895). In the chronotope essay, Bakhtin's focus is on the novel form; he does however refer to short fiction, and in fact to Chekhov as one of the main representatives of the provincial chronotope in Russian literature: 'It [cyclical everyday time] is familiar to us in many variants in Gogol, Turgenev, Gleb Uspensky, Saltykov-Shchedrin, Chekhov' (Bakhtin 2008, 248).[3] Bakhtin's prime example of the chronotope of the provincial town is Gustave Flaubert's novel *Madame Bovary* (1857), but he notes that the Flaubertian variant – which Chekhov can be seen as developing further – is only one among others, including the idyllic chronotope in the works of the provincialists.

The provincial chronotope appears particularly interesting when seen in the context of modern time-thought. The provincial town, as described in late nineteenth-century literature, can be seen as a negation of the modern world of the capital city. The provincial town is part of modernity but in a peculiar way: while life in the capital is considered to move forwards in a progressive and dynamic manner, the provincial town is characterized by stagnation and outdated ways of thought. In the following analysis I further develop the provincial chronotope, discussing it in connection with modern subjectivity and scrutinizing the narrative means whereby provincial time-spaces are constructed in Chekhov's short stories, in an attempt to explore how opportunities for action by the subject are represented spatio-temporally.

The Provincial Chronotope and the Idyll

In modernity, with its future-oriented linearity, time loses its previous close connection with human activities (the timing of tasks associated with natural cycles) and becomes abstract clock-time.[4] Repetition, associated with cyclicity, now easily takes on negative connotations and becomes associated with stagnation and non-autonomy (see also Moretti 1986). In the Chekhovian provincial chronotope, repetition and cyclicity pertain not solely to the everyday life described, to the present moment, but expand to cover whole lives and generations. Hence repetition is given a historical perspective which further underlines the societal stagnation of the storyworlds.

Generational repetition concerns female characters in particular. In 'The Betrothed' ('Nevesta', 1903), the central character Nadia is supposed to get married and in so doing live out the predictable female life cycle, during which a girl grows first into a bride, then a mother, and finally, into a bride's mother:

> 'Yes', said Nina Ivanovna [Nadia's mother], after a pause. 'Only the other day you were a little girl, and now you're almost a bride. Nature is in a constant state of metabolism. Before you know where you are you'll be a mother yourself, and then an old woman, with a troublesome daughter like mine.' (Chekhov 1979)[5]

In this sense, Nadia's lifespan (more precisely, the brief glimpse of a predictable lifespan that is possible within the limited narrative space of a short story) appears to repeat the past futures of previous generations. When repetition takes place not generationally but within a single lifespan, the question is of repeating oneself over and over again, without any noticeable development taking place in the character. These characters often lack education and appear as female *tabulae rasae*, whose void is filled by a man one after another.[6] In addition to 'The Betrothed', provincial stories where the female life cycle is represented as repetitive include 'The Darling' ('Dushechka', 1899), where the main character Olenka has no personal opinions, only those offered by her current companion. Once her lovers leave her one by one, her mind becomes empty: 'And what was worst of all, she had no opinions of any sort. She saw the objects about her and understood what she saw, but could not form any opinion about them, and did not know what to talk about. And how awful it is not to have any opinions!' (Chekhov 2004b).[7] Olenka may be a prime example of how the repetitive lives of Chekhov's female characters are associated with their insufficient autonomy. In 'The Betrothed', Nadia's mother Nina Ivanovna's lack of autonomy is underlined by her relationship to her own mother-in-law, on whom she depends financially as well. Nadia and her mother live in Nadia's matriarchal grandmother's house: 'Nadia's grandmother, or, as everyone in the house called her, Granny, a corpulent, plain old woman, with heavy eyebrows and a moustache, was talking loudly, and her voice and manner of speaking showed that it was she who was the real head of the house' (Chekhov 1979).[8]

These temporalities are opposed to progressive modern temporality, where the subject is seen to develop progressively in time by gaining new knowledge. Hence Reinhart Koselleck (1985), for example, sees modern subjectivity emerging in pace with modern time-thought. According to him, before the emergence of modernity people's space of experience and the horizon of expectation were in balance; in the cyclical perception of time, future expectations were determined by past experience. In modernity, the horizon of expectations is no longer congruent with the space of experience; the subject is now felt to acquire autonomy in relation to God, nature and society, due to processes of modernization such as secularization, the emergence of modern science, and democratization.[9]

The negative representation of cyclicity – as meaningless repetition and denoting non-autonomous thought – distances the provincial chronotope from the idyll, also discussed by Bakhtin in the chronotope essay (Bakhtin 2008, 224–36). According to Bakhtin, the characteristic temporality of the idyll is cyclic rhythmicalness (2008, 225). This emerges from the unity of place which characterizes this spatio-temporality:

> The unity of the life of generations (in general, the life of men) in an idyll is in most instances primarily defined by *the unity of place* [...] This unity of place in the life of generations weakens and renders less distinct all the temporal boundaries between individual lives and between various phases of one and the same life. (Bakhtin 2008; emphasis in the original)

Several of Chekhov's provincial stories contain traces of the idyll. However, here the idyll, and the spatio-temporal features characteristic of it, are represented in a different manner from that found in the work of provincialist writers, where the characters do not yearn for another kind of life somewhere else but feel content with what they have in their familiar space. Likewise in the novels of Goncharov or Tolstoy, the pastoral life often takes on positive connotations.[10] It might indeed be claimed that in some of his stories Chekhov is aiming precisely at a critique of the Tolstoyan version of the idyll. In the idyll the subject is represented as connected both with other subjects and – importantly – with nature; in *Anna Karenina*, for example, Konstantin Levin feels that in working with the peasants he is becoming part of nature. The Chekhovian subject, in contrast, feels alien to his or her surroundings and wishes to escape from them. Where in Tolstoy agricultural labour is represented as reuniting man with nature, the Chekhovian character either merely dreams of labouring in a Tolstoyan manner, or – if he or she actually gets to work with the soil – ends up feeling frustrated and yearning for another sort of life. In 'My Life (The Story of a Provincial)' ('Moia zhizn: Rasskaz provinciala', 1896), for example, the protagonist Misail and his wife Mariia move to the countryside, hoping to cultivate the peasants as well as themselves according to Tolstoyan principles. Their endeavour results in a catastrophe: they know agriculture only from books, and the peasants laugh at them and completely ignore their aims of cultivating them. In the end, Mariia decides to leave both countryside and husband and travel to America to make a career as a pianist. Similarly, in 'The Duel' ('Duel', 1892) the protagonist Laevskii and his mistress Nadezhda Fedorovna move to the south of Russia to live according to Tolstoyan principles:

> We pictured our future like this: to begin with, in the Caucasus, while we were getting to know the people and the place, I would put on the Government uniform and enter the service; then at our leisure we would pick out a plot of ground, would toil in the sweat of our brow, would have a vineyard and a field, and so on. (Chekhov 2004b)[11]

The plan, however, is never accomplished, and the couple end up living in the local seaside resort according to completely different ideals. This life too is permeated by repetition: days in the sun follow a similar schedule – a late breakfast, strolling down the boulevard, swimming, dinner and gossiping, nightly discussions and encounters with lovers – but these cycles appear to the characters meaningless and non-organic.

The comparison of the idyllic and the provincial chronotope is interesting from the vantage point of modernity: it reveals that the first is strongly associated with premodern temporality and subjectivity, while the latter connotes modern temporality and subjectivity. While in the provincial chronotope such features as repetition and cyclicity appear negative qualities, in the idyll, on the contrary, they have positive connotations. The idyll includes no longing for escape because within it the subject is content with the predictable repetition and cyclicity that permeate this spatio-temporality; it is as if he or she did not know about ways of the modern world. In contrast, in the provincial time-space the characters already know about life beyond the familiar sphere and start yearning for this other sort of life, whatever that may be. In this sense, the provincial town appears as the negation of the modern, dynamic city and cannot exist without its antithesis.

The Provincial *Poshlost*

The modernity of Chekhov's provincial time-spaces is also manifested in the way in which authoritative attitudes and non-autonomous thought is represented in them. In 'The Betrothed' authoritarian values are associated with arts and architecture. Nadia finds provincial architecture oppressive: the dwelling that her fiancé Andrei Andreich has chosen for himself and his future wife haunts Nadia as much as the 'low ceilings' of her grandmother's house.

Where Nadia's childhood home is dominated by the matriarchal grandmother, this future home is similarly dominated by the huge photographic portrait of Andrei Andreich Sr, her fiancé's father and, as the local cathedral priest, the patriarchal head of the town:

> In the ballroom, with its gleaming floor, painted to look like parquet, were bentwood chairs, a grand piano, a music-stand for the violin [...] On the wall was a large oil-painting in a gilt frame – a picture of a naked lady beside a purple vase with a broken handle. 'Beautiful picture', said Andrei Andreich with an awed sigh. 'It's by Shishmachevsky.' [...] Over the sofa hung an enlarged photograph of Father Andrei with all his medals on, wearing a tall ceremonial hat. They passed into the dining-room with its sideboard, and from there into the bedroom. Here, in the half-light, stood two beds side by side, and it looked as if those who had furnished the bedroom had taken it for granted that life would always be happy here, that it could not be otherwise. Andrei Andreich conducted Nadia through the rooms, never removing his arm from her waist. And she felt weak, guilty, hating all these rooms and beds and chairs, while the naked lady made her sick [...] He had his arm round her waist, spoke to her so kindly, so humbly, was so happy, walking about his home. And all she saw was vulgarity, stupid, naive, intolerable vulgarity, and his arm round her waist seemed to her cold and rigid, like an iron hoop. (Chekhov 1979)[12]

The combination of paternal authoritative guidance and *poshlye* elements is interesting here.[13] The *poshlost* of the quotation is strengthened by the connection with the Orthodox Church in the character of Andrei Andreich Sr, whose authoritative presence in his son's life can be seen even in the latter's name.[14] This mentality is further associated with sexuality, as in Nadia's experience Andrei Andreich's warm feelings for her blend with the explicit sensuality of the portrait of the naked woman. By putting his arm around her 'like an iron hoop', Andrei Andreich binds his future wife to the vulgar mentality and pseudo-artistic eroticism that he himself, his house and his taste for art represent in a very concrete way. The way in which Nadia, as the focalizer of the above example, feels bound to *poshlost* is further underlined by narrative repetition: the fact that the future husband has his arm around her waist is reported three times.

In 'The Betrothed', the exteriors and interiors of the provincial town in question are linked with certain kinds of worldviews and affect the characters' possibilities of acting; hence social localities appear not as mere background to human action but indeed as contributing towards this action. Similarly in the story 'My Life', the narrow-minded mentality of the provincial town is embodied in its oppressive and unimaginative architecture, designed mainly by the central character Misail's father, an architect, who has produced a whole town of identical labyrinthine houses which in turn form the mentality of the town: 'And somehow all the houses built by my father were like each other, and vaguely reminded me of a top hat, and the stiff, obstinate back of his head. In the course of time the people of the town grew used to my father's lack of talent, which took root and became our style' (Chekhov 2004e).[15] As in 'The Betrothed', in 'My Life' too the authoritarian mentality is transmitted to the next generation. Both Misail and his sister Kleopatra strive for change and autonomy in relation to their father and the moral double standard of the provincial town. Kleopatra's efforts towards independence are represented as particularly futile, and indeed as doomed from the very outset:

> My father introduced the style into my sister's life. To begin with, he gave her the name of Cleopatra (and he called me Misail). When she was a little girl he used to frighten her by telling her about the stars and our ancestors; and explained the nature of life and duty to her at great length; and now when she was twenty-six he went on in the same way, allowing her to take no one's arm but his own, and somehow imagining that sooner or later an ardent young man would turn up and wish to enter into marriage with her out of admiration for his qualities. And she adored my father, was afraid of him, and believed in his extraordinary intellectual powers. (Chekhov 2004e)[16]

Kleopatra's struggle towards autonomy starts with her dreams of becoming an actress: she tries her luck at the local amateur theatre, and fails. The amateur theatre – a typical *fin-de-siècle* institution of *poshlost*[17] – is represented as a space for women to try their wings, but only within certain limits. When Kleopatra falls in love with a married man and becomes pregnant, it is the enlightened theatre ladies who are the first to condemn her.

The issue of provincial *poshlost* may also be linked with painting, more particularly with art collecting and decoration, which in Chekhov's work are often further connected with *meschanstvo*. In 'The Betrothed', painting is described in terms of decoration. Andrei Andreich's reference to the renowned painter ('It's by Shishmachevsky') emphasizes the status-related position of art and thus connotes his philistine values.[18] The same can be said of the employment of photographs in the story: Andrei Andreich Sr's huge photograph contributes to the *poshlost* of the house; at the same time, it speaks of the authoritarian values that the object of the photograph represents. The photograph also makes the object of description eternal – this is something mentioned by Bakhtin in the fragmented essay 'O Flobere' ('About Flaubert') from 1944. Of Flaubert's work, Bakhtin focuses on *The Temptations of St. Anthony* (*La Tentation de Saint Antoine*, 1874) but he also gives some thought to provincial themes. According to Bakhtin, *poshlost* and the model of *poshlost* is '[t]ransforming things that defy every trait of eternity into eternal' (1996, 132).[19] In some stories, the acknowledgement of socially regulated ways of admiring art may even grow into a critique of such endeavours and show the way towards intellectual independence. Thus in the story 'Three Years' ('Tri goda', 1895) the main female protagonist, Juliia Sergeevna, starts to criticize the appetite of her husband Laptev – a well-off merchant – and his friends for art, after finding in a gallery a modest painting that shows the way for her later development towards intellectual independence:

> She kept looking at the picture with a mournful smile, and the fact that the others saw nothing special in it troubled her. Then she began walking through the rooms and looking at the pictures again. She tried to understand them and no longer thought that a great many of them were alike [...] And after that the gilt cornices, the Venetian looking-glasses with flowers on them, the pictures of the same sort as the one that hung over the piano, and also her husband's and Kostia's reflections upon art, aroused in her a feeling of dreariness and vexation, even of hatred. (Chekhov 2004f)[20]

The *poshlost* of the provincial town seems to deny any historical change, let alone change in the characters living in this time-space. This concerns female characters in particular. Nevertheless, when the chronotope is interpreted as a space for possible human action and is seen from the vantage point of modernity, it appears that it does allow, at least potentially, for action towards change. What characterizes the Chekhovian provincial people is their longing for departure and life in the capital city: they do know about other ways of life, even if they may have only a faint idea what this otherness might be. They start to yearn for another sort of life, to dream about it, but in most cases they will never be able to realize it – and if they do, their new life turns out to be different from their expectations. Growth towards intellectual independence begins with acknowledging the narrow-mindedness of the dominant ways of thought in the provincial sphere, as discussed above. This process of gaining independence with respect to provincial mentality is described narratively in terms of predictability and unpredictability (see also Popkin 1993), and can be best illuminated by analysing certain minor chronotopes in which this problematic is crystallized.

Provincial Longing and Narrative (Un)predictability

In 'The Betrothed', Nadia's yearning is aroused with the help of Sasha, the foster-son of the family, who encourages Nadia to leave the provincial town and move to St Petersburg to study.[21] After Sasha's advice, Nadia begins to hesitate and consider other possibilities for her life. This process becomes associated with the family garden, which is about to awaken to spring; Nadia's development likewise appears as a gradual process of awakening. Traditionally, the springtime garden connotes a bridal theme as such; in this respect, it can be seen as a predictable plot element, strengthening the reader's expectations of a story about a young woman getting married. In this story, however, the garden turns out to serve as a space of transformation, connected both to the provincial world and to the prospect of Nadia's alternative future.

The nocturnal garden is the space that allows Nadia to spend time on her own. The events that take place in the garden are correlated with her development and are strongly associated with springtime: when Nadia prepares herself for the wedding, the apple trees are about to blossom; the garden shares in Nadia's nightly thoughts; and the sounds of the garden set the pace for her process of coming to a decision. Finally, when Nadia's contemplations result in her decision to leave the town and Andrei Andreich, this decision is juxtaposed with the devastation of the garden after the storm: when there is no bride, there is no blossoming garden. Thus the garden functions not only as the symbol of a young woman, but also as that of a young woman who is compliant with what is expected of her. At the beginning of the story it is noted that somewhere else, in the natural world beyond the garden walls, springtime has already arrived; this is a reference both to the on-going processes of modernization and to Nadia's individual search for authenticity:

> It was cool and still in the garden, and dark shadows lay peacefully on the ground. *From a long way off, probably outside town*, came the distant croaking of frogs. There was a feeling of May, the delightful month of May, in the air. One could draw deep breaths, and imagine that *somewhere, far beyond the town*, beneath the sky, above the treetops, in the fields and woods, *the spring was beginning its own life*, that mysterious, exquisite life, rich and sacred, from which sinful mortals are shut out. It almost made one want to cry. (Chekhov 1979; emphasis by T. K.)[22]

The garden is also physically connected to Nadia's childhood home and is mentioned in connection with other markers of stagnation in the provincial town: 'Nadia walked about the garden and the streets, looking at the houses and the drab fences, and it seemed to her that the town had been getting old for a long time, that it had outlived its day and was now waiting, either for its end, or for the beginning of something fresh and youthful' (Chekhov 1979).[23] In this respect, the garden in 'The Betrothed' has a similar function to the famous garden of *The Cherry Orchard* (*Vishnevyi sad*, 1904): in both texts the garden is juxtaposed with the degenerate way of life.[24]

If in 'The Betrothed' Nadia looks for a way to escape from the provincial *poshlost* by dreaming about studying in St Petersburg, several of Chekhov's female characters seek a solution from love affairs, in a way reminiscent of Flaubert's provincial longing.[25] Kleopatra's case in 'My Life', discussed above, is typical, and so is Anna Sergeevna's in 'The Lady with a Dog' ('Dama s sobachkoi', 1899). In the first part of the story, Gurov, an experienced womanizer from Moscow, seduces the provincial beauty Anna Sergeevna in the seaside resort of Yalta. Gurov's and Anna Sergeevna's emerging love affair takes place from the very beginning as a holiday romance, which Gurov anticipates as a brief adventure with no further consequences. The milieu of the story underlines the predictability of the plot: it is widely known that at the turn of the century Yalta was regarded as a stereotypical setting for a conventional liaison, a sort of Ibiza of the *fin-de-siècle*, and at the outset of the story there is thus a powerful anticipation of a typical holiday affair. For the visitors, Yalta means a short break from the dull everyday life, possibly an amorous adventure; however, also this break is characterized by regulation and predictability: the affair should not go too deep but remain within the limits of a socially acceptable short holiday romance. This is why Gurov finds Anna Sergeevna's behaviour immediately after their love-making unsuitable – it goes beyond the unspoken but generally accepted conventions of a holiday love affair:

> But in this case there was still the diffidence, the angularity of inexperienced youth, an awkward feeling; and there was a sense of consternation as though some one had suddenly knocked at the door. The attitude of Anna Sergeevna – 'the lady with the dog' – to what had happened was somehow peculiar, very grave, as though it were her fall – so it seemed, and it was strange and inappropriate. Her face dropped and faded, and on both sides of it her long hair hung down mournfully; she mused in a dejected attitude like 'the woman who was a sinner' in an old-fashioned picture.
>
> [...]
>
> Gurov felt bored already, listening to her. He was irritated by the naïve tone, by this remorse, so unexpected and inopportune; but for the tears in her eyes, he might have thought she was jesting or playing a part.
>
> 'I don't understand', he said softly. 'What is it you want?' (Tchekhov 2004b)[26]

'The Lady with a Dog' bears an obvious resemblance to Flaubert's *Madame Bovary*. Anna agrees to have an affair in her longing for something else; passionate love appears for her, as for Emma Bovary, a way to escape from the dull provincial everyday life and the 'lackey-like' husband. Similarly, in the relatively early 'The Lights' ('Ogni', 1888), the female protagonist, whom the intradiegetic narrator Ananev calls Kisochka ('Pussycat'), tries to escape from her unhappy, perhaps even violent marriage by starting an affair. Ananev begins to feel like having a light-hearted adventure with his schoolday object of desire, who still lives in the seaside resort town of their youth. Kisochka epitomizes the relationship between provinciality and non-autonomous female subjectivity. Her worldview is limited and the mere presence of a worldly man confuses her. After becoming Ananev's mistress she immediately starts to work on making him her next husband, as Emma Bovary does with Léon:

> What was for me an ordinary amatory episode was for her an absolute revolution in her life. I remember, it seemed to me that she had gone out of her mind. Happy for the first time in her life, looking five years younger, with an inspired enthusiastic face, not knowing what to do with herself for happiness, she laughed and cried and never ceased dreaming aloud how next day we would set off for the Caucasus, then in the autumn to Petersburg; how we would live afterwards. (Chekhov 2004d)[27]

The seaside resort can be seen as a variant of the chronotope of the provincial town, in the sense that both these time-spaces embrace repetitive, predictable temporality. However, it diverges from the provincial chronotope in its association with adventure time, with its promises of light-hearted affairs in the sun. Nevertheless, the seaside resort town as a time-space also connotes predictability, since the action associated with it is well-known to everyone in advance.

Chekhov's provincial stories may describe stagnant time-spaces, but at the narrative level they aim at evoking unpredictability. In the case of 'The Betrothed', for instance, the reader, after seeing the title, is prepared to read a story about a young woman getting married. Nadia never gets married but leaves her fiancé and escapes to St Petersburg; it is her decision *not* to get married that is the climax of the story. In terms of narrative, 'The Betrothed' gains its force from this conflict between the expectations that emerge from the title of the story and the actual course of events.[28]

However, it is important to note that both in this story and in the others discussed, even the unpredictable is represented in terms of ambiguity. In 'The Lady with the Dog', the event structure of the story after the episode at Yalta centres on the unpredictable awakening occurring in Gurov's consciousness. Gurov starts to think of his affair with Anna Sergeevna not as a temporary arrangement but perhaps indeed as the love of his life. It is at this point that the real departure from his normal habit occurs. This change taking place in Gurov is represented with ambiguity: it may well be that he has gone through similar processes earlier and that the current one with Anna Sergeevna is merely the most recent. Similarly in 'The Lights', the unpredictable climax of the story is when Ananev describes to his comrades that he considers the decision to return to Kisochka the moment from where his life began. Even here the situation is ambiguous: Ananev may be telling the story just to convince the younger comrade of the superiority of his knowledge. In 'The Betrothed', Nadia's view at the close of the story of the radical change that has taken place in her life is represented as limited and liable to change, since the narrator-focalizer suggests that Nadia's new life may not be as completely cut off from her past as it now appears to her:

> She realized clearly that her life had been turned topsy-turvy, as Sasha had wanted it to be, that she was lonely, alien, unwanted here, and that there was nothing she wanted here, the past had been torn away and vanished, as if burned by fire, and the ashes scattered to the winds. She went into Sasha's room and stood there.
>
> 'Good-bye, dear Sasha', she thought [...] She went upstairs to pack, and the next morning said good-bye to her family, and left the town, gay and full of spirits – *as she supposed, forever.* (Chekhov 1979; emphasis by T. K.)[29]

Nadia herself appears to see her future life as radically different from the past; in this sense, her view follows the pattern of Sasha's idealistic thought. In the light of the narrator's subtle comment, however, this experience is questioned as youthful and naïve. The subtlety and indeed the mere *brevity* of the narrator's addition underline his ironical distance from Nadia's limited perspective.

The ambiguous process of awakening in 'The Betrothed' follows the typical Chekhovian narrative structure, which Vladimir Kataev has named 'it seemed – it turned out' (*kazalos – okazalos*) (e.g. Kataev 2002, 20–22). Indeed, as Kataev observes, the story is a prime example of this structure: at first it seems to Nadia that Sasha's advice is original and the right idea to follow, but then it turns out that Sasha's viewpoint is limited as well. The same holds true of Nadia's relationship with her mother: at first she finds her interesting and wise, but after having a glimpse of life in the capital she sees her in all her provinciality. It might be added that this structure is also to be found in the narrator's final comment, suggesting that in an undetermined future to come Nadia may discover that her thoughts about a radical new beginning were illusory, and may refigure her future in the light of this new information. Even Nadia's impression, on the very first page of the story, of the infinite repetition ahead of her can be seen in the light of the revelatory structure of *kazalos – okazalos*: 'And it *seemed* as if things would go on like this, without changing, for ever and ever' (Chekhov 1979; emphasis by T. K.).[30] This view is later questioned, in Nadia's decision to leave the provincial town and its endless repetition. The future-oriented conception of subjectivity that emerges from narrative temporalities of the story speaks of a situation-based perception, which is liable to shift with new knowledge. Nadia's future expectations are not permanently fixed but, to employ Koselleck's terms, are due to change according to the future spaces of experience she is to gain.

To conclude: when analysed from the viewpoint of the acting subject, Chekhovian provincial chronotopes connote meaningless repetition and cyclicity, further associated with non-autonomous subjectivity. This negative representation of repetition distinguishes the provincial chronotope from the idyllic one, where cyclicity appears as a positive feature: in the idyll, cyclicity is perceived as an organic connection with nature, while in the provincial chronotope it is distanced from this connection. This is where the fundamental modernity of the Chekhovian provincial chronotope, its 'borderlessness' (cf. Sukhikh 2007, 290–91) is revealed: in comparison with the idyll, the longing for the capital city extends this literary time-space towards the movement of history and modernization.

The Chekhovian provincial chronotope can be seen as further developing Flaubert's provincial time-spaces in the short-story genre by paying even more attention to the stagnant repetition, the petit-bourgeois values and the social hierarchies associated with this topos. With regard to the discourses of predictability and unpredictability in the stories discussed in this chapter, by means of these Chekhov seems to allow the possibility of moving beyond the vulgarizing provincial mentality. In so doing, the stories also include a glimpse of a progressive time and change. Nevertheless, the *poshlost* of the social localities greatly determines the characters' possibilities of action. The possibility of leaving the provincial time-space behind is represented with a strong dose of irony: the characters view the changes taking place in their lives in terms that appear rhetorically ambiguous. This temporality is represented as a continuous, situationally determined and unfinalized temporal process, i.e. as thoroughly modern.

Notes

1 The essay was written in 1936–37, published for the first time in Russian in 1975, and in English in 1981. The concluding remarks were written in 1973. I refer in the main to the English translations of Bakhtin's texts, but where necessary the references are to the original, published in Bakhtin's Collected Works (*Sobranie sochinenii*; hereafter, also SS).
2 In the English translation, 'doings'. The Russian original *byvaniia* might better be translated as 'occurrences' or 'happenings'; it does not imply an acting subject but refers to things that merely happen or take place.

3 As Igor Sukhikh observes, Chekhov was never at the centre of Bakhtin's interests. Even if this reference is made in passing and is not developed any further, it is the only major reference to Chekhov in the whole of Bakhtin's oeuvre (cf. Sukhikh 2007, 285–6).

4 It does not, however, follow from this that cyclicity will completely fade away; it survives in everyday routines as well as in the biological rhythms and natural cycles that form the basis of human life.

5 «– Да, – сказала Нина Ивановна, помолчав. – Давно ли ты была ребенком, девочкой, а теперь уже невеста. В природе постоянный обмен веществ. И не заметишь, как сама станешь матерью и старухой, и будет у тебя такая же строптивая дочка, как у меня.» (Chekhov 1962c, 259)

6 This concerns not only the provincial stories but also narratives that take place in Moscow, such as 'Aniuta' ('Aniuta', 1887), where the title character turns from one relationship to another. In Aniuta's case, the repetitive chain of her life appears a financial necessity; she earns her living by serving medical students as mistress and housewife.

7 «А главное, что хуже всего, у нее уже не было никаких мнений. Она видела кругом себя предметы и понимала всё, что происходило кругом, но ни о чем не могла составить мнения и не знала, о чем ей говорить. А как это ужасно не иметь никакого мнения!» (Chekhov 1962b, 139)

8 «Бабушка, или, как ее называли в доме, бабуля, очень полная, некрасивая, с густыми бровями и с усиками, говорила громко, и уже по ее голосу и манере говорить было заметно, что она здесь старшая в доме» (Chekhov 1962c, 250).

9 In his *Futures Past: On the Semantics of Historical Time* (1985; *Vergangene Zukunft: Zur Semantik geschichtlicher Zeiten*, 1979) Reinhart Koselleck employs the metahistorical categories of 'the space of experience' and 'the horizon of expectation' to define the human experience of historical time and possible histories. By 'experience' Koselleck relates to 'present past, whose events have been incorporated and can be remembered. Within experience, a rational reworking is included, together with unconscious modes of conduct which do not have to be present in awareness' (Koselleck 1985, 259). 'Expectation' takes place similarly in the present and is both interpersonal and person-specific: '[I]t is the future made present; it directs itself to the not-yet, to the nonexperienced, to that which is to be revealed. Hope and fear, wishes and desires, cares and rational analysis, receptive display and curiosity; all enter into expectation and constitute it' (Koselleck 1985, 259).

10 This difference between Chekhov and his predecessors is what Igor Sukhikh seems to have in mind in his discussion of the writer's work in relation to the Bakhtinian chronotope. Sukhikh notes that Chekhov's time-spaces actually contradict Bakhtin's notion of the provincial chronotope; while in Gogol, Turgenev and the other Russian writers mentioned in Bakhtin's list of typical provincial chronotopes the town described is still a closed, 'epic entity' (*epicheskaia celostnost*), in Chekhov it opens up towards the outer world and is characterized by 'borderlessness' (*neogranichennost*) in a fundamental way (Sukhikh 2007, 284–301, esp. 290–91).

11 «Будущее наше рисовалось нам так: вначале на Кавказе, пока мы ознакомимся с местом и людьми, я надену вицмундир и буду служить, потом же на просторе возьмем себе клок земли, будем трудиться в поте лица, заведем виноградник, поле и прочее» (Chekhov 2006, 99).

12 «В зале блестящий пол, выкрашенный под паркет, венские стулья, рояль, пюпитр для скрипки […] На стене в золотой раме висела большая картина, написанная красками: нагая дама и около нее лиловая ваза с отбитой ручкой.

– Чудесная картина, – проговорил Андрей Андреич и из уважения вздохнул. – Это художника Шишмачевского. […] Над диваном большой фотографический портрет отца Андрея в камилавке и в орденах. Потом вошли в столовую с буфетом, потом в спальню; здесь в полумраке стояли рядом две кровати, и похоже было, что когда обставляли спальню, то имели в виду, что всегда тут будет очень хорошо и иначе быть не может. Андрей Андреич водил Надю по комнатам и всё время держал ее за талию; а она чувствовала себя слабой, виноватой, ненавидела все эти комнаты, кровати, кресла, ее мутило от нагой дамы. […] Он держал ее за талию, говорил так ласково, скромно, так был счастлив, расхаживая по этой своей квартире; а она видела во всем одну только пошлость, глупую, наивную, невыносимую пошлость, и его рука, обнимавшая ее талию, казалась ей жесткой и холодной, как обруч.» (Chekhov 1962c, 256–7)

13 The Russian term *poshlost* means 'vulgarity', 'philistinism', 'banality', 'triviality' or 'kitsch'. As Vladimir Nabokov puts it, *poshlost* – or 'poshlust', an amusing term he developed from the English words of 'posh' and 'lust' – is '[c]orny trash, vulgar clichés, Philistinism in all its phases, imitations of imitations, bogus profundities, crude, moronic and dishonest pseudo-literature' (1961). The concept has a certain erotic layer to it, which may be connected with the spiritual: according to Svetlana Boym, *poshlost* appears as 'the Russian version of banality, with a characteristic national flavouring of metaphysics and high morality, and a peculiar conjunction of the sexual and the spiritual. This one word encompasses triviality, vulgarity, sexual promiscuity, and a lack of spirituality' (1994, 41). As Gennadi Obatnin (2012, 183) notes, *poshlost* is often defined from rather subjective vantage points and its connotations have varied greatly during its two-hundred-year existence; it is characteristic of the concept to be recognizable but to escape definition. From the mid-nineteenth century onward, the concept is connected with *meschanstvo*, ('petty bourgeoisie', 'philistinism'; e.g. Obatnin 187–8); this connection is clear in Chekhov.

14 The son declares his obeisance to his father even when there is no apparent reason for this: '"I love my old Dad", said Andrei Andreich, patting his father on the shoulder. "Dear old man. Good old man!"'(Chekhov 1979). In declaring his passion for Nadia, he chooses a sentence that Nadia feels 'to have heard long, long ago, to have read it in some novel, some old, tattered volume which no one ever read anymore' (Chekhov 1979; «ей казалось, что это она уже давно слышала, очень давно, или читала где-то […] в романе, в старом, оборванном, давно уже заброшенном» [Chekhov 1962c, 255]). This kind of reproduced rhetoric is often employed in Chekhov to mark the reproductive everyday temporality; the Latin teacher Kulygin, Masha's normative husband in *The Three Sisters* (*Tri sestry*, 1901), is a particularly well-developed example of a walking dictionary of quotations and catchphrases.

15 «И почему-то все эти, выстроенные отцом, дома, похожие друг на друга, смутно напоминали мне его цилиндр, его затылок, сухой и упрямый. С течением времени в городе к бездарности отца пригляделись, она укоренилась и стала нашим стилем.» (Chekhov 1977a, 198)

16 «Этот стиль отец внес и в жизнь моей сестры. Начать с того, что он назвал ее Клеопатрой (как меня назвал Мисаилом). Когда она была еще девочкой, он пугал ее напоминанием о звездах, о древних мудрецах, о наших предках, подолгу объяснял ей, что такое жизнь, что такое долг; и теперь, когда ей было уже двадцать шесть лет, продолжал то же самое, позволяя ей ходить под руку только с ним одним и воображая почему-то, что рано или поздно должен явиться приличный молодой человек,

которы́й пожела́ет вступи́ть с не́ю в брак из уваже́ния к его́ ли́чным ка́чествам. А она́ обожа́ла отца́, боя́лась и ве́рила в его́ необыкнове́нный ум.» (Chekhov 1977a, 198)

17 In contemporary discussions on *poshlost*, amateur plays were mentioned alongside with other things *poshlye* (see Obatnin 2012, 193).

18 Likewise Stephen Hutchings (1997, 249, n15) notes that Chekhovian *poshlost* draws sustenance from the falsely aesthetic, referring specifically to the painting of the naked woman in 'The Betrothed'.

19 «Жизнь и о́браз жи́зни, по́шлость и о́браз по́шлости (увекове́чение того́, что лишено́ вся́ких вну́тренних прав на ве́чность)».

20 «Она́ всё смотре́ла на пейза́ж с гру́стною улы́бкой, и то, что други́е не находи́ли в нем ничего́ осо́бенного, волнова́ло её; пото́м она́ начала́ сно́ва ходи́ть по за́лам и осма́тривать карти́ны, хоте́ла поня́ть их, и уже́ ей не каза́лось, что на вы́ставке мно́го одина́ковых карти́н. [...] И по́сле того́ золоты́е карни́зы, венециа́нские зеркала́ с цвета́ми и карти́ны вро́де той, что висе́ла над роя́лем, а та́кже рассужде́ния му́жа и Ко́сти об иску́сстве уже́ возбужда́ли в ней чу́вство ску́ки и доса́ды, и поро́й да́же не́нависти.» (Chekhov 1977b, 66)

21 The core of Sasha's advice for Nadia is to get an academic education: "'If only you would go away and study", he said. "Enlightened, saintly people are the only interesting ones, the only ones who are needed'" (Chekhov 1979). The rhetoric Sasha employs is parodic to such an extent that it is impossible for the reader not to be aware of its markedness. As Stephen Hutchings (2007, 44–5) observes, even if Sasha speaks against the crowd mentality, in rhetorical terms his words echo Dostoevsky's utopian characters. There is also a great discrepancy between Sasha's rhetoric and his action. As Popkin (1993, 37) observes, even if Sasha acts as the catalyst for Nadia's personal revolution, his own everyday life represents the same repetitive and predictable pattern of existence that Nadia hopes to escape. His advice to Nadia speaks for a progressive temporality that can become available through education. His own development, however, contradicts this: even though he has studied architecture, he keeps reproducing lithographs in a factory – and repeating the same words of enlightenment to Nadia year after year. Moreover, his attitude to Nadia is perhaps no less authoritative than is Andrei Andreich Jr's; in his manners, Sasha closely resembles a biblical figure and a demagogue.

22 «В саду́ бы́ло ти́хо, прохла́дно, и тёмные поко́йные те́ни лежа́ли на земле́. Слы́шно бы́ло, как *где́-то далеко́, о́чень далеко́, должно́ быть, за го́родом*, крича́ли лягу́шки. Чу́вствовался май, ми́лый май! Дыша́лось глубоко́ и хоте́лось ду́мать, что не здесь, а где́-то под не́бом, над дере́вьями, *далеко́ за го́родом*, в поля́х и леса́х, *разверну́лась тепе́рь своя́ весе́нняя жизнь*, таи́нственная, прекра́сная, бога́тая и свята́я, недосту́пная понима́нию сла́бого, гре́шного челове́ка. И хоте́лось почему́-то пла́кать.» (Chekhov 1962c, 248)

23 «На́дя ходи́ла по саду́, по у́лице, гляде́ла на дома́, на се́рые забо́ры, и ей каза́лось, что в го́роде всё давно́ уже́ состаре́лось, отжи́ло и всё то́лько ждёт не то конца́, не то нача́ла чего́-то молодо́го, све́жего» (Chekhov 1962c, 265).

24 In *The Cherry Orchard*, the cutting down of the orchard in order to build dachas for town-dwellers symbolizes the intermingling of social estates that takes place in the process of Russian modernization. The idealist Trofimov's partly socialist vision of the future of the orchard as open to everyone contributes to the same effect. In 'The Betrothed', the garden is not cut down but its apple trees fall in the storm while in blossom. The storm of course symbolizes the process Nadia is currently going through and the falling, blossoming apple trees the decision she is about to make. Thus, where in *The Cherry Orchard* the garden

connotes the changing socio-historical paradigm, in 'The Betrothed' the garden and its devastation refer more straightforwardly to the development of the main character: to her personal liberation from the grandmother's house and its tameness.

25. Provincial female characters often do not go that far, but find satisfaction in fiction *about* tragic liaisons – similarly to Flaubert's Emma, whose affairs start from models offered by romantic literature. Thus for example in 'Women's Kingdom' ('Babe carstvo', 1893), another provincial story, Anna Akimovna bases her ideal of passion on her reading of romantic literature. Indeed, in this story Anna's problem with love lies precisely in her romanticized view of passion. She absorbs books about romantic affairs, and eagerly listens to her male guest's report of the Maupassant novel he has read; the excited conversations at dinner, together with the experience of the heightened and adventurous life of a fictional character, finally arouse in her a passion for the working-class man Pimenov.

26. «Но тут всё та же несмелость, угловатость неопытной молодости, неловкое чувство; и было впечатление растерянности, как будто кто вдруг постучал в дверь. Анна Сергеевна, эта «дама с собачкой», к тому, что произошло, отнеслась как-то особенно, очень серьезно, точно к своему падению, – так казалось, и это было странно и некстати. У нее опустились, завяли черты и по сторонам лица печально висели длинные волосы, она задумалась в унылой позе, точно грешница на старинной картине.

    [...]

    Гурову было уже скучно слушать, его раздражал наивный тон, это покаяние, такое неожиданное и неуместное; если бы не слезы на глазах, то можно было бы подумать, что она шутит или играет роль.

    — Я не понимаю, — сказал он тихо, — что же ты хочешь?» (Chekhov 1962a, 177–8)

27. «Ставши моей любовницей, Кисочка взглянула на дело иначе, чем я. Прежде всего она полюбила страстно и глубоко. То, что для меня составляло обыкновенный любовный экспромт, для нее было целым переворотом в жизни. Помню, мне казалось, что она сошла с ума. Счастливая первый раз в жизни, помолодевшая лет на пять, с вдохновенным, восторженным яйцом, не зная, куда деваться от счастья, она то смеялась, то плакала и не переставала мечтать вслух о том, как завтра мы поедем на Кавказ, оттуда осенью в Петербург, как будем потом жить...» (Chekhov 1967, 557)

28. Cathy Popkin (1993, 33–8; esp. 37) employs this story as a prime example in the line of Chekhov's stories that 'minimize the maximum'; in other words, narratives that channel the reader's attention in one direction, towards an apparently significant event, which then turns out to be non-eventful. In the case of 'The Betrothed' it is the predictable future for a young woman living in the provinces that appears the 'maximum' of the story, to employ Popkin's terms. The future that the title implies, and that is open to Nadia at the beginning of the story, thus confirms the reader's expectations.

29. «Она ясно сознавала, что жизнь ее перевернута, как хотел того Саша, что она здесь одинокая, чужая, ненужная и что всё ей тут ненужно, всё прежнее оторвано от нее и исчезло, точно сгорело и пепел разнесся по ветру. Она вошла в Сашину комнату, постояла тут.

    «Прощай, милый Саша!» – думала она. [...] Она пошла к себе наверх укладываться, а на другой день утром простилась со своими и, живая, веселая, покинула город – *как полагала, навсегда*.» (Chekhov 1962c, 265)

30. «И почему-то *казалось*, что так теперь будет всю жизнь, без перемены, без конца!» (Chekhov 1962, 248).

References

Bakhtin, M. M. 1996. 'O Flobere'. In *Sobranie sochinenii*, vol. 5, 131–7. Moscow: Russkie slovari.

———. 2007 [1986]. 'The *Bildungsroman* and Its Significance in the History of Realism (Toward a Typology of the Novel)' ('Roman vospitaniia i ego znachenie v istorii realizma'). In *Speech Genres and Other Late Essays*. Edited by Caryl Emerson and Michael Holquist, translated by Vern McGee, 10–59. Austin: University of Texas Press.

———. 2008 [1981]. 'Forms of Time and of the Chronotope in the Novel' ('Formy vremeni i khronotopa v romane: Ocherki po istoricheskoi poetike'). In *The Dialogic Imagination*. Edited by Michael Holquist, translated by Caryl Emerson and Michael Holquist, 84–258. Austin: University of Texas Press.

———. 2012. 'Formy vremeni i khronotopa v romane: Ocherki po istoricheskoi poetike'. In *Sobranie sochinenii*, vol. 3, 341–503. Moscow: Iazyki slavianskikh kultur.

Boym, Svetlana. 1994. *Common Places: Mythologies of Everyday Life in Russia*. Cambridge, MA: Harvard University Press.

Chekhov, Anton Pavlovich. 1962a. 'Dama s sobachkoi'. In *Izbrannye proizvedeniia*, vol. 3, 173–89. Moscow: Gosudarstvennoe izdatelstvo khudozhestvennoi literatury.

———. 1962b. 'Dushechka'. In *Izbrannye proizvedeniia*, vol. 3, 132–43. Moscow: Gosudarstvennoe izdatelstvo khudozhestvennoi literatury.

———. 1962c. 'Nevesta'. In *Izbrannye proizvedeniia*, vol. 3, 248–66. Moscow: Gosudarstvennoe izdatelstvo khudozhestvennoi literatury.

———. 1967. 'Ogni'. In *Izbrannye proizvedeniia v trekh tomakh*, vol. 1, 531–66. Moscow: Khudozhestvennaia literatura.

———. 1977a. 'Moia zhizn'. In *Polnoe sobranie sochinenii i pisem v tridcati tomakh*, vol. 9, 192–280. Moscow: Nauka.

———. 1977b. 'Tri goda'. In *Polnoe sobranie sochinenii i pisem v tridcati tomakh*, vol. 9, 7–92. Moscow: Nauka.

———. 1979. 'The Betrothed'. In *Anton Chekhov's Short Stories*. Translated by Ivy Litvinov. http://www.eldritchpress.org/ac/betroth.html (accessed 28 January 2012).

———. 2006. 'Duel'. In *Palata No 6*. Moscow: Eksmo.

Hutchings, Stephen. 1997. *Russian Modernism: The Transfiguration of the Everyday*. Cambridge: Cambridge University Press.

Kataev, Vladimir. 2002. *If Only We Could Know! An Interpretation of Chekhov*. Chicago: Ivan R. Dee.

Koselleck, Reinhart. 1985. *Futures Past: On the Semantics of Historical Time* (*Vergangene Zukunft. Zur Semantik geschichtlicher Zeiten*, 1979). Translated and with an introduction by Keith Tribe. Cambridge, MA: MIT Press.

Moretti, Franco. 1986. 'The Moment of Truth'. *New Left Review* 1, no. 159: 39–48.

Nabokov, Vladimir. 1961. *Nikolai Gogol*. New York: New Directions.

Obatnin, Gennadi. 2012. '"Two Hundred Years of Poshlost": A Historical Sketch of the Concept'. In *Understanding Russianness*, 183–209. Edited by Risto Alapuro et al. London and New York: Routledge.

Popkin, Cathy. 1993. *Pragmatics of Insignificance. Chekhov, Zoshchenko, Gogol*. Stanford: Stanford University Press.

Sukhikh, Ivan. 2007 [1987]. *Problemy poetiki Chekhova*. St Petersburg: SPbGU.

Tchekhov, Anton. 2004a. 'The Darling'. In *The Tales of Chekhov*, vol. 1. Translated by Constance Garnett. http://www.gutenberg.org/cache/epub/13416/pg13416.html (accessed 28 January 2012).

_____. 2004b. 'The Duel'. In *The Duel and Other Stories*. Translated by Constance Garnett. http://www.gutenberg.org/cache/epub/13505/pg13505.html (accessed 28 January 2012).

_____. 2004c. 'The Lady with the Dog'. In *The Tales of Chekhov*, vol. 3. Translated by Constance Garnett. http://www.gutenberg.org/cache/epub/13415/pg13415.html (accessed 28 January 2012).

_____. 2004d. 'The Lights'. In *The Tales of Chekhov*, vol. 13. Translated by Constance Garnett. http://www.gutenberg.org/cache/epub/13414/pg13414.html (accessed 28 January 2012).

_____. 2004e. 'My Life'. In *The Tales of Chekhov*, vol. 8. Translated by Constance Garnett. http://www.gutenberg.org/cache/epub/13418/pg13418.html (accessed 28 January 2012).

_____. 2004f. 'Three Years'. In *The Tales of Chekhov*, vol. 1. Translated by Constance Garnett. http://www.gutenberg.org/cache/epub/13416/pg13416.html (accessed 28 January 2012).

LIST OF CONTRIBUTORS

Edward Gieskes is associate professor of English at the University of South Carolina. His research interests range from Shakespeare, early modern drama and theatre history to Bakhtin, genre theory and Bourdieu. He has published a monograph entitled *Representing the Professions: Administration, Law and Theatre in Early Modern England* (University of Delaware Press, 2006), co-edited the essay collection *Writing Robert Greene: New Essays on England's First Notorious Professional Writer* (Ashgate, 2008) and written several articles on early modern English theatre.

Tintti Klapuri is a PhD student at the Finnish Graduate School for Literary Studies and is based at the University of Turku, Finland. Her dissertation concerns temporality and modernity in the work of Anton Chekhov. She has published articles dealing with Chekhov, Bakhtin and contemporary Russian literature, and has co-edited the books *Genre and Interpretation* (2010) and *Kenen aika? Esseitä venäläisestä nykykirjallisuudesta* (2012, 'Whose time? Essays on contemporary Russian literature').

Aino Mäkikalli is a post-doctoral research fellow at the Department of Comparative Literature, University of Turku. She has published a monograph, *From Eternity to Time: Conceptions of Time in Daniel Defoe's Novels* (Peter Lang, 2007), and has co-edited a volume entitled *Positioning Daniel Defoe's Non-Fiction: Form, Function, Genre* (Cambridge Scholars Publishing, 2011), along with articles on, for instance, Ian McEwan and Wladimir Kaminer.

Mikhail Oshukov is associate professor of English at Petrozavodsk State University, Russia, and a PhD student at the Department of Comparative Literature, University of Turku. His candidate of philology dissertation deals with the American transcendentalists, and he is currently working on a PhD dissertation on Russian and American modernist poetry. He has published several articles on Ezra Pound, e. e. cummings and T. S. Eliot.

Christian Pauls is a research assistant and lecturer at the University of Marburg, Germany. His PhD thesis concerns the contemporary English poet Peter Reading, whose works he analyses using the approach established by Bakhtin for the analysis of polyphony and its emergence in Dostoevsky's novels. Along with this interest in modern English poetry and Bakhtinian theory, Pauls' other research interests include literary theory, the modern novel and the theatre of the absurd.

Liisa Steinby (until 2007 Liisa Saariluoma) is professor of comparative literature at the University of Turku. She has published ten monographs on different aspects of the modern novel or on literary theory, including *Der postindividualistische Roman* (Königshausen und Neumann, 1994), *Nietzsche als Roman: Über die Sinnkonstituierung in Thomas Manns "Doktor Faustus"* (Niemeyer 1996), *Erzählstruktur und Bildungsroman: Wielands "Geschichte des Agathon", Goethes "Wilhelm Meisters Lehrjahre"* (Königshausen und Neumann, 2004), *Wilhelm Meisters Lehrjahre und die Entstehung des modernen Zeitbewusstseins* (Wissenschaftlicher Verlag Trier, 2005) and *Kundera and Modernity* (Purdue University Press, 2013). Her main research interests include the problematics of modernity in the novel from the eighteenth century to the present and related issues in literary theory.

www.ingramcontent.com/pod-product-compliance
Lightning Source LLC
Chambersburg PA
CBHW021832300426
44114CB00009BA/404